Spenser, Marvell, and Renaissance Pastoral

Spenser, Marvell, and Renaissance Pastoral

Patrick Cullen

Harvard University Press
Cambridge, Massachusetts
1970

© Copyright 1970 by the President and Fellows of Harvard College

All rights reserved

Distributed in Great Britain by Oxford University Press, London

Library of Congress catalog card number 76-123566

SBN 674-83195-0

Printed in the United States of America

To My Parents

Preface

To some, Spenser and Marvell may seem a curious combination
of authors. Seventy-five years separate "The Garden" from the
Shepheardes Calender, and in that time of course poetry and ideas
had in many respects diverged far from the Elizabethans. My choice
of pastoralists is not meant to suggest a paradigm of pastoral in
evolution or to establish a historical or "source" relationship between
the two writers, but instead to demonstrate how Spenser and Marvell
received and used what is one of the most varied and complex traditions of European literature. What brings these two, among the greatest, English pastoralists of the Renaissance together is, therefore, more
general than specific: they both demonstrate the malleability and complexity pastoral had attained by the time of the Renaissance. In this
respect, the two pastoralists serve somewhat as case studies in the
problem of interpreting pastoral. Pastoral is a highly fluid and protean
tradition: neither Marvell nor Spenser was always doing the same
thing with pastoral; nor, what is the deterministic fallacy of much
genre criticism, were they always doing what their predecessors in
pastoral had done. Failure to perceive this has resulted in much critical
obtuseness. Spenser's eclogues in the *Calender* are commonly interpreted as an exposition "sage and serious" of a single, moralistic
perspective in the manner of Mantuan; but such a reading obscures
the comedy whereby the moralism is tempered, and it goes counter
to the central purpose and technique of the work: a juxtaposition
of different perspectives whereby pastoral experience is evaluated.
Similarly, Marvell criticism has increasingly viewed poems as dissimi-

lar as "The Garden" and "Damon the Mower" as though they were the same kind of pastoral and employed the same kind of poetic technique to the same end. As a result, a comic amorous pastoral like "Damon the Mower" becomes a sober imitation of the consequences of Adam's Fall, a portrayal of the grave disorder passion introduces into the world; and that, it seems to me, is far from the target. Pastoral is not all of a piece, nor are the pastorals of Spenser and Marvell; that is the point from which my analysis begins.

Contents

Spenser, Marvell, and

Renaissance Pastoral

Introduction:
The Pastoral Context

When in the late 1570's Spenser chose pastoral as the mode for his first important work, he chose it no doubt in part because Virgil had chosen it, and because "So flew Mantuane, as being not full somd. So Petrarque. So Boccace; So Marot, Sanazarus, and also diuers other excellent both Italian and French Poetes."[1] Spenser also chose it for the same reason Virgil had chosen it: pastoral provided a mode for the juxtaposition of contending values and perspectives. The conception of pastoral as the airy froth of the retreating imagination, however true of some of the lesser and frailer pastorals, was not Spenser's conception. This is not to say that Spenser did not and could not associate aspects of pastoral *life* with a kind of escapist retreat from reality: obviously he did, for example, in "June" when he placed the partially naive Hobbinol in a somewhat artificial Arcadia; and obviously the whole point of locating Leicester in a pastoral setting in "Virgil's Gnat" was to suggest that Leicester had permitted his idyllic illusions to blind him to reality. But while pastoral can portray an escape from reality, or a desire to escape reality, the pastoral *mode* itself from Theocritus onward involved, implicitly or explicitly, a critical exploration and counterbalancing of attitudes, perspectives, and experiences. However differently values may be weighed, however

1. "Dedicatory Epistle" to the *Shepheardes Calender,* in *The Works of Edmund Spenser: A Variorum Edition,* ed. C. G. Osgood and H. G. Lotspeich (Baltimore, 1943), VII, *The Minor Poems,* pt. 1, p. 10.

1

differently perspectives may be encompassed, this is an attribute of pastoral from its inception; an attribute that culminates in the Renaissance with the extreme opposition of values in the pastorals of Mantuan and his imitators.

Spenser used not only pastoral, but also a division within pastoral, as a means of portraying and exploring a conflict of values. While the pastoral tradition Spenser inherited undeniably possessed continuity, it was from one perspective divided—at the very core, in the conception of the ideal pastoral life. By the time of the Renaissance one can discern two different, though related, strands within pastoral, the "Arcadian" and the "Mantuanesque."[2] Arcadian pastoral for the most part takes as the pastoral ideal the *pastor felix* and the soft life of *otium;* correspondingly, it locates its characters in a landscape of varying degrees of idealization, a landscape originating in Theocritus' idylls, named "Arcadia" by Virgil, and explored by the Renaissance, a landscape lush and pleasant but at the same time almost always vulnerable and precarious. Mantuanesque pastoral, however minor it may be in the whole history of pastoral, was a major strand in the Renaissance. Emerging in part from the pastoral polemics of Petrarch and Boccaccio on the corruption of church and court, it found its culminating and definitive expression in the ten eclogues of Battista Spagnuoli. Widely read, lauded to the point that his name rivaled his master Virgil's, a required staple in English schools of the sixteenth century,[3] he influenced and was imitated by the two English pastoralists immediately preceding Spenser, Alex-

2. These two pastoral perspectives are not intended to encompass and describe the whole pastoral tradition, though what I describe as the Arcadian tradition does seem to me to be the mainstream of pastoral. The two perspectives illustrate a division within pastoral, but not necessarily within *all* pastoral. Pastoral is so diverse—encompassing birthday eclogues, dream eclogues, myth eclogues—that no generalization can justifiably claim to account for all pastoral. Nor is my aim that lofty; what follows is a sketch of suggestions for a modification of our conception of pastoral. I should add, too, that the two perspectives are not always as "pure" or unmixed as, for the purpose of clarity, I may seem to describe them—the pastorals of Petrarch and Boccaccio, not to mention Spenser, testify to this. Finally, I refer largely only to pastoralists who antedate Spenser, and I have limited my discussion of Mantuanesque pastoral to Mantuan and his English imitators and chosen to ignore pastoralists like Petrarch and Boccaccio who undoubtedly point the way toward him, simply because Mantuan, as W. W. Greg, *Pastoral Poetry and Pastoral Drama* (London, 1906), p. 26, says, provided the "definitive form" and model for this kind of pastoral. On neo-Latin satirical and didactic pastoral, see W. Leonard Grant, *Neo-Latin Literature and the Pastoral* (Chapel Hill, N.C., 1965), ch. 12.

3. See the Introduction to *The Eclogues of Baptista Mantuanus,* ed. Wilfred P. Mustard (Baltimore, 1911), pp. 30-40.

ander Barclay and Barnabe Googe. Mantuanesque pastoral takes as its ideal the Judaeo–Christian *pastor bonus,* the shepherd unwaveringly committed to the flock and to the requirements for eternal salvation, and consequently one largely opposed to the shepherd of worldly felicity. In the light of this ideal, the function of pastoral became one of enlightening man on the virtues of the *pastor bonus* and the vices of the *pastor malus.* Poggioli, in his parenthetical notice of Christian moralistic pastoral, admittedly oversimplifies but does none-theless strike a fundamental truth: "Christian imagination . . . was able to use consistently the pastoral convention only as an allegorical travesty and satirical mask. The allegorical pastoral, starting with Battista Mantovano's Latin eclogues, is primarily a polemical tool: the religious mind uses the form to indict the bad shepherds or the wolves in sheep's clothing who mislead and destroy the Christian flock."[4] That is to say, we are caught up in the Judaeo–Christian opposition of good shepherds and bad shepherds, and all the grave sense of duty, work and good works, distrust of the worldly and the natural that accompany that opposition. Accordingly, the pastoral ideal of the good shepherd becomes *the* ideal, *the* value, and there is painfully little sense of the limitations of that ideal and painfully few variants possible within it. It is in this respect, as well as in the conception of the ideal life, that Arcadian and Mantuanesque pastoral differ. Of course all pastoral, including Mantuanesque pastoral, is constantly implying, introducing, juxtaposing disparate values, values other than pastoral—the heroic, the urban, the courtly. But whereas in Mantuanesque pastoral the confrontation of disparate values involves a polemical antagonism of opposites, in Arcadian pastoral it involves a "tension between opposites."[5] Arcadian pastoral can and does satirize the artifices and corruptions of the nonpastoral world, indeed in the very fact of withdrawal from that world criticism is implicit; but there is, implicitly or explicitly, a counterpoising aware-ness of the limitations of pastoral values and with that a greater sense of the multivalence of experience, a sense of the potential legiti-macy of urban and heroic modes which seem to contradict, but some-times actually mesh with, its own—opposite modes in terms of which

4. Renato Poggioli, "The Oaten Flute," *Harvard Library Bulletin* (*HLB*), 11 (1957), 164.
5. The phrase is Gilbert Lawall's, *Theocritus' Coan Pastorals: A Poetry Book* (Cambridge, Mass., 1967), p. 5. Lawall is, of course, speaking of Theocritus, but his remark, it seems to me, holds true for much of the rest of pastoral.

it is constantly evaluating itself, as it perceives in the pastoral experience (and poetic mode) a reformation in retreat for a return engagement, a preliminary to higher things. In Arcadian pastoral, then, there is a greater ambivalence in the relationship of disparate values.

Perhaps the most obvious indication of the multivalence I have been speaking about is the fact that, from Virgil on, pastoral is often made as an offering to the heroes and leaders of the world of greater things. Virgil of course dedicates poems to Varus, Pollio, and Gallus, while Calpurnius dedicates sycophantic poems to Nero. Later, Sannazaro dedicates his fourth piscatorial eclogue to Ferdinand of Aragon, Marot and Ronsard dedicate a number of eclogues to members of the French court, Garcilaso dedicates his first eclogue to Don Pedro, Viceroy of Naples, "splendidly armed, representing on earth fierce Mars" (13-14),[6] and Spenser dedicates his *Calender* "to the noble and vertuous Gentleman most worthy of all titles both of learning and cheualrie M. Philip Sidney."

Yet, not only is pastoral dedicated to members of the nonpastoral world, it also has as one of its prime functions the praise of that world. The court pastoral has been one of the major types of pastoral since its beginnings, with Theocritus' encomium to Ptolemy in his seventeenth idyll. Virgil's fourth, the famous golden-age eclogue, provided possibly the most influential model for this type of pastoral. The speaker's praise of the ruler and the child suggests a continuum, not a doctrinaire opposition, between the pastoral and nonpastoral worlds. Both father and son will be among heroes, and the son will guide the father's kingdom into a new golden age when peace returns and hard labor is made unnecessary. Significantly, the return of the ideal *otium* of the Arcadian pastoral golden age is brought about not by shepherds but by heroes, men of action. The heroic is celebrated as the means of realizing the pastoral ideal; yet the relationship between pastoral and heroic is not one-sided, for if the heroic is celebrated as the means to the realization of the pastoral ideal, it has in the process been remolded by that ideal, directed away from injury, whether done through war or through the eviction of landowners, to happiness. Neither heroic values nor pastoral values are all-sufficient, and in the golden age the best aspects of each are married. At any rate, Virgil's court eclogue established a model for

6. Citations from Garcilaso's eclogues are to *Obras,* Clásicos Castellanos, ed. T. Navarro Tomás (Madrid, 1963). Translations, when given, are my own.

the use of pastoral to praise the heroic and active life, and it reveals a strain of hero-worship that manifests itself repeatedly in the pastoral tradition in, for example, Calpurnius' praise of Nero, the Carolingian court eclogues, Petrarch's praise of the rebellion of Cola in his "Pietas Pastoralis," Boiardo's epic-like panegyric of the Duke of Calabria, Marot's two imitations of Virgil's fourth, and Ronsard's court eclogues—to mention only some of the more obvious later celebrations of the world of action.

Pastoral's praise may, however, contain pastoral's censure as well. One may well feel criticism implicit in the golden-age eclogue's praise of what the heroic *could* become; certainly it is a part of Virgil's first eclogue, which reveals pastoral functioning as an instrument to praise and to criticize both the pastoral and the nonpastoral worlds. Because the poem is structured largely around the advantages of the pastoral life and the disadvantages of the nonpastoral life, it is commonly viewed as an illustration of the virtues of rustic *otium,* and to some extent this view is accurate: Meliboeus' prospective hard life in distant lands obviously contrasts unfavorably with the cool shade and gentle breezes of the shepherd's world. But such a reading is incomplete; for *otium,* while undeniably an ideal envied and desired, is not an exclusive ideal. The first eclogue, after all, is a celebration not only of pastoral *otium* but also of the grandeur of Rome. Tityrus informs Meliboeus, "the man to whom I owe this happy leisure is a god" (6); and that god is not pastoral Pan but a young prince of augustly heroic Rome. Indeed, the urban world of Rome far surpasses the pastoral market towns the shepherds in their ignorance know. Rome stands out above all other cities as the cypress stands out above the undergrowth, and it is in Rome that the great prince Augustus lives:

. . . neque servitio me exire licebat
nec tam praesentes alibi cognoscere divos.
hic illum vidi iuvenem, Meliboee, quotannis
bis senos cui nostra dies altaria fumant.
hic mihi responsum primus dedit ille petenti:
"pascite, ut ante, boves, pueri; submittite tauros."

(40-45)

[There was nowhere else than Rome where I could bring my serfdom to an end or find a god so able to protect me. It was there, Meliboeus, that I saw the young man for whom my altar is going to smoke on twelve days in the year. There too that I had from him the first kind answer to my suit. "Lad," he said, "let your cattle graze, as you have always done, and put your bulls to stud."][7]

Pastoral *otium,* then, is not attained by the pastoral world's excluding itself from the nonpastoral world, for it is actually the urban world that has enabled Tityrus to attain *otium.* But it must be added that just as the celebration of pastoral *otium* is not all of the poem, neither is the celebration of the urban and heroic; for while the great hero and the great city have granted Tityrus his ease, they have had exactly the opposite effect on Meliboeus and the remainder of the countryside: "every farm in the whole countryside [is] in such a state of chaos" (11-12). Panegyric of Augustus and Rome though the poem is, it is also an indictment; the poem looks perhaps to the same resolution as the golden-age eclogue, a reforming of the heroic according to pastoral ends and uses, and to the rebuilding of society for peaceful order and rest.

The ambivalence behind pastoral's countermovements—its longing to regress coupled with its longing to progress, to anticipate greater things—further manifests itself in its combined tendencies to depreciate itself as a lowly genre and, according to the Virgilian progression from pastoral to epic, to see itself as a preliminary to a higher style. Just as many of the shepherds in pastoral retire to the pastoral world only to prepare for a renewed encounter with the outer and greater world, so too the pastoral poet turns to pastoral for his projected encounter with epic. Consequently, one finds within pastoral recurring intimations of greater things. Such is the intimation of Virgil's invocation to the messianic eclogue:

Sicelides Musae, paulo maiora canamus.
non comnes arbusta iuvant humilesque myricae;
si canimus silvas, silvae sint consule dignae.

(1-3)

[Muses of Sicily, let us attempt a rather more exalted theme. Hedgerow and humble tamarisk do not appeal to all. If we must sing of woodlands, let them be such as may do a consul honour.]

The compliment is clear, and it is one that recurs throughout pastoral, that the lowly pastoral may be unworthy of the great man; but the corollary is equally clear, the pastoral poet himself deserves a greater

7. Citations from Virgil's Eclogues are to *Virgil: The Pastoral Poems,* ed. and trans. E. V. Rieu (Baltimore, 1954).

style and subject. Certainly this is the implication behind the material that follows, as Virgil strives to go beyond the limitations of pastoral in a celebration of the heroes—perhaps Pollio and his son, perhaps simply the present rulers and the future generation—who will bring about a great new age. As John Coolidge, speaking of this eclogue, has suggested, there is in the pastoral regression to a past golden age the countermovement of heroic progression to greater things: "The longing to go back is gratified in terms of the history of the race at the same time that the desire to move forward towards greatness is being gratified in terms of the individual life."⁸ It is perhaps not too fanciful to add that just as the messianic child holds the promise of growing into a maturity in which he will dwell among heroes and be one, so too the aspiring poet.

Intimation of greater things to come is the central concern of Virgil's introduction to the sixth eclogue. His first muse, Thalia, we are told, inhabited the forests; but when he later thought to sing of kings and battles, Cynthius, or Apollo, admonished him: " 'Tityrus, a shepherd ought to let his sheep grow fat, but court a slender Muse' " (4-5); and Tityrus, addressing Varus, says there will be poets enough to praise him and write of unhappy war and he will stick to pastoral stuff. "Non iniussa cano," he says (9); "I do not sing what I have not been bidden." But the disclaimer gives the lie to itself, and the desire for precisely that *iussum* to bold new enterprise is transparent. That the poet awaits, with obvious impatience and eagerness, a bid to the heroic, whether from Apollo or from a patron, is clear, as it was in the fourth eclogue, from the material that follows: the description of Silenus' song about the creation of the world and about great mythical and legendary events. The celebration of Gallus, the pastoral singer, by Apollo's choir and his receiving a reed pipe from Linus, "godlike singer of the countryside" (67), may seem a curious inclusion among these greater events unless we realize how much the eclogue is concerned with Virgil's own poetic ambitions, his own receiving of the favors of Apollo. The fact that Gallus and Linus are celebrated as pastoral poets would seem to confirm the speaker's own disclaimer of higher ambitions, to assert that pastoral can itself do great things. The greatness of pastoral is being celebrated, but—once again the ambivalence—so

8. John S. Coolidge, "Great Things and Small: The Virgilian Progression," *Comparative Literature* (*CL*), 17 (1965), 12. Coolidge's essay is filled with good things, and I am indebted to it for a number of insights and apt phrases.

is the heroic. Silenus is a poet of things beyond the woods, a poet of the cosmos, of myth, of legend, of heroes, a poet of verses with more than woodland ring:

Omnia quae Phoebo quondam meditante beatus
audiit Eurotas *iussit*que ediscere laurus,
ille canit (pulsae referunt ad sidera valles),
cogere donec oves stabulis numerumque referre
iussit et invito processit Vesper Olympo.

(82-86; my italics)

[Indeed, he gave them all the songs that once upon a time Eurotas, happy river, heard from Phoebus' lips and bade his laurels get by heart. All these Silenus sang. The music struck the valleys and the valleys tossed it to the stars—till the lads were warned [bade] to drive home and to count their sheep, by Vesper, as he trod unwelcome into the listening sky.]

We are, I think, referred back to Virgil's "non iniussa cano" of the introduction in this concluding focus on two different bids—the bid received by the river's laurels, and by implication Silenus, to sing all the songs Eurotas heard Apollo sing; and the much more limited bid received by the two shepherd boys simply to return and count their flocks. The conclusion of the sixth eclogue, then, focusses on what has been implicitly its subject all along, the limitations of pastoral and the desire for greater things. Suggested in the ambivalent disavowal of heroic ambitions in the introduction, the theme is embodied in the very form of Virgil's song. We never hear Silenus sing, and this is a crucial point. We are given merely an account of what was sung, and perhaps of what Virgil might sing; but an account is all we have, and is all we can have within the limitations of the pastoral form. The vast scope of Silenus' song, its myriad subjects, cannot be compressed within pastoral; they do not fit. The shepherd boys, like the pastoral itself, can only awaken the poet to greater things; they do not repeat Phoebus' song, and are bade to return to the much more limited world where sheep are counted, and the much more limited form in which they (and Virgil–Gallus) may make the valleys with their song Apollo's pride but yet may not with their music reach the stars. The concluding contrast between the narrow limits the shepherd boys must accept and the cosmic freedom Silenus has, his songs echoing to the stars, is, then, a contrast between the smaller things of pastoral and the greater things Virgil awaits the bid for, and strains toward in this poem: greater theme, greater scope, greater argument. Gallus and the shepherd boys thus serve to define Virgil's ambivalence toward pastoral, its greatness and its limitations. In terms of the poem's figures, Virgil-Gallus awaits the bid to become Virgil-Silenus; and until that bid comes, we will not hear Silenus sing.

In Virgil, pastoral is aware of its limits and strains against them; so, too, after him. Calpurnius' Corydon expresses the commonplace pastoral longing for greater things:

carmina iam dudum, non quae nemorale resultent,
volvimus, o Meliboee; sed haec, quibus aurea possint
saecula cantari, quibus et deus ipse canatur,
qui populos urbesque regit pacemque togatam.

(IV. 5-8)[9]

[For long, Meliboeus, have I been pondering verses, verses of no woodland ring but fit to celebrate the golden age, to praise even that very god who is sovereign over nations and cities and toga-clad peace.]

But Meliboeus, speaking to the decorum that both justifies and depreciates pastoral, reminds Corydon of the limits of pastoral, that "the divinities of mighty Rome are not to be extolled in the same style as the sheepfold of Menalcas" (10-11). This same ranking of genres, in which pastoral always comes out at the bottom of the totem pole, induces Renaissance pastoralists, too, to speak disparagingly about the unworthiness of the pastoral style. As a result, we have Boiardo, for example, as Orfeo in the tenth eclogue, claiming that the high fountain between Cyrra and Nysa is not enough for the undertaking he has in mind; his matter goes beyond the pastoral customs of singing, and he must sing "with better voice and verses in another style"; epic, of course, and he goes on to *Orlando Innamorato*. So, too, Garcilaso asks Maria not to disdain "this coarse aspect of my style" (III. 35-36) and to listen to "the humble sound of my coarse pipes" (42), though he adds the common apology that

. . . a las veces son mejor oídos
el puro ingenio y lengua casi muda,
testigos limpios de ánimo inocente,
que la curiosidad del elocuente.

(45-48)

9. Citations from Calpurnius Siculus are to *Minor Latin Poets*, Loeb Classical Library, ed. and trans. J. Wight Duff and Arnold M. Duff (London, 1934).

[at times it is better to hear the pure mind and almost silent tongue, honest witnesses of the innocent soul, than the elaborateness of the eloquent.]

And in his dedication of his first eclogue to Don Pedro de Toledo, Garcilaso promises that when he has the leisure, he will be able to offer a work more worthy of the fame and glory of the hero; epic, of course:

luego verás ejercitar mi pluma
por la infinita innumerable suma
de tus virtudes y famosas obras.

(I. 24-26)

[then you will see my pen exercised for the infinite, innumerable sum of your virtues and famous deeds.]

As much as the Renaissance admired pastoral poetry, as much as it praised its naturalness and simplicity, it was at the same time aware that the aspiring poet, like the great men celebrated in and by pastoral, deserved and required a higher style, a greater argument. Pastoral is, then, repeatedly aiming at something greater, at ascending the scale of generic progression: from pastoral, Petrarch goes on to the *Africa,* Boiardo to *Orlando Innamorato,* Ariosto to *Orlando Furioso,* Sannazaro to *De Partu Virginis,* Spenser to the *Faerie Queene,* and similarly "diuers other excellent both Italian and French Poetes." From this same impulse ultimately comes, in the Renaissance, the expansion of pastoral into the larger forms of epic (or something akin to epic)—the Arcadias of Sannazaro, Lope, and Sidney, for example, or the *Diana* of Montemayor, or even the sixth book of the *Faerie Queene*—and drama, Poliziano's *Orfeo,* for example, or Tasso's *Aminta,* Guarini's *Il Pastor Fido,* Peele's *Arraignment of Paris.*

If pastoral is ambivalent in its attitude toward the world of greater things, it is ambivalent too in its attitude toward the lowly rustic life. The pastoral poet is, after all, a city man, not a country man; consequently, he looks at rustic life with a characteristic admixture of sentimentality and comic irony. Whereas the urban poet promotes the sentimental illusion that the innocence of the rustic enables him to appreciate things unperceived by the more sophisticated and cultivated eye of the urbanite, at the same time the poet is often deflating the illusion, portraying this innocence as a naiveté comically incapable of perceiving and adapting to the complexities of experience. Rejection provides the context for one of the more common comic situations

of rustic life, the naive self-praise of the unrequited shepherd. Rejection forces the shepherd into a situation in which, to our own detached
perspective, the shepherd is comically naive in the lack of self-con-
sciousness in which he examines himself. Try as he will, the shepherd
cannot see himself as others see him; like Virgil's Corydon, for example, in the second eclogue:

"despectus tibi sum nec, qui sim, quaeris, Alexi,
quam dives pecoris, nivei quam lactis abundans:
mille meae Siculis errant in montibus agnae;
lac mihi non aestate novum, non frigore defit.
canto, quae solitus, si quando armenta vocabat,
Amphion Dircaeus in Actaeo Aracyntho.
nec sum adeo informis: nuper me in litore vidi,
cum placidum ventis staret mare; non ego Daphnim
iudice te metuam, si numquam fallit imago."

(19-27)

["Alex, you despise me. You do not even ask what sort of man I am,
what flocks I may possess, how rich I am in snowy milk. Yet a thousand
lambs of mine range Sicilian hills; summer and winter I have fresh
milk in plenty.
  "And I can sing, as once upon a time Theban Amphion used to
sing when he was calling home the cows on Attic Aracynthus.
  "Nor am I as ill-favoured as all that. Down by the sea the other
day, I saw myself reflected when the dying wind had left the water
calm. You could compare me even with Daphnis, and I should have
no fears—if mirrors do not lie."]

We are charmed as Nemesianus' rejected Alcon muses in hurt bewilderment how Donace could conceivably reject so much. Like Corydon, he too is a lover of the pleasing images he imagines himself
to possess: "the radiance of my cheeks, the milky neck, the laughter
in my eyes and the comeliness of my manhood" (II. 80-81).[10] Caught
up in his emotions, the rustic lover from Theocritus on cannot view
himself and his state objectively. Disoriented by love, Theocritus'
Bucaeus, for example, attempting to defend the depth of his passion
to the elder Milon, childishly remarks: "But I've been in love, Milon,
the better part of ten days."[11] We smile, and at his expense; we
smile also at the singing matches in which one shepherd vies with
another in a childish fashion to see who has more wealth, who gives

10. Citation from Nemesianus is to *Minor Latin Poets* (London, 1934).
11. Citations from Theocritus are to *The Greek Bucolic Poets*, ed. and trans.
J. M. Edmonds, rev. ed. (London, 1928).

the better gifts (lizards or oak leaves), who has the better voice, and so on. We smile, too, at the verbal fisticuffs of the combatants as they remark cattily on the bugs in the opponent's location and the skinniness of his flock. Ironic and sentimental perspectives coexist, as we at once realize the limitations of the shepherd and his charm. In a work like *Daphnis and Chloe,* in fact, the tension between these two perspectives provides almost the whole basis for its appeal; as we observe with combined admiration and amusement, the two rustics move from innocent groping attempts at sex—what Longus calls, with the condescending affection of the urbanite looking on, "mere pastoral play"[12]—to the real thing. Longus clearly finds value in the naturalness and simplicity of the bucolic world; for when his characters have discovered their respectable higher birth, he has them remain for most of their lives in the pastoral world. But this pastoral world is by no means all-sufficient. Indeed, Longus' portrayal of Daphnis and Chloe is often at the expense of the real rustic world: the two characters as children "revealed a beauty more exquisite than became shepherds," and when Chloe doffs her pastoral gear for city clothes she appears "so much handsomer to everyone that even Daphnis scarcely recognized her"; and of course they are both given proper, that is, urban, parents. Longus thus takes a relatively balanced view of the merits of urban and rustic life: the city may be the home of a pederast like Gnathon, but it is also the residence of kind benefactors and masters; the country may afford a more natural and simple life, but it also lacks—sometimes comically, sometimes crassly—the refinement of the city. Daphnis and Chloe must go to the city to mature, to rid themselves of a naiveté that while comic is nonetheless limiting; and returning to the world of their childhood, they return as something more than shepherds, and more than children.

In its comedy and sentimentality, in its straining to break its own bonds to attach itself to, or progress to, greater things, pastoral manifests an ambivalence, a tension between opposing values. This ambivalence is perhaps even more obvious in Renaissance pastoral than in classical pastoral; for the issues involved in pastoral—art and nature, the active life and the contemplative life, complexity and simplicity—were possibly even more acute then than in classical times. I would like to conclude this discussion on the ambivalence of Arcadian pas-

---

12. Longus, *Daphnis and Chloe,* in *Three Greek Romances,* trans. Moses Hadas (New York, 1953; repr. 1964).

toral by focusing on two exemplary Renaissance works, Sannazaro's *Arcadia* and Garcilaso's second eclogue.

No better example can be found than Sannazaro's *Arcadia* of the difficulty the Renaissance poet had in reconciling the idealizations of pastoral with both the real pastoral world and his own aspiration for greater things. The work opens with all the sentimental clichés justifying pastoral, that its naturalness and simplicity please more than "refined verses on the smooth papers of gilded books"; and goes on to disclaim ambition for greater things:

> Onde io, se licito mi fusse, più mi terrei a gloria di porre la mia bocca a la umile fistula di Coridone, datagli per adietro da Dameta in caro duono, che a la sonora tibia di Pallade . . .
>
> (Proemio)

> [Wherefore, I, if it were allowed me, would hold it a greater glory to set my mouth to the humble reed of Corydon, given him as a costly gift by Damoetas, than to the sounding pipe of Pallas.][13]

The commonplace defense; and yet, as everyone knows, Renaissance thinking is often uncertain about the relationship of nature and art.[14] To commit oneself to nature may lead to praiseworthy innocence and simplicity, but it may also lead to rustic rudeness or worse, to man's loss of his position in the hierarchy superior to nature's and thus to a failure to fulfill his function of improving nature. To ally oneself with nature may make of one a divine innocent or a foolish beast. It is hardly surprising, therefore, to find Sincero–Sannazaro longing for the nobility of Naples from which he is exiled and identifying Arcadia as a world fit for beasts, not men:

> Massimamente ricordandomi in questa fervida adolescenzia de' piaceri de la deliciosa patria, tra queste solitudini di Arcadia, ove, con vostra pace il dirò, non che i giovani ne le nobili città nodriti, ma appena mi si lascia credere che le selvatiche bestie vi possano con diletto dimorare.
>
> (VII)

> [Above all I remember in this fervid adolescence the pleasures of my delicious homeland, among these solitudes of Arcadia, where, by your leave I will say it, I can scarcely believe that wild beasts, much less youths brought up in the noble city, can dwell with pleasure.]

13. Citations from Sannazaro's *Arcadia* are to *Opere di Jacapo Sannazaro*, ed. Enrico Carrara (Torino, 1952). My translation.

14. A good discussion of this and related points is that of E. W. Tayler, *Nature and Art in Reniassance Literature* (New York, 1964), especially pp. 11-37.

Even in Sannazaro's Arcadia—which is as idealized as any with its perpetual games, picturesque sights, and simple rural joys—the shadow of bestiality, man's avoiding a loftier mission, casts its darkness on the pastoral world. Sincero's opinions are echoed by Carino, who like Sincero has retired from urban life to cure himself of love and who also looks ultimately to a return to the city:

> Con la quale spero che, se da li Fati non ti è tolto, con più alto stile canterai gli amori di Fauni e di Nimfe nel futuro. E sì come insino qui i principii de la tua adolescenzia hai tra semplici e boscarecci canti di pastori infruttuosamente dispesi, così per lo inanzi la felice giovenezza tra sonore trombe di poeti chiarissimi del tuo secolo, non senza speranza di eterna fama trapasserai.
>
> (VII)

> [With this I hope that, if it is not prevented by the Fates, you will in the future sing in a loftier style the loves of Fauns and Nymphs. And if up till now you have fruitlessly spent the beginnings of your adolescence among the simple and rural songs of the shepherds, from now on you will pass your fortunate youth among the sounding trumpets of the brightest poets of your age, not without hope of eternal fame.]

The ambivalent attitude of the *Arcadia* toward the values of the pastoral and nonpastoral worlds is repeated in the parting address of Sincero to his sampogna. Though he himself is leaving Arcadia, Sincero repeats to his sampogna all of the sentimental arguments in defense of pastoral both as a poetic mode and as a way of life. The sampogna is "worthy because of [its] lowness," and should feel fortunate not to have to go seeking "the shadowy favors, or the windy glories, most vain cajolery, false enticements, stupid and obvious adulations of the fickle mob"; its "humble sound" would ill be heard among the "royal trumpets." His last words are merely Horatian chestnuts:

> Conciosiacosa che chi non sale, non teme di cadere; e chi cade nel piano, il che rare volte adiviene, con pícciolo agiuto de la propria mano senza danno si rileva. Onde per cosa vera et indubitata tener ti puoi, che chi più di nascoso e più lontano de la moltitudine vive, miglior vive; e colui tra' mortali si può con più verità chiamar beato, che senza invidia de la altrui grandezze, con modesta animo de la sua fortuna si contenta.

[Inasmuch as he who does not climb does not fear falling, and he who falls on the plain, which rarely happens, lifts himself up with his own hand with little assistance and with little injury, you can take it as an unquestionable truth that he who lives more hidden and apart from the multitude lives better; and that man who lives without envy of the greatness of others and who in modest spirit is content with his fortune, can most truly call himself blessed among mortals.]

Sincero's sentimental defense of his abandoned friend is pathetic but only partly convincing. This is only part of the story; we have heard him and Carino speak on this matter before. But even here in his sentimental parting, ambivalence emerges from Sincero's apology for pastoral lowness. If, he says, the sampogna feels it must defend itself, then let it remember that it was made by a man who came into Arcadia "not as a rustic shepherd but as a highly cultivated young man"; and almost in the same breath he adds that "in other times there have already been shepherds so bold that they have advanced their style even to the ears of Roman Consuls." In Sannazaro, the tension between pastoral and nonpastoral, nature and artifice, primitivism and civilization is never finally resolved. With Sincero at once idealizing the primitive and labeling it bestial, at once denouncing the city and yet longing to return to it, at once urging pastoral simplicity upon the sampogna and praising himself as a cultivated man, the attitudes in the *Arcadia* remain quite openly contradictory. Indeed this contradiction is embodied in the very development and structure of the work itself. Not just Sincero, but the *Arcadia* itself moves from pastoral at the beginning to epic at the end. In the tenth prose section, Sincero and his shepherd friends discover hanging from a pine tree a large seven-piped sampogna which, as Enareto explains, is the instrument made by Pan, passed on to Theocritus and then to Virgil; but Virgil, having by nature a mind disposed to "higher things" (*più alte cose*) and not contenting himself with "so humble a sound," replaced one of the pipes with a larger pipe in order to sing of "greater things" (*le cose maggiori*) and to make the forests "worthy of the highest consuls of Rome." That pipe is, of course, the pipe of Virgil's fourth eclogue, in which Virgil, who was later to show how far the pastoral poet himself could go (to georgic and epic), attempted a higher style worthy of greater things and in so doing took pastoral itself as far as it could go. This section on pastoral orders the entire conclusion of the *Arcadia,* as the remainder of the work strains increasingly to encompass, and its prospective epic poet, Sincero–Sannazaro, to experience, "le cose maggiori." Enareto's description of how he will effect Clonico's cure in love—how he will call the gods "in the high heavens, on the wide earth and in the rolling sea; and the most exalted Oceanus, universal father of all things," "the dark kingdoms of the underground gods . . . the triple Hecate . . . deep Chaos, most powerful Erebus and the infernal Eumenides, inhabitants of the Stygian waters"—bursts far beyond the confines of Arcadia and pastoral; and resembles, to my mind at any rate, the similar bursting forth into mythic and cosmic matter in Virgil's sixth eclogue. This breaking of the bonds of pastoral, manifested in the work itself with the imitation of the funeral games of the *Aeneid* (Book V), which takes up section eleven, and Sincero's Virgilian-Dantesque descent into the underworld, which takes up section twelve, is manifested as well in the poet-hero's own separation from Arcadia and his return to the city. Listening to Selvaggio's description of the Sebeto ("il mio napolitano Tevere") and Chalcis (home of the founders of Naples) brings to Sincero's mind once again memory of "the magnificence of my noble and most generous homeland," its "abundant treasures," "honored people," "high towers, rich temples, proud palaces"; and his descent into the underworld, rich with reminiscences of the *Aeneid* and the *Inferno,* ultimately concludes with a vision of the god of the Sebeto and of Barcinio lamenting the fate of Naples, "your Naples is no longer Naples." The progress from pastoral to epic concludes for the work as for its hero where it must, in the city. Sannazaro's *Arcadia,* like its hero, moves into Arcadia that it may ultimately move out of Arcadia, to the city and to epic, in its final sections straining toward, reaching toward, both of these, encompassing in the pastoral mode the very promise of "le cose maggiore" for which the mode must be abandoned.

The tension between the ambivalent countermovement of pastoral into Arcadia and out of it, from lesser things to greater, does not seem to me ever finally resolved in Sannazaro's work; primarily because it continues to present, unmodified, the stock pastoral clichés while at the same time, from as early as the seventh section, the work itself and its hero are clearly headed in a direction contradicting all these clichés. Garcilaso in his second eclogue escapes this contradiction (as do Sidney, Shakespeare and other Renaissance pastorialists) by reducing the pastoral idea to a cliché which neither we nor the poet fully accepts. We are aware from the beginning of the work that the voice of conventional pastoral wisdom, Salicio's, is hardly entirely credible. When we first encounter Salicio, he is wandering in a forest paraphrasing Horace's "beatus ille":

¡Cuán bienaventurado
aquel puede llamarse
que con la dulce soledad se abraza,
y vive descuidado,
y lejos de emparcharse
en lo que al alma impide y embaraza!

(38-43)

[How blessed the man can consider himself who embraces sweet solitude and lives without care, far from being disturbed by whatever impedes and interferes with the soul!]

Salicio's literary man of pastoral contemplation, like Sannazaro's sampogna, disdains the false pursuits of ambition and gold, "baja y vil," for the true pleasures of "dulce sueño" and of nature; correspondingly, for Salicio the nonpastoral world, the world of the court, is portrayed conventionally as a world for flatterers, insecure and at the mercy of fortune. It is a sweet picture, this simple contrast of peace and frenzy, and some pastoral literature might leave it at that. But Garcilaso's vision is more sophisticated, and Salicio's pretty moralizing is not the final word on the matter. Salicio is ironically unaware that, while he is celebrating the carefree nature of the pastoral world into which he has withdrawn, the disturbed and troubled Albanio, who has lain himself down to die, is sleeping only a few feet away. Hearing the sound of the hidden figure breathing, Salicio takes his cue and begins another of his windy apostrophes, this time to sleep: sleep that relaxes the tensions of mind and desire, sleep that makes the body sane and quiets the agonies of the heart. Beautiful commonplaces, but naive, divorced from reality: Albanio ironically sleeps in the hope of death, and when he awakens he is, rather than being rested, near madness. Salicio is thus portrayed ambivalently, and the same is true of the pastoral and moral commonplaces he represents. His conventional wisdom is a bit like Polonius': adequate perhaps for the normal, everyday world but inadequate, sometimes ludicrously so, when applied to the abnormal world of Albanio's passion. Like Polonius, too, he likes the sound of his wisdom, is generous with his windy and pompous moralizing. It is not so much that his wisdom is false, but that it is inappropriate and incomplete; his pastoral idealization, somewhat like Hobbinol's in a similar confrontation in "June," are naively irrelevant. "Salicio amigo, cese este lenguaje; / cierra tu boca," orders Albanio (392-393), "Salicio, friend, cease this rambling; shut your mouth," and the reproach is not undeserved. By portraying Salicio in this fashion, Garcilaso has effectively established limitations on the universal verity of pastoral truth. The partly ironic portrayal of Salicio does not permit idealization, and Salicio's version of pastoral does not, therefore, become the exclusive ethic of the work as it contradictorily does and does not in Sannazaro. Consequently, when Garcilaso, like Sannazaro, takes his work beyond pastoral things to a lengthy and laudatory account at the end of the epic deeds of Don García de Toledo, Don Fadrique, and Don Fernando, it is not epic contradiction of pastoral fact. Pastoral and epic exist side by side in the same work, as two equally justified aspects of life and truth, neither necessarily excluding the other.

Pastoral, therefore, is something other than, more than the simplistic apotheosis of pastoral life and the disparagement of the world of greater things; for there is in pastoral, as I have attempted to show, a multiform ambivalence. Pastoral mode and experience are celebrated as humble and natural; they are also disparaged as low and unworthy, existing as they do under the shadow of the heroic and the poet's own hope for greater things. Rusticity is one side of the coin, rudeness the other; similarly contrasted are naturalness and bestiality, innocence and naiveté. Pastoral can acknowledge the virtues of conquerors; it can even on occasion, as in Boiardo's tenth eclogue and Garcilaso's second, actually assimilate epic events and style; it can celebrate cities, rulers, men of action, and all the rest that we ordinarily conceive of as opposed to pastoral. Pastoral has, at least potentially, a considerable power of discrimination between disparate values. The country life has certain virtues; it has other disadvantages. The city life may incorporate more vice, but it is also more cultivated and more grand; it may cause the hardship of dispossession but then it also has the power to give us "haec otia." Pastoral can lament the fact of war, and yet at the same time praise men in the field of action. It can idealize the naturalness and simplicity of the shepherd, and simultaneously expose the naive limitations of his conception of himself and sometimes ours of him. From the beginnings, then, when Theocritus first cloaked his rustics with literary clothing, pastoral has manifested a recognition, implicit or explicit, of a plurality of values.

In some important respects, what has been said of Arcadian pastoral applies as well to Mantuanesque pastoral—and not surprisingly, since Virgil was the chief model for Mantuan as he was for Sannazaro. Mantuanesque pastoral is not a separate entity unto itself, but rather a branch from the main stalk of pastoral. Like Arcadian pastoral, Mantuanesque pastoral involves a counterpointing of disparate values, and it, too, is constantly concerned with the nonpastoral world of the city, court, and church. Indeed, perhaps even more than Theocritus, Virgil, or Lope, the Mantuanesque pastoralists testify to the fact that pastoral is at least as much "about" nonpastoral life as it is "about" pastoral life. Similarities, then, there are; but there are also, as I suggested at the opening of this chapter, important differences: the pastoral ideal is different, not *pastor felix* but *pastor bonus,* and it is also more rigid; as a result, pastoral life is portrayed in an almost uncompromising opposition with the life of the city and court. As an instrument of Christian polemics, pastoral's sense of multivalence, its tension in opposition, is transmuted into simplistic Christian conflict of good and evil.

The distinction I am trying to draw here is especially reflected in the different portrayals of the urban world. Arcadian pastoral of course uses pastoral as a means whereby the city can be criticized, but, while the city may be the locus of misplaced values and frustration from which the urbanite must retire to be cured, it is still the world to which he returns. In Mantuanesque pastoral, the city takes on Christian implications of the World, and all that that image suggests from Augustine to Bunyan. Mantuan, for example, devotes his sixth eclogue to a polemical attack on the vices of the city, its corrupt pursuit of gold, worldly ambition, and fleshly pleasures: "(Pray) where is whoredome usde, / manslaughter and uprore?" asks Cornix (VI. 165); and the answer is not simply the city, but the mutable city of man, the World. Of course Rome, as we see in the ninth eclogue, is for Mantuan the chief example of urban worldliness preying on virtue:

19

Hoc est Roma viris avibus quod noctua: trunco
insidet et tamquam volucrum regina superbis
nutibus a longe plebem vocat. inscia fraudis
turba coit, grandes oculos mirantur et aures,
turpe caput rostrique minacis acumen aduncum;
dumque super virgulta agile feruntur
nunc huc, nunc illuc, aliis vestigia filum
illaqueat, retinent alias lita vimina visco,
praedaque sunt omnes veribus torrenda salignis.

(IX. 120-128)

[Rome is to men as the birds
    the Owle with visage wide,
She sits upon a flocke,
    and like a stately Queene
With loftie becks she cals a farre
    the Birds that nie hir beene.
The route suspecting nought
    togither come apace,
They maruell at his picked eares
    and gastly glewing face,
And at hir Monstrous head
    and crooked bending byll:
While thus (I say) they hoppe about
    not mynding any yll,
From spring to spring, from bough
    to bough, from tree to tree,
Some threaded are with limed lace,
    with twigs some other bee
Ycaught: thus all as pray
    unto the Broach do goe.][15]

Rome, instead of leading man from this world, ensnares him in it
(it may be significant, in this respect, that the owl is often symbolic
of Satan). Barnabe Googe also portrays the city as the locus of ensnar-
ing "Vice [which] hath euery place posseste, / and Vertue thence
is flowne" (III);[16] but by far the most astringent attack on the city
and the court is in Alexander Barclay's three eclogues, based on the
Miseriae Curialium of Aeneas Sylvius. Containing an absolutely fan-
tastic array of vices, the urban world is repeatedly portrayed as Hell.

15. Citations from Mantuan in the original are to *The Eclogues of Baptista
Mantuanus*, ed. Mustard; and in translation, to *The Eclogues of Mantuan*, trans.
George Turbervile (1567), ed. Douglas Bush (New York, 1937).
16. Citations from Barnabe Googe are to *Eglogs, Epytaphes, and Sonettes* (1563),
ed. Edward Arber (London, 1910).

It is "the bayting place of Hell" (I. 586), "an ymage infernall, / Without fayre paynted, within vggly and vile" (I. 1260-1261), and is the dwelling place of the false gods of lust, ambition, and avarice (I. 477-481, 877-878; II. 569-570, 572-578). Barclay, in fact, goes so far as to identify the court and city with "all sin," the Flesh, the World, and the Devil. There are, Cornix claims, five lures of the court:

> The first is honour, I tolde thee of this same,
> The seconde is laude, hye name or worldly fame,
> The thirde is power might or aucthoritie,
> The fourth is riches chiefe roote of dignitie,
> The fifte is pleasour, lust and voluptuousnes.[17]

(I. 643-647)

These lures correspond to a familiar pattern in medieval and Renaissance theology and art, the triple temptations or the inclusive triad of vices, variously formulated but usually gluttony or *concupiscentia carnis*, avarice, and vainglory.[18] These were the Devil's three lures which he used to tempt the First Adam and the Second Adam, and which he uses to tempt all men (the connection to all men was made through I John 2:16, "For all that is in the world, the lust of the flesh, the lust of the eyes, and the pride of life, is not of the Father, but is of the world"). Barclay's first two lures—worldly honor and praise or fame—accord with *vanagloria*. The third and fourth, authority and riches, accord with *avaritia;* for as Gregory claimed, along with a host of theologians and Chaucer's Pardoner, "Avarice is not only for money but also for high station."[19] The fifth lure is of course *concupiscentia carnis*. The entire structure of Cornix's tirade against the city, from I. 850 to II. 1062, is in fact organized around this inclusive triad of vices: *vanagloria*, I. 850-910 (a continuation

17. Citations from Alexander Barclay are to *The Eclogues of Alexander Barclay* (c. 1515), ed. Beatrice White (London, 1928).

18. The pervasiveness of this pattern has been demonstrated by Elizabeth Marie Pope, *"Paradise Regained": The Tradition and the Poem* (New York, 1947), pp. 51-69 *et passim*, and by Donald R. Howard, *The Three Temptations* (Princeton, 1966), pp. 41-75 *et passim*. The triad also plays an important role in the first two books of the *Faerie Queene*. See Samuel C. Chew, "Spenser's Pageant of the Seven Deadly Sins," in *Studies in Art and Literature for Belle da Costa Greene* (Princeton, 1954), p. 46, and *The Pilgrimage of Life* (New Haven, 1962), ch. 4; Robert M. Durling, "The Bower of Bliss and Armida's Palace," *CL*, 6 (1954), 337-338; and my own "Guyon *Microchristus*," to be published in *English Literary History* (*ELH*) in 1970.

19. Gregorius Magnus, *XL homiliarum in evangelia, Patrologia latina* (*PL*), 76:1136. This is the classic text.

of the discussion of I. 457-492); *avaritia,* I. 911-1076 (*avaritia alti-tudinis*), I. 1087–1308 (*avaritia pecuniae*); and *concupiscentia carnis,* II. 1-1062. In making the connection between the city and the Flesh, the World, and the Devil, Barclay to be sure out-Mantuans Mantuan, but the connection testifies to how far the impulse of Christian moralism could take this kind of pastoral away from the generally more balanced criticism of the mainstream of pastoral.

The same *contemptus mundi* which colors Mantuanesque pastoral's perspective on the city and court colors as well its perpective on love, so different from that found in Arcadian pastoral. While the portrayal of love in Arcadian pastoral is extremely diverse—delicacy of sentiment juxtaposed to brute physicality, unrequited love to requited love, boy-love to girl-love, for example—love, though often a cruel god, is almost always accepted as a normal and necessary part of experience. As Hallett Smith remarks, "Pastoral emphasizes the irrationality of love . . . but there is no blame imputed to anyone for falling in love. It is irrational but unavoidable."[20] Shepherds are sometimes advised to leave their love, but that is not because love per se is wrong but because that particular love is frustrating or *indignus.* The tragedy that involves, or threatens to involve, Sincero, Carino, Tasso's Aminta, or Garcilaso's Albanio, as they are led to madness, despair, or suicide, occurs outside the moral arena. From Theocritus' Comatas to Tasso's Aminta, ordinarily more love, not less, is the solution to the problem of love in Arcadian pastoral: "There is no drug for Eros—nothing to drink or to swallow and no spells to chant—but only kisses and embraces and lying together with naked bodies";[21] and the golden age was golden, says Tasso's famous chorus, not for rivers running with milk but because Honor, "idol d'inganno,"

> Che di nostra natura il feo tiranno,
> Non mischiava il suo affano
> Fra le liete dolcezze
> De l'amoroso gregge.[22]

(I. ii)

[which became a tyrant over our nature, did not mix its affliction with the happy pleasures of the amorous flock.]

20. Hallett Smith, *Elizabethan Poetry* (Cambridge, Mass., 1952), p. 17.
21. Longus, *Daphnis and Chloe,* in *Three Greek Romances,* p. 22.
22. Citations from Tasso's *Aminta* are to the volume edited by Pia Piccoli Addoli (Milan: Rizzoli, 1955). My translation.

The attitudes toward love in Arcadian pastoral are, for the most part, precisely those that Mantuanesque pastoral repudiates. Mantuanesque pastoral agrees with Arcadian pastoral on one point, love is irrational; but from this initial agreement, it reaches antierotic conclusions very much at odds with the mainstream of pastoral. Underlying the Mantuanesque attitude toward love is the fear that love, since it involves a loss of reason, is an instrument of the devil, seducing man through woman-Eve into error and sin. Even in Mantuan's first eclogue, which concerns Faustus' lawful and supposedly happy love, love is seen as "aliquis daemon" deceiving the senses and dulling the eyes: "Love . . . blinds the senses sore, / it guiles the gazing eyes"; "Love is not as they say / A heavenly God, but bitter gall, / and errour from the way" (I. 48-52). The next two eclogues, which tell the tale of Amyntas' tragic and lawless love, provide a moral exemplum for Fortunatus' point that "A hatefull thing is Love" (II. 167). Love is seen not as a force refining man, as it is in Tasso's *Aminta,* where in the prologue Amore states, "I will inspire noble feelings in rude breasts," but instead as a Circean force that "makst us brutish seeme to sight": "What cuppe of *Circes,* or *Calipso* / So might with this compare?" (III. 158-159). The danger of love is that *sensus* takes supremacy over *mens,* and consequently man is led into sin and becomes a bad shepherd. Love must be avoided "If you will have / your Cattle well to fare" (IV. 173), concludes Alphus, after having told the tale of how a sheepboy abandons his flock through love of a woman, and after having gone into a polemical attack against women as "Vile, greedy, catching, quareling aye / and strouting full of hate" (IV. 126). The antierotic, antifeminist impulse behind Mantuan's pastorals culminates in the seventh eclogue. Pollux, a love-sick youth, is told by the Virgin Mary in a vision of the two paths he may take, the path of pleasure which leads to Hell and the path of religion and virtue which leads to Heaven. The youth awakes, cured of his secular love, and turns to the cloister and *amor dei.*

Mantuan's distrust of love and pleasure as powers seducing man away from reason, responsibility to the flock, and eternal things is featured even more prominently in Googe's eclogues, all but one of which portray the folly of love and youth. As in Mantuan's seventh eclogue, the love of "fickle fadynge forme" leads the soul to lose "the Skyes aboue" and gain Hell instead. Speaking from the flames of Hell, Dametas in the fourth eclogue points the obvious moral:

> A fonde Affection lead me then,
>   When I for God dyd place,
> A Creature, cause of all my Care,
>   a flesshye fletynge face.

The eighth and final eclogue provides the inevitable culmination of the antieroticism underlying Googe's collection of eclogues. It focuses on the Augustinian opposition found in the previous eclogues between true love, *caritas* and *amor dei,* and false love, *amor concupiscentiae.*[23] in other words, the opposition between the good shepherd of Christian love and the bad shepherd of worldly love. Calling all men to repentance, Cornix implores shepherds to replace the false god of love, Cupid, with the true God of love. Where should man's love be placed, where but in Him who gave and asks nothing but love?: "I aske no more but onely loue," says Christ, but man, loving lesser things, forces Christ to "turne awaye [His] eyes." For the youth who foolishly "Pleasure makes his Mariner" and sails "the seas of sin," "Contynuall torment . . . awaytes":

> Loe. This the end, of euery suche
>   as here lyues lustylye
> Neglectyng God thou seest, in vyce.
>   do lyue. in syn do dye.

The moral upon which this final eclogue concludes might well be the epigraph for the entire series: it epitomizes the Pauline attitude towards the flesh and "womens loue," the stark opposition of this world and the next, of *amor mundi* and *amor dei,* of the bad shepherd and the good shepherd, that pervade Googe's eclogues.

Mantuanesque pastoral, influenced as it was by the medieval *contemptus mundi,* has, then, at best a parenthetical and begrudging tolerance of love. It may concede, as does the antierotic *senex* Amintas in Googe's first eclogue that

> rather wolde I (thoo it be muche)
> that thou shuldest seeke the fyre,
> Of lawfull Loue, that I have tolde,
> than burne wyth suche desyre,

23. See, for example, Augustine, *Ennaratio in Psalmum,* XXXI, ii. 5, *PL,* 36:260; or CXXII, i, *PL,* 37:1629.

but this is a parenthesis which is minor in the overall context of Mantuanesque antierotic polemics. It is more likely to be said instead, as does Googe's Silvanus, "Gyue ouer pleasures now, / Let neuer Ioye the please" (VII). Whereas one of the main concerns of Mantuanesque pastoral is to restrain eroticism, one of the central, if not *the* central concern of Arcadian pastoral is to satisfy it. Correspondingly, Arcadian pastoral, in the Renaissance especially, exists in praise of woman and the joys of satisfied love, and its ideal in love is generally a kind of impassioned delicacy of feeling worthy of woman. Mantuanesque pastoral, on the other hand, is astringently antifeminist. The vice of woman in Mantuanesque pastoral is that she is too unchaste, too unreluctant, too "salax" (Mantuan, IV. 130); whereas in Arcadian pastoral her vice, more often than not, is not that she is of the devil's party but of Diana's.

Mantuanesque pastoral thus takes pastoral's criticism of the city and transmutes it into an attack on the life of the World, takes pastoral's portrayal of the irrationality of love and transmutes it into a contrast of secular love and Christian love, takes pastoral's tension of values and transmutes it into a vices-and-virtues antagonism. Pastoral's criticism of values and its reforming impulse are modified according to the polemical and doctrinal interests of Mantuanesque pastoral, the interest that man may be "saued by councell sapient / Out of hell mouth and manyfolde torment" (Barclay, II. 1367-1368). Poggioli's observation, therefore, that the shepherd is "obsessed by neither temptation nor guilt," that he "is free from the sense of sin,"[24] while largely true of the mainstream of pastoral, simply does not hold for Mantuanesque pastoral, which perceives the world as an unceasing combat between virtue and vice, *mens* and *sensus,* pastoral and nonpastoral. Whereas the Arcadian tradition creates, or attempts to create, a world in which man's instincts and desire for *otium* can be satisfied, Mantuanesque pastoral creates a largely predatory world from which only religion and eternity promise relief: the city, the court, Eros, all are instruments of the devil preying upon man, luring him to the loss of his soul; and against these vices there can be no ambivalence. While the *otium* of Arcadian pastoral stipulates a retreat from the arena, Mantuanesque pastoral has merely substituted one arena for another, the arena of Christian combat for the arena of secular society. Seeing the world as it does, as a constant

24. Poggioli, *HLB,* 11 (1957), 153.

testing-ground for the soul, Mantuanesque pastoral identifies the Arcadian pastoral ideal of the soft life, of the easy indulgence of the senses, the surcease from toil, as a temptation to the pastoral life. In Mantuanesque pastoral there is no room for Arcadia.

The pastoral tradition Spenser inherited was thus divided in its vision. To pastoral had graviated many of the crucial and unresolved conflicts of Renaissance thinking: nature and art, otherworldliness and secularism, Christianity and paganism, reason and emotion. Not only was pastoral a vehicle for these divisions in thinking, it was itself marked by that division. This division in pastoral is, I believe, the proper starting point for any analysis of the *Calender*. The work is not an exposition of a single pastoral perspective, though it has often been made to seem that way; it is instead a critique of pastoral, through a confrontation of conflicting pastoral perspectives.

That, at any rate, is the assumption upon which chapter 1 will operate. The first section will take up the function of the moral debates as, largely, a dramatic pitting together of versions of the Mantuanesque and Arcadian pastoral perspectives. The second will examine the contending attitudes towards love in terms of the tragic and comic polarities of portrayal. The third will consider the April eclogue as the golden age of Spenser's pastoral world, a mythic and ideal resolution of the contention and conflict of the real or iron-age world of the *Calender*. Throughout this analysis, one thing above all becomes clear: in the *Calender*, as in his later works, we will find Spenser constantly making distinctions, weighing different values, exploring perspectives. For even at this stage in his career, Spenser possessed those qualities of mind that we have increasingly found in him, a pragmatic and mature awareness of a plurality of values, a continuous capacity for discrimination, his " 'most goodly temperature.' "[25]

25. Edmund Spenser, *Amoretti,* XIII; Spenser's phrase is aptly applied to the *Amoretti* by Louis L. Martz in his cogent reading, "The *Amoretti:* 'Most Goodly Temperature,' " in *Form and Convention in the Poetry of Edmund Spenser* (New York, 1961), pp. 146-148.

I. Edmund Spenser

1. The Shepheardes Calender and the Variety of Pastoral

THE MORAL DEBATES AND THE CONFLICT
OF PASTORAL PERSPECTIVES

More often than not, the moral debates of the *Shepheardes Calender* have been read in light of E.K.'s rather lopsided moralistic interpretation of their "Satyrical bitternesse": "February's" satire involves the "reuerence dewe to old age"; "May's," "coloured deceipt"; "July's" and "September's," "dissolute shepherds and pastours"; and "October's," the "contempt of Poetrie and pleasaunt wits."[1] Obviously satire does inform some parts of the *Calender,* but the really astringent satire is generally directed at figures other than the disputants themselves; moreover, whatever satire is directed at the disputants is directed at both, not merely one, and this satire is usually comic and genial, not harsh and bitter. The moral debates are real and exploratory, not staged, debates between pastoral perspectives of varying

1. For a thorough survey of these opinions, see *The Works of Edmund Spenser: A Variorum Edition* (hereafter referred to as the Variorum Edition) ed. C. G. Osgood and H. G. Lotspeich (Baltimore, 1943), VII, *The Minor Poems,* pt. 1, pp. 253–266. Among the more important recent readings of the *Calender,* note especially A. C. Hamilton, "The Argument of Spenser's *Shepheardes Calender,*" *English Literary History* (*ELH*), 23 (1956), 171–268, and Robert Allen Durr, "Spenser's Calendar of Christian Time," *ELH,* 24 (1957), 269–298, both of which, it seems to me, tend to assume a too narrow morality on Spenser's part. The tendency of much recent criticism, however, especially Virgil Whitaker, *The Religious Basis of Spenser's Thought,* Stanford University Publications, Language and Literature, VII, no. 3 (Stanford, 1950), and Paul McLane, *Spenser's "Shepheardes Calender": A Study in Elizabethan Allegory* (Notre Dame, 1961), is to view Spenser as more concerned with the orderly success of the Anglican Compromise, that is, with some reforms, than with the imposition of a rigid or ascetic ethic.

but plausible legitimacy; they are a balanced portrayal of the different and often conflicting attempts by man to strike a balance between aspects of his contradictory nature, between his role as a creature of the world who must make practical provision to survive in that world and his role as a creature of eternity with eternal obligations. The characters of the debates are thus involved in coming to terms with conflicting demands and ideals: love and asceticism, age and youth, heroic aspiration and pastoral humility, self-seeking and self-sacrifice, participation and withdrawal.

The contending perspectives within the debates are to a considerable extent reflections of the contending perspectives we have seen within pastoral. Embodying the Mantuanesque pastoral perspective are Thenot, Piers, Thomalin, and Diggon Davie, with their exacting demands on human nature and capabilities: Thenot demands that youth restrain itself; Piers demands that reason restrain instinct; Thomalin demands that caution restrain ambition; Diggon Davie demands a constant vigil against wolves; and Piers in "October" demands that the poet ignore practical necessity for the lofty rewards of his calling. Their moralistic vision tends to see life, as Mantuanesque pastoral largely does, always under the threat of winter and destruction: life is mutable, precarious, and untrustworthy, and man must therefore place his confidence in things outside this world or in the things of this world that are most stable and permanent. Their moral imperative is Mantuan's: rational duty.

Countering the rigid moralism of the Mantuanesque shepherds is the more pragmatic pastoral perspective of, above all, Hobbinol; but Cuddie, Palinode, and Morrell also represent various sides, various versions, and at times various perversions of what I have described as the dominant perspective of pastoral into the Renaissance, the Arcadian perspective. The Arcadian shepherds are vastly more aware than their Mantuanesque opponents of man as a creature of and within nature, a creature with desires and instincts that must be satisfied. As a creature within the world, the shepherd must accommodate himself to the world. Cuddie, therefore, defends youth and procreation as part of nature; Palinode defends natural instinct and the pleasures of youth; Morrell speaks for man's ambitions in this world; Hobbinol defends man's psychological need to relax the permanent vigil; and Cuddie in "October" insists upon the satisfaction of man's physical needs, material provision and an age to inspire.

The Arcadian shepherds attempt to capture what there is in the world of Arcadian spring and *otium;* the ideal of the *pastor bonus* is tempered by, and sometimes admittedly endangered by, the ideal of the *pastor felix.* On the other hand, the Mantuanesque shepherds, always preparing for winter, view man's participation in nature and spring with distrust, as a potentially disastrous, if not sinful, deviation from moral austerity. The Arcadian shepherds possess a pragmatic understanding of man's psychological and physical limits and a willingness to accept the pastoral and human need for *otium* to transform life from a dreary and austere struggle. The pragmatic ideal of Hobbinol is thus appropriately that of moderation. It is a flexible, if potentially timeserving, ideal, adaptable to personalities and circumstances: Hobbinol can celebrate his retreat of pastoral *otium* and at the same time urge Colin to pursue an ambitious course. In contrast to the Mantuanesque shepherds, whose contentious orthodoxy requires either than man revise the world radically or that he withdraw from it, Spenser's Arcadian shepherds want to share in whatever fun and joy that world may have to offer.

It is the major purpose of the moral debates, therefore, to explore the conflict of perspectives and meanings that, by the time of the Renaissance, pastoral was fitted to express. In not all of these debates, however, do we find a representative of both Mantuanesque and Arcadian perspectives. In "July," while Thomalin is clearly Mantuanesque in his repudiation of ambition and in his invective against the abuses of power, Morrell's defense of ambition does not really fall strictly within the province of the Arcadian pastoral vision. At the same time, much Arcadian pastoral can accommodate itself to ambition, though it does not usually celebrate ambition as part of the pastoral world, as Morrell does. In this one instance it would be misleading to conceive of Morrell as representing Arcadian pastoral; more precisely, he represents an aspect of experience that the Arcadian vision could come to terms with, as we can tell from Hobbinol's encouraging Colin in "June" to climb "*Parnasse* hyll." In the rest of the debates, however, both pastoral perspectives are represented. From their confrontation emerges an ambivalence in which neither perspective can claim to the whole truth.[2] In "February,"

2. There has been some recognition, extremely scattered, of the possible ambivalence in the moral debates. H. S. V. Jones, for example, *A Spenser Handbook* (New York, 1930), p. 47, remarks that "the tradition of the debate, that had long been accommodated to the pastoral, was all in favor of a well-balanced rather

Thenot's Mantuanesque restraint and Cuddie's youthful *otium* are both limited, the one running the risk of sterility, the other running the risk of overweening pride and ambition. Cuddie's practical awareness of man's need to participate in the natural world, to procreate, is a necessary counter to Thenot's wintry wisdom of withdrawal and restraint. In "May" there is a similar opposition of the desires of youth and the requirements of age, with Piers taking the Mantuanesque imperative of duty and responsibility, a withdrawal from the temptation of nature, and Palinode articulating the Arcadian desire to satisfy instinct and nature, but the eclogue's exemplary fable suggests that while distrust of instinct is a necessary part of caution and restraint, carried too far it may also extinguish the good in instinct—sympathy, compassion, and so on. In "July" Morrell's knowledge of the potential value of aspiration is a valuable counter to, and is valuably countered by, Thomalin's Mantuanesque awareness of humility and the danger of ambition. In "September" the Arcadian Hobbinol's practical understanding of human nature, his realization that the shepherd is a man like other men, is a useful qualification of the Mantuanesque Diggon Davie's wild-eyed, lofty but unrealistic demand for perpetual vigilance. And finally, in "October," Cuddie's realistic awareness that the poet, for all the praise, must survive hunger like other men is a necessary foil to Piers's idealistic demand that the praise should be enough, that eternal rewards are all-important.

The moral debates, then, are not simply debates between good and bad shepherds, but between two perspectives, each limited, each containing a potential for either good or evil. What has misled criticism into making the debates a black-and-white confrontation is in part an almost uniform failure to realize that the debate and the fable (or the invective) are not necessarily equivalent: Cuddie is not the Briar, though his perspective contains the dangerous possibility

---

than a one-sided argument," but he fails to carry this through convincingly. Although Isabel G. MacCaffrey's sensitive and illuminating article, "Allegory and Pastoral in *The Shepheardes Calender*," *ELH*, 36 (1969), 88–109, came to my attention too late to make use of it, and although her reading of the *Calender* differs from mine on many points, she, too, discovers in the *Calendar* "a balance of attitudes held in equilibrium" (p. 105). See also William Nelson, *The Poetry of Edmund Spenser* (New York, 1963), p. 46, and William Nicolet, "Edmund Spenser's *Shepheardes Calender:* An Interpretation" (Ph.D. dissertation, Brown University, 1964), pp. 181–230.

of the Briar's solitary self-assertion; Palinode is not the Kid, though his perspective runs the risk of the Kid's naiveté. Similarly, Morrell is not the moral equivalent of the corrupt, flock-devouring prelates described by Thomalin, nor is Hobbinol in "October." Although it is possible, perhaps more than possible, that Spenser sympathized more with the Mantuanesque than with the Arcadian pastoral perspective, the point still remains: the debate frameworks of the moral eclogues portray a legitimate conflict—"normal" disagreement—while the fables, or the invective passages, illustrate a totally unacceptable and generally corrupt extreme.

Failure to recognize the human comedy involved especially in the framework has also obscured the ambivalence in the debate. The comedy ranges from the verbal fisticuffs characteristic of the singing-contest and the pastoral debate to a more sophisticated comedy of character. In "February," the comedy emerges from the conflict of generations, the perennial inability of youth and age to communicate. Cuddie's petulant taunts, Thenot's stuffy aphorisms represent a well-known situation, part of the absurdity underlying human behavior and relationships. The comic situation in "May" shifts from "February's" plight of youth's desire to be mature and participate in the sexual rites, to the mature man's desire to be young. In "July," the comedy is in part a comedy of verbal abuse, but it is primarily a comedy of misperception: the rustic's fear of having the wool pulled over his eyes; the literal-minded naiveté that leads to an argument's playing into the opponent's hands; the inflexible conviction that makes all other positions totally unbelievable. The comedy in "September" depends on both Hobbinol's open-eyed naiveté and Diggon Davie's wild-eyed, breathless account of the evils he has seen. Finally, "October's" comedy emerges from the innocence of Piers's idealism and from Cuddie's pretentious pose as the poet who, unlike the mere theorist, knows what the scene is. Piers is gradually driven into a corner with his arguments (from wars to God) while Cuddie, indeed the "perfecte paterne of a Poet," tosses aside, one after another, the uninformed suggestions of the mere aficionado. The comedy in the debates is, therefore, a comedy of character and misperception, of talking at cross-purposes on different wave-lengths, of naive literal-mindedness, and of exaggerated argument. This is not to say that the issues are unimportant, obviously that is not so; the point is that the debates are debates between personalities as well as perspectives, and that Spenser employs comedy to point to the limitations of both the disputant and his perspective. Even the characters who are often taken to represent Spenser's own opinions, like Thenot, Piers, and Diggon Davie, are not immune to seeming naive, stuffy, literal-minded, or quaint. Thinking himself the possesser of the whole truth, no character is immune to Spenser's irony and its insistence on the limitations of our vision. The poem's technique is thus an extension of its recurring emphasis on the recognition of a plurality of values, a necessity for discrimination: the medium illustrates the message.

"February"

The debate that frames the February eclogue is a portrayal at once comic and serious of the perennial conflict of age and youth. The debate opens with the youthful Cuddie, identifying himself with the oncoming spring, raging against "these bitter blasts" of "rancke Winters rage." To the aged Thenot, Cuddie's complaint is only the ignorance of a "laesie ladde." With the pat fatalistic moralisms of one that "gently took, that vngently came. / And euer my flocke was my chiefe care," the Mantuanesque Thenot admonishes Cuddie to shut up and realize that the world must "wend in his common course / From good to badd, from badde to worse." Cuddie replies sarcastically that it is no wonder Thenot can bear winter, he is so much like winter himself:

> No marueile *Thenot,* if thou can beare
> Cherefully the Winters wrathfull cheare:
> For Age and Winter accord full nie,
> This chill, that cold, this crooked, that wrye.
> And as the lowring Wether lookes downe,
> So semest thou like good fryday to frowne.
> But my flowring youth is foe to frost,
> My shippe vnwont in stormes to be tost.

$$(25\text{-}32)$$

Winter clearly has more than a seasonal meaning for Cuddie. Identifying himself with the fertility of spring, he likewise identifies winter with parental discipline, with age's dampening of youth's desire. Similarly, Thenot identifies spring with the carelessness, the lack of discipline of youth. The debate over winter and spring is thus symbolic of the psychological power struggle between age and youth. Thenot's reply is psychologically true; he resents the rebelliousness of youth:

> So loytring liue you little heardgroomes,
> Keeping your beastes in the budded broomes:
> And when the shining sunne laugheth once,
> You deemen, the Spring is come attonce.
> Tho gynne you, fond flyes, the cold to scorne,
> And crowing in pypes made of greene corne,
> You thinken to be Lords of the yeare.
> But eft, when ye count you freed from feare,
> Comes the breme winter with chamfred browes,
> Full of wrinckles and frostie furrowes.
>
> . . . . . .
>
> Then is your careless corage accoied,
> Your carefull heards with cold bene annoied.
> Then paye you the price of your surquedrie,
> With weeping, and wayling, and misery
>
> (35-50)

Thenot's reply is comically typical of age's desire to keep youth in check by moralizing on the carelessness, the irresponsibility of youth. His argument is an old one, and Cuddie's reply no younger: Thenot is simply envious of the fact that he's no longer young, and, using the briar and tree images of the tale Thenot will later tell, Cuddie complains:

> Now thy selfe hast lost both lopp and topp,
> Als my budding braunch thou wouldest cropp:
> But were thy yeares greene, as now bene myne,
> To other delights they would encline.
> Tho wouldest thou learne to caroll of Loue,
> And hery with hymnes thy lasses gloue.
> Tho wouldest thou pype of *Phyllis* prayse:
> But *Phyllis* is myne for many dayes:
> I wonne her with a gyrdle of gelt,
> Embost with buegle about the belt.
> Such an one shepeheards woulde make full faine:
> Such an one would make thee younge againe.
>
> (57-68)

One does not need Freud to understand the sexual (comically so) undercurrent in Cuddie's fear that Thenot would crop off his budding branch and in his taunt that Thenot himself has lost "lopp and topp." Cuddie is challenging Thenot on his most vulnerable ground, his virility. To this youthful taunt, Thenot offers an aged aphorism: "Thou art a fon, of thy loue to boste, / All that is lent to loue, wyll be lost." But love, while it is not timeless, is also an essential part of nature. Cuddie produces his evidence and argument from their flocks. His flock, now that spring approaches, feels the natural urges of procreation:

> Seest, howe brag yond Bullocke beares,
> So smirke, so smoothe, his pricked eares?
> His hornes bene as broade, as Rainebowe bent,
> His dewelap as lythe, as lasse of Kent.
> See howe he venteth into the wynd.
> Weenest of loue is not his mynd?
>
> (71-76)

Thenot's flock, on the other hand, is deficient in nature; it is bedraggled and lifeless, like its master indifferent to the procreative urges of spring:

> Seemeth thy flocke thy counsell can,
> So lustlesse bene they, so weake so wan,
> Clothed with cold, and hoary wyth frost.
> Thy flocks father his corage hath lost:
> Thy Ewes, that wont to haue blowen bags,
> Like wailefull widdowes hangen their crags:
> The rather Lambes bene starued with cold,
> All for their Maister is lustlesse and old.
>
> (77-84)

To which age responds with aphorisms:

> For Youngth is a bubble blown vp with breath,
> Whose witt is weakenesse, whose wage is death,
> Whose way is wildernesse, whose ynne Penaunce,
> And stoopegallaunt Age the host of Greeuaunce.
>
> (87-90)

The portrayal here of age as the penalty for foolish youth is an amusing contradiction to Thenot's picture of age, a minute or two before, as "the lusty prime." But Cuddie is also not immune to contradiction. When Thenot offers to tell a tale of Tityrus', Cuddie enthusiastically praises everything that Tityrus made as "so wise"; but having heard the tale of the Oak and the Briar, he interrupts Thenot's ponderous moralizing with the comic petulance typical of youth, complaining against long-winded age:

> Now I pray thee shepheard, tel it not forth:
> Here is a long tale, and little worth.
> So longe haue I listened to thy speche,
> That graffed to the ground is my breche.
>
> . . . . . .
>
> But little ease of thy lewd tale I tasted.
> Hye thee home shepheard, the day is nigh wasted.

(239-246)

The framework of the February eclogue thus portrays the human comedy of the conflict of generations. The comedy of course resides largely in the typicality of character and situation: youth's perennially impatient and somewhat petulant desire to participate in life, to be "grown up"; and age's perennial resentment of youth's rivalry, rebelliousness, impatience, and follies. Petulant taunts alternate with bromidic aphorisms, and each disputant naturally believes himself the holder of all truth. We enjoy the absurdity here, we have seen this confrontation before; there is no need to mourn or moralize. Spenser is portraying the comic absurdity underlying one of the common situations of human experience, the human comedy with its contradictions and conflicts, as natural as the conflict of winter and spring traditionally associated with the month of February.[3] When Cuddie protests impatiently against "Winters rage" and age's fatalistic formulas, and when Thenot replies with the confident contempt of one who feels that age and experience provide the ultimate vision, the disputants symbolize and reflect in human terms the struggle of winter and spring within the natural year and the natural order. Were Cuddie not to protest, feeling his oats, and were Thenot not to feel the need to restrain him, then they would represent disorder by being alien to nature's potential, if precarious, balance of opposites.

Both Thenot and Cuddie have a share of wisdom and folly. Both represent a way of living that, being incomplete in itself, must find some potential measure of completeness in its opposite. There is wisdom in Thenot's restraint of his protégé and in his realization that

---

3. February is at once both the last month of the old year (by the old calendar) and the first month of spring according to the popular calendar. For further details, see chapter 2, "The Unity and Design of the *Shepheardes Calender*."

man must control himself if he is to endure the winter rather than be its victim; for,

> Comes the breme winter with chamfred browes,
> Full of wrinckles and frostie furrowes:
> Drerily shooting his stormy darte,
> Which cruddles the blood, and pricks the harte.
> Then is your careless corage accoied,
> Your carefull heards with cold bene annoied.
>
> (43-48)

Cuddie's "flowring youth" needs this caution. But there is bias as well as wisdom in Thenot's advice: bias in Thenot's contention that old age is "the lusty prime" man should live his life for, bias in his unwillingness or inability to see that spring and procreative love are as much the function of youth and life as restraint is the function of age. Moreover, Cuddie, in asserting himself as the child of spring, affords an important complement to Thenot's wintry wisdom—an awareness of the necessity of procreation and natural impulse within the natural world. There is an obvious aphoristic truth in the aged Thenot's contention that "All that is lent to loue, wyll be lost," but there is no less wisdom in Cuddie's instinctive knowledge of the function and value of spring and youth, fertility and procreation. If youth wastes itself without the wise restraint of age and experience, life itself is wasted, and age becomes sterile if youth is spent withdrawing from experience and procreation. The ideal here is a balance, lest age become sterility and youth be vainly spent.

One of the chief errors of previous interpretations of the February eclogue is the assumption that the fable of the Oak and the Briar is either a refutation of Cuddie's ignorance or, more flexibly, a parallel to the Thenot-Cuddie framework.[4] In actuality they are not parallels

4. In this tale, as in others, I prefer a reading "rather morall and generall, then bent to any secrete or particular purpose." For a survey of the various attempts at either general religious and political allegory or specific personal identification, see the Variorum Edition, VII, pt. 1, pp. 254-255, 261-262. Among the most influential theories are Edwin Greenlaw's "The Shepheardes Calender, II," Studies in Philology (SP), 11 (1913), 3-25, that the fall of Catholicism was symbolized in the fall of a great tree, and E. De Selincourt's, The Poetical Works of Edmund Spenser (Oxford, 1912), p. xvi, that the Oak, "once a goodly tree," is the "true spirit of Christianity degenerated under the influence of Romist superstition" and the Briar is "the irreverent and godless temper of the new clergy, whose irreligion offered so bold a contrast to the simple piety of pure Christian faith." More recently, A. C. Hamilton, ELH, 23 (1956), 178, has contended that the Oak is "the Catholic Church which suffers reform by the Established Church under

but foils to each other. The framework of the fable portrays, with a comedy of age's pat aphorisms and youth's rigid denials, the healthy rite of spring; but the fable portrays a tragic and wasteful perversion of the healthy contest of age and youth. Like Colin's wintry mind, sterile not wise, turbulent not restrained, the fable of the Oak and the Briar reveals the tragic distortion of true, valid accommodation to the year. The fable is a parody of the order and balance contained in the framework.

The Oak and the Briar, like Thenot and Cuddie, have the incompleteness of age and youth, respectively. As in the framework, both parties have a partial claim to truth. The Briar does in fact have just cause for complaint against the Oak, once an image of fertility in youth ("mochell mast to the husband did yield") but now an image of sterility:

Whilome did bene the King of the field,
And mochell mast to the husband did yielde,
And with his nuts larded many swine.
But now the gray mosse marred his rine,
His bared boughes were beaten with stormes,
His toppe was bald, and wasted with wormes,
His honor decayed, his braunches sere.

(108-114)

The Briar, again with the partial justification of Renaissance figures who speak with "painted words," accuses the Oak of tyranny, of blighting his fertility; complaining to his sovereign husbandman, he begs his "right":

Was not I planted of thine owne hand,
To be the primrose of all thy land,
With flowring blossomes, to furnish the prime,
And scarlot berries in Sommer time?
How falls it then, that this faded Oake,

. . . . . .

Elizabeth"; and Robert Durr, *ELH*, 24 (1957), 275, has argued that the Oak "in its religious aspect . . . represents the Catholic Church, as the briar does the extreme Puritan faction." William Nicolet, "Edmund Spenser's *Shepheardes Calender*," p. 193, suggests that the fable is "a warning against the dangers of factionalism," with the Briar representing the energetic and ambitious middle-class counselors and the Oak the less energetic older nobility. Spenser would, therefore, be suggesting the need for a common front against the dangers of the elements (France and Spain, for example) and the need for cooperation between the dissident factions of the old and new nobility. Of the topical readings, this seems to me probably the most consistent and sensible.

Vnto such tyrannie doth aspire:
Hindering with his shade my louely light,
And robbing me of the swete sonnes slight?
So beate his old boughes my tender side,
That oft the bloud springeth from wounds wyde:
Vntimely my floweres forced to fall,
That bene the honor of your Coronall.
And oft he lets his cancker wormes light
Vpon my braunches, to worke me more spight:
And oft his hoarie locks downe doth caste,
Where with my fresh flowretts bene defast.
     · · · · · ·
Nought aske I, but onely to hold my right.

(165-186)

Even Thenot, who can hardly be considered partial to the ambitions and vitality of youth and whose narration is interspersed with comments disparaging the Briar, relates that the Oak

. . . had bene an auncient tree,
Sacred with many a mysteree,
And often crost with the priestes crewe,
And often halowed with holy water dewe.
But sike fancies weren foolerie,
And broughten this Oake to this miserye.
And nought mought they quitten him from decay.

(207-213)

Age's reverence for tradition has been perverted by the Oak into superstition, while youth's self-assertion of its fertility has been perverted by the Briar into ambition destroying itself and others. It is the last lines that tell the tale and point the moral:

Now stands the Brere like a Lord alone,
Puffed vp with pryde and vaine pleasaunce:
But all this glee had no continuance.
For eftsones Winter gan to approche,
The blustring Boreas did encroche,
And beate vpon the solitarie Brere:
For nowe no succoure was seene him nere.
Now gan he repent his pryde to late:
For naked left and disconsolate,
The bying frost nipt his stalke dead.
     · · · · · ·
Such was thend of this Ambitious brere,
For scorning Eld

(222-238)

The fable of the Oak and the Briar points the same moral as that in the debate between Thenot and Cuddie: age and youth are both incomplete; they need each other. Neither is self-sufficient. But whereas in the debate the contest of Thenot and Cuddie was part of the natural order, in the fable the Briar (unlike Cuddie) destroys his opponent, upsets the precarious harmony of opposites, refuses compromise, and "solitary" insists upon his self-fulfillment and thus "solitary" dies. The fable illustrates the dangers of Cuddie's position taken to an extreme, but indirectly it also shows the dangers of Thenot's, the perversion of reverence for age into mere superstition. Neither the old nor the new, neither youth nor age, neither spring nor winter, is sufficient unto itself. They must have the balance-in-opposition of the natural year, its harmonious whole, or both perish. This is the teaching for the month of February.

"May"

The debate in the May eclogue centers around the role of the priest in the world, with Palinode defending a more worldly priesthood and Piers a more otherworldly priesthood. Here, as in "February" and the two succeeding eclogues, the focal issue is man's participation in spring. In "May" the conflict between withdrawal and participation is appropriately defined by the disputants' differing attitudes toward the Maytime festivities. Palinode, desiring the *otia* of classical pastoral, responds to the seasonal instinct to participate in the Maytime flourishing of nature, and longs to join youth in its rites of spring:

> Yougthes folke now flocken in euery where,
> To gather may buskets and smelling brere:
> And home they hasten the postes to dight,
> And all the Kirke pillours eare day light,
> With Hawthorne buds, and swete Eglantine,
> And girlonds of roses and Sopps in wine.
> Such merimake holy Saints doth queme,
> But we here sytten as drownd in a dreme.

(9-16)

Piers, however, takes a more austere, Mantuanesque view. Like Thenot in "February," he declares that he pities youth's folly. Nonetheless, Piers, at least initially, appears sufficiently flexible to admit a certain ethical decorum, what is fit for youth is not necessarily fit for priests and older men:

> For Younkers *Palinode* such follies fitte,
> But we tway bene men of elder witt.
>
> (17-18)

After Palinode has accused him of speaking spitefully just because he is jealous and because he does not realize that "Good is no good, but if it be spend: / God giueth good for none other end," Piers's rebuttal again takes the form of decorum:

> But shepheards (as Algrind vsed to say,)
> Mought not liue ylike, as men of the laye:
> With them it sits to care for their heire,
> Enaunter their heritage doe impaire:
> They must prouide for meanes of maintenaunce,
> And to continue their wont countenaunce.
> But shepheard must walke another way,
> Sike worldly souenance he must foresay.
>
> (75-82)

But Piers's actual judgment is not always as flexible as his doctrine of decorum would suggest. In practice, he fails to apply his doctrine consistently. After Palinode has expressed his envy of youth's great sport (19-36), Piers, who in his speech immediately before had tolerated if not recommended youthful foibles ("For Younkers *Palinode* such follies fitte"), begins a tirade against youth. He accuses them of irresponsibility in their pleasures and condemns them as "shepeheards for the Deuils stedde." The follies or foibles fit for youth have now become contradictorily part and parcel of Satanic temptation. Moreover, Piers, failing to preserve his earlier distinction between age and youth and his later distinction between the clergy and the laity, lumps together youth's delight in May with the sins of the clergy:

> Those faytours little regarden their charge,
> While they letting their sheepe runne at large,
> Passen their time, that should be sparely spent,
> In lustihede and wanton meryment.
> Thilke same bene shepeheards for the Deuils stedde,
> That playen, while their flockes be vnfedde.
> Well is it seene, theyr sheepe bene not their owne,
> That letten them runne at randon alone.
> But they bene hyred for little pay
> Of other, that caren as little as they,
> What fallen the flocke, so they han the fleece
> And get all the gayne, paying but a peece.
>
> (39-50)

Piers has shifted the issue from Palinode's question of the pleasures of youth to the problem of the clergy and benefices. The May festivities of young shepherd's boys become one and the same with the sins of those who substituted for the absent clergy. The flexibility in Piers's decorum thus seems more technical and intellectual than practical. Confronted with a situation in which he must apply that flexibility, the basic rigidity of his character, its underlying ascetic abhorrence of the world and pleasure, take over. The theoretical issue between Palinode and Piers is whether some men, the priesthood, should be required to reject the things of the world: that is, to what extent is the priest a man like other men? But one wonders if this issue is not less well marked and defined for Piers on an emotional level; for despite his theoretical disclaimer, in practice he imposes on all of mankind his own monastic and artificial code.

Piers's ideal, like that of many Puritans and of Protestants in general, is that of primitive Christianity, when shepherds had no inheritance, no money and land except "what might arise of the bare sheepe . . . which they did keepe":

> Nought hauing, nought feared they to forgoe.
> For *Pan* himselfe was their inheritaunce,
> And little them serued for their mayntenaunce.
> The shepheards God so wel them guided,
> That of nought they were vnprouided,
> Butter enough, honye, milke, and whay,
> And their flockes fleeces, them to araye.

(110-116)

This ideal Christian golden age is a foil to the conventional pagan Arcadian golden age, where rivers ran with milk and honey, where pleasures were free and easy, where the sheep took care of themselves and man had little toil to do. Indeed it is precisely the pagan golden age's *otia* that undermine Piers's Mantuanesque golden age of austerity and duty:

> But tract of time, and long prosperitie:
> That nource of vice, this of insolencie,
> Lulled the shepheards in such securitie.
>
> . . . . . .
>
> Tho gan shepreards swaines to looke a loft,
> And leaue to liue hard, and learne to ligge soft.

(117-125)

The prosperity and soft life that underlie the pagan golden age are the same factors that undermine the Mantuanesque golden age.

For Palinode, however, Piers's ideal of austerity and restraint is impractical, if not absurdly masochistic:

What? should they [shepherds] pynen in payne and woe?
Nay sayd I thereto, by my deare borrowe,
If I may rest, I nill liue in sorrowe.
  Sorrowe ne neede be hastened on:
For he will come without calling anone.
While times enduren of tranquillitie,
Vsen we freely our felicitie.

(149-155)

He adds, with some cogency, that Piers's open and vehement protest against the way of life of some shepherds may bring about the collapse of the whole profession (that is, the Church itself):

And sooth to sayne, nought seemeth sike strife,
That shepheardes so witen ech others life,
And layen her faults the world beforne,
The while their foes done eache of hem scorne.
Let none mislike of that may not be mended:
So conteck soone by concord mought be ended.

(158-163)

There is something more behind Palinode's argument than simple hedonism. Both his points are reasonable, practical qualifications on the reforming zeal of Piers, who in his intransigence will "none accordaunce make / With shepheard, that does the right way forsake" and would prefer him his enemy rather than his friend.

In this prefatory debate, then, we are presented with two incomplete points of view, the conservative and the reformer, if you will.[5]

5. Most older commentary has concluded that Piers represents Spenser's own view, that he is his mouthpiece (for a survey of this scholarship, see the Variorum Edition, VII, pt. 1, 290–295). More recently, Hallett Smith, *Elizabethan Poetry* (Cambridge, Mass., 1952), p. 43, has found an apparently clear-cut opposition between "the gay, irresponsible pastoral life and the conscientious tending of sheep," a position similar to that taken by Robert Durr, *ELH*, 24 (1957), 280–282, who considers Palinode little more than a degenerate spokesman for *carpe diem* and Acrasia's bower. A. C. Hamilton, *ELH*, 23 (1956), 179, contends that "May" is another example of Spenser's argument for the rejection of the pastoral world, with Piers as spokesman. The few older commentators who found ambivalence of some sort in the debate include, especially, Francis Palgrave, "General Introduction to the *Shepheardes Calender*," in *Works of Edmund Spenser*, ed. Alexander Grosart, IV (London, 1882–84), xlvii–xlix, and E. Legouis, *Edmund Spenser* (Paris, 1923), pp. 26–28, both of whom find the debate an extension of the personal conflict

The complaints of the reformer are valid, and his contention that Palinode runs the risk of such corruption is equally true. It is not true, however, that Palinode himself represents that corruption. Even for Piers, Palinode contains the seeds of corruption rather than corruption itself. The debate is not between Puritan and Roman, but between two sides of the Anglican clergy, one more Romanist, the other more Puritanical; it is improbable that either is Roman or Puritan. In all of the ecclesiastical eclogues the debating shepherds tend neighboring flocks and speak of a single ideal about which the debate centers for a single priesthood. Moreover, if Piers thought Palinode a Roman or a thoroughly corrupt shepherd like those he denounces, he would quite clearly be inconsistent in keeping fellowship with him. Palinode is not an equivalent to the wolf or fox of the succeeding exemplum, but a potential victim of wolves. In Piers's tale, if Palinode is to be equated with any figure, it is with the Kid, a child ("Ah *Palinode, thou art a worldes childe*"), not the Roman Fox.

Piers's tale of the Fox and the Kid ostensibly describes only the limitations of Palinode's point of view; but we should remember that Spenser's moral tales do not always tell only what they seem to tell. Frequently they are a commentary on the speaker as well as his audience. In the debate framework, after all, are dramatized two conflicting and incomplete visions, the limitations of one complementing the limitations of the other, both of which are founded on some conception of a golden age. Palinode would like to act as though the world had never fallen; he lives in a child's world of innocence and pleasure. Piers's ideal, on the other hand, possesses an exaggerated awareness of the world as fallen, while at the same time it contradictorily ignores the practical limitations of fallen man, recalling him to an impossible golden age of Christian duty. Of the two, Piers's vision is probably the more complete; but if Palinode's childlike blindness to the foxes in the world is his flaw, Piers's flaw is its complement, that he may avoid the evil of the fox but still

in Spenser between the ascetic and the aesthetic. More recently, William Nelson, *The Poetry of Edmund Spenser*, p. 46, to some extent following H. S. V. Jones, *A Spenser Handbook*, p. 49, has observed sanely that the debate is not "as one-sided as the identification of the speakers with Protestantism and Catholicism would demand": Piers's contention is weightier and more emotional, but Palinode's, resembling Hobbinol's in "September," is not specious. "As Spenser uses it," writes Nelson, "the dialogue of a pastoral poem is not a Socratic demonstration but a valid disagreement in which the speakers explore what may best be said on either part." This is also my conclusion.

do no good. The dual limitations of teller and audience are, I believe, implicit in Piers's tale.

This tale describes how the Kid, despite the precautions of his widowed mother, is caught by a deceitful fox in pedlar's clothing. The Gate, wanting to see her son grow up "and florish in flowres of lusty head," warns him against the Fox, "master of collusion," and admonishes him at no cost to open the door while she is gone. When the Fox arrives, however, he appears not as the fox the Gate expected but as a poor suffering pedlar, for whom neither headache nor the gout will prevent his carrying around his bag of trifles. Previous commentators have all tended to blame the Kid's fascination for Roman toys (the things of this world) as the source of his demise. This is misleading and incomplete. There are actually two stages in the Kid's temptation: the first involves his natural sympathy for and interest in others, while the second involves a selfish interest in his own pleasures. The figure of the suffering pedlar elicits from the Kid an instinctive, natural sympathy for suffering; and in fact, only when the Kid looks out of a chink to see the source of the groaning does the Fox spot him and thus get an entree for his maudlin appeal:

> The Kidd pittying hys heauinesse,
> Asked the cause of his great distresse.
>
> (259-260)

The first stage of the Fox's seduction of the Kid is founded on two appeals to the Kid's natural sympathies: first, that he, the Fox, is "sicke, sicke, alas, and little lack of dead"; and second, that they are kin:

> And if that my Grandsire me sayd, be true,
> Sicker I am very sybbe to you:
> So be your goodlihead doe not disdayne
> The base kinred of so simple swaine.
> Of mercye and fauour then I you pray,
> With your ayd to forstall my neere decay.
>
> (268-273)

The second and conclusive stage of the seduction moves from an appeal to the Kid's natural sympathies for others to an appeal to self. The Fox takes a mirror (its narcissistic symbolism is obvious), and the Kid is "so enamored with the newell" that he opens the door. The Fox takes out all his wares but one, a bell, and when the Kid reaches into the basket to find it, the Fox pops him in and carries him off.

From his tale Piers derives this moral:

Such end had the Kidde, for he nould warned be
Of craft, coloured with simplicitie:
And such end perdie does all hem remayne,
That of such falsers freendship bene fayne.

(302-305)

Palinode of course disagrees: "Truly *Piers*, thou art beside thy wit." But he adds immediately, in what has seemed to some a contradiction, that he would like to borrow the tale to give to "our sir John":

For well he meanes, but little can say.
But and if Foxes bene so craft, as so,
Much needeth all shepheards hem to knowe.

(311-313)

A contradiction this is not, rather the comical second thought of a man prepared to disagree, momentarily convinced, and yet not willing to admit total defeat.[6]

It would be false to contend that either Piers or Palinode is beside his wit, and the customary conclusion that of the two Piers's argument is the more substantial is certainly partially true. But this debate, like others, is ambivalent: there is something to be said on both sides. In the first place, as I have indicated, the attitudes of neither contestant constitute a complete grasp of reality or the particular problem at hand. The liberal Palinode has a childlike naiveté, a blindness to the Fox and the evil in the world; yet at the same time, he does possess an awareness of natural man's limitations that the *senex* Piers unfortunately lacks. Furthermore, Palinode's fear that Piers's intransigence may contribute less to the reform than to the destruction of the Church is a practical, even if potentially timeserving, qualification of Piers's emotionalism. At the same time, Piers's vision is at least not blind to the Fox, however naive he is regarding human nature; even if his intransigence forces him to equate all pleasure with sin, at least he himself is less vulnerable to the seduction of sin.

6. Certainly C. H. Herford, *The Shepheards Calender* (London, 1895), p. 133 (Notes), is incorrect in attempting to account for the reversal on the grounds that "Spenser thus ingeniously gives a back-handed blow at the ignorant dullness of the Catholic clergy, while exposing their duplicity." Palinode is not a Catholic, and, although he is childlike, he is not involved in duplicity.

In the second place, Piers's own tale dramatizes the limitations of both contestants. The narrator's unwillingness to trust anyone potentially restricts his fellowship with even good men. Piers runs the risk of being a priest who, for fear of his own personal salvation, would never open the door, suffering pedlar or not. His fear of sin may actually confine his potential for good—his sins being those of omission rather than commission—and at the same time his morbid fear of sin at least partially precludes an effective and viable distinction between innocent and corrupt pleasures. There is, then, much to be said against Piers's puritanical obsession with sin, and there is something to be said for the Kid's responding to the suffering of the pedlar and to the pedlar's claim of kinship, however fraudulent. Piers's Mantuanesque tendency to repudiate the natural man for the intellectually percipient man of austere Christian duty runs the risk of ignoring the good in natural impulse as well as its potential folly. (Correspondingly, in the debate Piers finds it difficult on a practical basis to distinguish between the innocent pleasures of youth in May, their diversions away from their flocks, and the sinful practices of absentee clergymen.) If Palinode and the Kid run the risk of blindness to evil, Piers runs the risk of blindness to innocence.

The comic elements that run through this debate, moreover, contribute as in the other moral eclogues to an atmosphere that precludes too severe a moralistic evaluation of either protagonist. Palinode's weakness, for example, is portrayed not as moral depravity so much as a comic, if dangerous, silliness or triviality which runs the risk of tragic loss. Piers and Palinode may both be mistaken, but we are not permitted to assume from that that they are therefore immoral. In sharp contradistinction are those priests who devour their sheep; these are simply corrupt and immoral, and their corruption does not lend itself to comedy but to satire and violent invective. To a large extent, the human comedy here depends simply on the contrast between the childlike Palinode and the somewhat pompously moralistic Piers. The older man's envy of and nostalgia for the pleasures of youth have not uncommonly lent themselves to a comedy emerging from the seeming incongruity of "men of elder witt" indecorously longing to put aside their black robes. Palinode's naiveté, the childlike limitations of his vision, become comic as the characteristics of an older man. His long, almost Prufrockian speeches on the delights of youthful "merimake" evoke pathos and a smile at once:

To see those folkes make such iouysaunce,
Made my heart after the pype to daunce.

. . . .

(O that I were there,
To helpen the Ladyes their Maybush beare)
Ah *Piers*, bene not thy teeth on edge, to thinke,
How great sport they gaynen with little swinck?

(25-36)

Palinode also introduces a comedy of riposte and, at times, actual abuse. For example, having listened to Piers's long-winded nostalgic praise of a highly idealized golden age of Christianity, Palinode's riposte returns us to earth (if perhaps a bit too close to it): "Three thinges to beare, bene very burdenous, / But the fourth to forbeare, is outragious"—lustful women, an angry man, a thirsty man—"But of all burdens, that a man can beare, / Moste is, a fooles talke to beare and to heare." The outburst is human and natural, like Albanio's outburst against Salicio in Garcilaso's second eclogue, for all its naiveté. But that, it seems to me, is the function of this partly comic characterization of Palinode: comedy serves at once to define the limitations of Palinode's vision of life (his childlike inability to perceive the danger of wolves, his petulant unwillingness to accept Piers's frosty rigidity) and the limitations as well of Piers's vision. For Palinode represents human nature, with its natural desires and limitations, that Piers's lofty and impossible ideal fails to take into account. By making Palinode an at least partially comic and human figure, one not devoid of our sympathy, Spenser has removed him from the brunt of a too severely moralistic evaluation. Palinode's limitations are comic foibles; they are not, though they run the risk of being, the sins of corruption.[7]

7. The ambivalence in the "May" debate has been largely obscured by earlier critics' making Palinode a bad or corrupt Anglican or even a Roman, with Piers as the pure counterpart to Palinode's deep corruption. E.K.'s prefatory note that by "Piers and Palinodie, be represented two formes of pastoures or Ministers, or the Protestant and the Catholique" did much to establish this oversimplified relationship. Later critics have varied the formula, but not the spirit, of E.K.'s distinction, so that Piers becomes a Puritan or a Puritanical Anglican, while Palinode becomes an Anglo-Catholic or a representative of the orthodox clergy. Regardless of the ecclesiastical nomenclature, Palinode was black, Piers white. This, as I have suggested, is contrary to the literary and moral structure of the debates. The representative of the austere, Mantuanesque pastoral ethic in the debates in

"July"

Like the other moral eclogues, "July" is organized around a debate between two pastoral perspectives, the more flexible represented by Morrell, the more austere represented by Thomalin. The framework within which these perspectives are explored, however, has become that of the hills versus the plains, the high estate versus the low estate, rather than that of age versus youth in "February" or that of reason versus instinct in "May." Almost uniformly, the confrontation in "July" has been taken to be a clear-cut opposition between Morrell's overweening and corrupt ambition and Thomalin's true pastoral humility.[8] Thomalin, as a result, would be Spenser's mouthpiece, proclaiming absolute pastoral truth. But if, as I contend, the moral eclogues are explorations of conventional pastoral perspectives, neither of which is entitled to be sole arbiter of man's destiny and behavior, then this standard reading is a severe oversimplification. This oversimplification is of course in part a product of the older image of Spenser as ultra-Protestant or Puritan, but it is also a product of the failure

---

no instance regards his opponent as totally corrupt; his invective is instead directed primarily at the corrupt extreme he fears the follies of his antagonist may lead to. The whole thrust of Pier's argument, after all is to *prevent* Palinode's becoming corrupt, to *prevent* his becoming a seditious papist. Consequently, I think one is forced to conclude that, while Piers may be a Puritan (though more probably a Puritanical Anglican), Palinode is not and logically cannot be a Roman Catholic.

8. It is now generally agreed that Morrell represents Aylmer, Bishop of London (but for a full survey of suggestions regarding his identity as well as Thomalin's see the Variorum Edition, VII, pt. 1, pp. 325–326). Until Paul McLane's work, however, in his *Spenser's "Shepheardes Calender,"* pp. 188–202, Aylmer was usually portrayed as a grasping career man who, though he began as a reformer of the Church, became more and more a part of the orthodox Anglican establishment as it profited his career. He was, apparently, a man of greed rather than commitment. Such an image of Aylmer fit in well with the older interpretation of the *Calender* as Puritan satire. This interpretation established a clear-cut conflict between the degenerate papistical Anglican or Roman (Morrell) and the high-minded Puritan (Thomalin), who was identified with some contemporary Puritan figure like Thomas Wilcox or even Thomas Cartwright. McLane, however, has fortunately presented us with a much more balanced perspective, one based partly on knowledge of Aylmer as a historical figure and partly on the modern realization that Spenser was not a Puritan. McLane maintains that Spenser would be just as aware of Aylmer's virtues as of his defects: his stand in the Convocation of 1553, his scholarly assistance to Foxe, his great erudition, his care to provide qualified persons for the ministry, and his effort to make Elizabeth's ecclesiastical settlement work (he restrained Catholics as well as Puritans). Moreover, suggests McLane, Aylmer would have been sufficiently learned to appreciate "how, in the eyes of the Puritans, Morrell's cap fitted." McLane, working from a historical approach, thus reaches a conclusion similar to my own: "July" is a miniature drama of opposing pastoral perspectives in which Morrell, while not an ideal shepherd, is not simply the example of "proude and ambitious Pastours" E.K. makes him out to be.

to understand the precedents for "July's" debate between the hills and the valleys. In the pastoral eclogue, both the confrontation of shepherd and goatherd and the dispute over location have lent themselves to a comic as well as a moralistic treatment; while it would obviously be too much to claim that the debate is primarily comic, it is at least occasionally comic and, with Thomalin's invective against corrupt pastors aside, relatively good-natured. Certainly the disputants do not approach each other in a manner one would expect were their dispute a battle between good and evil. Moreover, whatever the limitations of Morrell's perspective, it is misleading to equate him with the pastors Thomalin inveighs against. Two issues are involved here, the danger of power and the dangers to power; and while Morrell may illustrate the second, he does not illustrate the first, In fact, as we shall see, Morrell shares Thomalin's fear of the danger in the corrupt use of power, though he rejects Thomalin's fear of the danger of falling from power. Finally, while it is true that the exemplum illustrates the dangers that can befall the man of high estate, the high estate occupied by Grindal is not intrinsically a place of corruption; for Grindal himself is portrayed throughout the *Calender,* as well as in "July," as an example of the good shepherd.

The discussion of the superiority of one location over another is one of the standard motifs of the pastoral eclogue. Most frequently, of course, it consists of little more than one shepherd's attempt to persuade another to exchange a less for a more comfortable location, to leave the heat for the shade or to leave a windy or chilly spot for a more sheltered one. In the *Calender,* "August" and "October," as well as others, illustrate this motif. For the most part it is only a motif, part of the genre's decorum which demands that the pastoral at least seem to be taking place in the country. In the singing-contest, however, what is elsewhere only a naturalistic detail sometimes becomes part of the debate. The most useful example of this, in that it most resembles "July," is the fifth idyll of Theocritus. The fifth idyll is an energetic contest between the shepherd Lacon and the goatherd Comatas in terms of both their singing ability and their personal merits. As in "July," one disputant is a goatherd, the other a shepherd. And also as in "July," the two disputants debate who has the better location. Lacon urges Comatas to come over and sit "under the wild olive and this coppice. There's cool water falling yonder, and here's grass and a greenbed, and the locusts at their prattling." The elder Comatas accuses Lacon of ingratitude to one "that had the teaching of you when you were but a child": "Nurse a wolf-cub,—nay rather, nurse a puppy-dog—to be eaten for't." "And when, pray, do I mind me to have learnt or heard aught of good from thee?" asks the younger shepherd. The two return to the original question of location, and not surprisingly the insulted Comatas is not disposed to accept the petulant upstart's suggestion. He answers indignantly:

> Thither will I never come. Here I have oaks and bedstraw, and bees humming bravely at the hives, here's two springs of cool water to thy one, and birds, not locusts, a-babbling upon the tree, and, for shade thine's not half so good; and what's more the pine overhead is casting her nuts.

> *Lacon:* An you'll come here, I'll lay you shall tread lambskins and sheep's wool as soft as sleep. Those buckgoat pelts of thine smell e'en ranker than thou. And I'll set up a great bowl of whitest milk to the Nymphs, and eke I'll set up another of sweetest oil.

> *Comatas:* If come you do, you shall tread here taper fern and organy all a-blowing, and for your lying down there's shegoat-skins four times as soft as those lambskins of thine. And I'll set up to Pan eight pails of milk and eke eight pots of full honeycombs.[9]

The similarity between this segment of the fifth idyll and the July eclogue is two-fold: one, the debate over location; two, the condescension of both shepherd and goathered toward the other's way of life (for Lacon, Comatas' pelts stink of goat; for Comatas, his goatskins are softer than Lacon's sheepskins). Of further significance is the comic portrayal of Lacon and Comatas, who like their counterparts in "July" often seem like children in their prideful convictions and taunts.

The pastoral comedy of taunts and self-preening also plays a role in Boccaccio's eclogue in the fourteenth chapter of the *Ameto*. This eclogue is an expansion of and elaboration on the debate over location and profession in Theocritus. In Boccaccio, however, virtually the whole subject of the eclogue becomes the debate over location. However, the eclogue, regardless of whatever allegorical meaning it may have, remains a singing-contest and an exchange of abuse just as it was in Theocritus. In addition, the debate over location has now

9. *The Greek Bucolic Poets*, ed. and trans. J. M. Edmonds (Cambridge, Mass., 1928), pp. 67–69.

taken on the form Spenser will use in "July," a debate over the respective merits of the mountains and the plains. For the greater part of the eclogue, the debate is comic. As in Theocritus, Alcesto and Acaten, the contestants, defend their way of life and abuse that of their opponent with a rigidity that, initially at least, is at once childish and comic. Caught up in attack and self-praise, they do not see themselves as others see them. As the eclogue progresses, the abuse grows increasingly bitter. Alcesto accuses Acaten of having shifted the ground for their song from who sings best to who is richer. Acaten, after a few more insults, retorts bitterly to the effect that, "That's what *you* say. I don't have to talk to you, for all you know is the mountains. Mere habit holds you back." Alcesto is furious: in Acaten's shelter there is no sense or value; he should shut up; he is an enemy of sheep more than a guard or herdsman, and for that he will go sad and a beggar. For all the highly moralistic sound of these closing lines, Boccaccio's debate is every bit as rhetorical and dramatic in its comic ritual as it is moralistic, there being no clear-cut association of virtue or vice with the plains or the mountains.

Mantuan's eighth eclogue is generally agreed to be the source, at least indirectly, of "July." As in Boccaccio's eclogue, the discussion is between two shepherds, not between a goathered and a shepherd. However, Mantuan's poem is not really a debate at all, and it naturally does not share the comedy of attack and counterattack found in the poems by Theocritus, Boccaccio, and Spenser. The eighth eclogue's discussion of the hills and vales is only a prelude and a framework to Candidus' personal experience with Saint Pollux. The framework is almost exclusively devoted to Candidus' praise of the hills. He disparages the plains for their stench, filth, gnats, and rats; they provide no marble for churches and no herbs and grass to cure disease. The hills, however, produce sturdy, hairy men, fit for life on the sea or, oddly enough for Mantuan, in the city; the hills are also closer to the stars and have been loved by the holy fathers. Alphus provides nothing by way of defense of the plains; he is simply an ignoramus who must be educated.

All in all, the work generally cited as the source for "July," while it provides some of Morrell's arguments, is only part of the tradition of pastoral debate that makes itself felt in that eclogue. Mantuan's eighth eclogue is not a debate or a contest, while Theocritus' fifth idyll and Boccaccio's *Ameto* eclogue clearly are. Comedy is non-existent in Mantuan, whereas it plays at least a slight role in the *Ameto* eclogue and a substantial role in Theocritus. Moreover, even the moralistic Mantuan ascribes no special symbolism to hills and vales. It may be too much to argue that elements of the location debate found in Theocritus and Boccaccio but largely absent in Mantuan are in any precise sense direct influences on Spenser's handling of the location debate in "July." But the similarity is there, less the result of precise imitation than of Spenser's general conception of the eclogue as a dramatic, often comic, characterization through the conflict of ideas rather than a simple exposition of ideas.

The pastoral debate in general, as well as the location debate, has, as I have indicated before, traditionally lent itself to various forms of rustic comedy. In the "July" framework Spenser continues to employ certain comic details to set the debate apart from the total seriousness of the invective against corruption. In part this comedy is a matter of verbal fisticuffs, mutual recrimination alternating with self-praise. But it depends as well on the simple quaintness of the abusive epithets the rustics throw at each other. If it was amusing to Spenser's audience to see the characters of formal and sophisticated bishops made the basis for rustic characters, it does not seem to me too fanciful to find the quaint rusticity of language and dialect, in addition to its function in terms of pastoral decorum, a related source of comedy. Critics, in defending Spenser's use of language, have perhaps unduly stressed how it could be justified by pastoral precedent and decorum, and too little revealed the comedy emerging from the quaint rusticity of this language. Spenser is most like Theocritus in his ability to capture some of the comedy of rustic language and behavior. When Thomalin bluntly retorts to Morrell's naive claim that the hills being nearer to heaven enable the hill-dweller to pass more readily to heaven, "Syker thou speakes lyke a lewde lorrell, / of Heauen to demen so," we are to enjoy the quaintness of his expression as well as the aptness of his observation. More comic if less apt is Morrell's recrimination:

> Syker, thous but a laesie loord,
>   and rekes much of thy swinck,
> That with fond termes, and weetlesse words
>   to blere myne eyes doest thinke.

(33-36)

The quaintness of the blunt frontal assault, the rustic's fear of having the wool pulled over his eyes—this is part of the Theocritean comedy of the rustic debate, and to enjoy it we must *hear* it—the tones of shock, contempt, or total disbelief that an antagonist could possibly take his argument seriously. Equally a part of rustic comedy is its play with the literal and naive perceptions of the rustic. In pastoral literature, and especially in Spenser, the shepherd's innocence is at once the strength and the weakness of his vision. While both Thomalin and Morell have something important and serious to say as shepherds, they are not immune to the comic literal-mindedness associated with the rustic. Morrell, for example, as part of his defense of the hills, remarks naively:

> Hereto, the hills bene nigher heuen,
>   and thence the passage ethe.
> As well can proue the piercing leuin,
>   that seeldome falls bynethe.

(89-92)

These lines do not involve any attempt on Morrell's part to deceive Thomalin. Instead, they are a comic revelation of the rustic literal-mindedness of Morrell's mind and his quaint adherence to an absurd myth. Morrell's inability to see that his "proof" that the hills are closer to heaven since lightning strikes them more often actually plays right into Thomalin's hands is part of the pastoral comedy of the limited, literal-minded, and naive perception of the rustic we have been talking about. Failure to appreciate this comedy of perception and misperception may lead us to give exaggerated moralistic weight to Thomalin's contention that Morrell's herd has strayed:

> Is not thilke same a goteheard prowde,
>   that sittes on yonder bancke,
> Whose straying heard them selfe doth shrowde
>   emong the bushes rancke?

(1-4)

E.K.'s observation that the "straying heard" represents those "which wander out of the way of truth" is a trifle beside the point. Thomalin's remark, made when he first spies Morrell on the hill, is another example of the comedy emerging from the limited and inflexible perceptions of the rustic, the "seely shepherds swayne": the comedy consists simply of Thomalin's bewilderment that someone would actually *intend* goats to be on a hill; he cannot conceive of anyone's actually choosing the hills, so that of course to his eyes they have "strayed." Although I do not wish to make "July" into a totally comic eclogue (it clearly is not), it does seem important to me that we realize how Spenser uses traditional comic details taken from the pastoral debate to temper the conflict of pastoral perspectives portrayed. Thomalin and Morrell are engaged in a serious dispute over values, but it is a dispute between two perspectives each sufficiently just that comedy can affect both. In this respect, the debate is quite different from Thomalin's long invective against corruption in the Church. Here as elsewhere in the moral eclogues the Theocritean exchange of abuse, which is at least partly comic, must be distinguished from the invective, which is exclusively moral.

In "July," as in the other moral eclogues, neither contestant can lay claim to the full truth. Just as in the debates in "February" and "May," none of the contending pastoral perspectives is fully complete, so too in "July's" debate between ambition and the low estate.[10] The argument progresses in three overlapping stages: the first stage deals with the dangers of the hills and the plain; the second, with the traditional associations with hills and the plain; the third, with the exemplum of Algrind. Thomalin opens his Mantuanesque argument with the medieval and Renaissance theme of the dangers of ambition:

This reede is ryfe, that oftentime
   great clymbers fall vnsoft.
In humble dales is footing fast,
   the trode is not so tickle:
And though one fall through heedlesse hast,
   yet is his misse not mickle.

(11-16)

Thomalin's first point, and the one he will put forth most strenuously and persistently, is simply that if one trips on a hill one has a great deal farther to fall than on the lowly plain. Moreover, by dwelling on the hills one lays himself open to disease and death:

10. H. S. V. Jones, *A Spenser Handbook,* p. 49, claims that "July" contains a "clear-cut issue of pride and humility," and this opinion has been generally accepted and elaborated on by more recent critics. Hallett Smith, for example, in his *Elizabethan Poetry,* p. 48, claims that Morrell "represents the Catholic or Anglican clergy gloating in worldly pomp"; he is the aspiring mind, while Thomalin is the mean estate, "the central theme of pastoralism." Robert Durr, *ELH,* 24 (1957), 284, discovers a similarly clear-cut opposition: the central issue revolves around "*superbia* and worldly ambition versus *humilitas* and the contentment of the tried estate." Holding like views are William Nelson, *The Poetry of Edmund Spenser,* pp. 46–47, and A. C. Hamilton, *ELH,* 23 (1956), 180.

The rampant Lyon hunts he ["the Sonne"] fast,
    with Dogge of noysome breath,
Whose balefull barking bringes in hast
    pyne, plagues, and dreery death.
Agaynst his cruell scortching heate
    where last thou couerture?
The wastefull hylls vnto his threate
    is a playne ouerture.

(20-27)

Morrell accuses Thomalin of preferring the plains because he is too lazy and too afraid to climb the hills. "Thous but a laesie loord," he scolds, and a few lines later he taunts Thomalin with being "affrayed,/to climbe this hilles height." What Morrell says of Thomalin could in fact be fairly applied to Colin in "June": Colin rationalized his poetic slothfulness, his failure to "presume to *Parnasse* hyll" by resorting to the Mantuanesque argument that "With shepheard sittes not, followe flying fame: / But feede his flocke in fields, where falls hem best"; if the danger of the high estate is pride and a precipitous fall, the danger of the low estate is passivity and inactivity.

Morrell initiates the second state of the argument by enumerating the favorable mythological and religious (mainly Roman) associations hills have had. There are "holy hylles . . . sacred vnto saints" like Saint Michael's mount and Saint Bridget's bower in Kent; there is Parnassus, where goatherds dwell beside a learned well (an allusion providing another link with "June"). Indeed, Christ himself, "the great God *Pan*," fed his "blessed flocke of *Dan*" on Mount Olivet. Morrell's rebuttal continues by reference to the simple facts of nature: the Medway, whose waters serve the dales, has its source in the hills, and herbs good for the health of goats, Malampode and Teribinth, grow there. Morrell concludes his argument, as we saw earlier, with the naive and literal-minded statement that since lightning strikes hills more often than the plains, the hills must be nearer heaven; and if the hills are nearer heaven, it necessarily follows that hill-dwellers have an easier passage to heaven.

In his lengthy rebuttal, Thomalin continues to pursue the "de casibus" theme: "he that striues to touch the starres, / oft stombles at a strawe." He argues from the typical Protestant perspective that, although he adores the holy hills, it is not for themselves but for the saints and their example of meekness, humility, and sacrifice. Indirectly and ironically, Thomalin is receding from his earlier rigid rejection of the hills and hill-dwellers: not only proud but also great and humble men have lived thereon. Thomalin then proceeds to enumerate examples of good shepherds: Abel "the first shepheard," the twelve sons of Jacob, and Moses. Like Piers in "May," Thomalin contrasts a golden past of shepherding with the inglorious present:

> Whilome all these were lowe, and lief,
>   and loued their flocks to feede,
> They neuer strouen to be chiefe,
>   and simple was theyr weede.
> But now . . .
>
> (165-169)

But now shepherds dress "in purple and pall," not plainly. Ambitious, they abuse and take advantage of their sheep; greedy, they fatten themselves and make their sheep fast. Thomalin's indictment, it is important to see, is not an indictment of Morrell but of Rome and Romanism in the Anglican Church. Moreover, the invective is directed not at the high estate as such but at a misuse of the high estate, in which shepherds take the profits of others' labors, accumulate wealth for themselves, and pamper themselves in pleasures. Thomalin's invective is much like Piers's in "May": it illustrates the dangers of his antagonist's position, but it does not identify the antagonist himself with the actual abuses. There are, then, two main points to Thomalin's argument, the danger to power and the danger of power; and failure to distinguish between them can only blur the moral position of Morrell. For even Morrell, who rejects the first part of Thomalin's thesis, the danger to power, can at least half-agree with him on the dangerous abuses of power: "Here is a great deale of good matter," he admits, though like most of the worldly disputants in the *Calender* he has his reservations:

> Thou medlest, then shall haue thanke,
>   to wyten shepheards welth:
> When folke bene fat, and riches rancke,
>   it is a signe of helth.
>
> (209-212)

In a purely material sense, there is of course some truth to this; but the moral flaw of the worldly shepherd is nonetheless apparent.

The disputing shepherds are by no means so far apart as their critics have made them. That there is some common moral ground between them is clear from Morrell's partial concession to the complaints of Thomalin's invective. The two are brought even closer together, however, in their common sympathy for Algrind. The considerable controversy over interpreting this exemplum of an eagle that mistook Algrind's white head for chalk and therefore dropped a shellfish on his head should not cause us to lose sight of the fact that the fable is primarily a "morall and generall" exemplum of the danger of the high places and of the irrationality of human fate.[11] No matter what historical equation we use to interpret the fable, this fact is a constant, regardless of whether the mistake illustrated is the fault of Algrind, Elizabeth, or the shellfish. Furthermore, it is important to note that the fable cannot be used to support Thomalin's association of sinful ambition with the hills. What is exemplified in the fable is not the sinfulness of ambition but its dangers. Algrind, after all, is a good man. He is injured not because his lofty station involved him in sin but simply because it exposed him to danger.

If the exemplum illustrates the dangers of the high places and the irrationality of man's fate, it also establishes a common bond of agreement between the two contestants. Whatever their disagreement over high and low places, they are united in their sympathy for Algrind. This fact, along with Morrell's earlier half-agreement with Thomalin on the abuses of power, thoroughly contradicts any attempt to paint Morrell entirely black. The chief difference between the two men is less in terms of the abuses of the high places than on the dangers of the high places. This division in Morrell's own opinions is reflected in his last speech:

Ah good *Algrin,* his hap was ill,
    but shall be bett in time,
Now farewell shepheard, sith thys hyll
    thous hast such doubt to climbe.

(229-232)

11. It is generally agreed that this little allegory involves Elizabeth's sequestering of Archbishop Grindal for refusing to suppress the prophesyings. The specifics of the allegory are still controversial, however. C. H. Herford, *The Shepheards Calender,* p. 217 (Notes), reads it as follows: "Elizabeth (the she-eagle) desiring to crush the Puritans (the shell-fish), sought to make Grindal, the newly-appointed archbishop, the instrument of the blow." Even now this is still probably the most widely accepted reading. Percy Long, however, in "Spenser and the Bishop of Rochester," *PMLA,* 31 (1916), 734–735, has argued that because a golden scallop dominates the Bishop of Rochester's coat of arms, it is Bishop Young, not the Puritans, who is meant by the shell-fish: "Spenser in effect declares that Elizabeth's command to suppress 'prophesyings' contemplated specifically a removal of abuses for which Young was responsible." This reading seems unlikely in light of the fact that Spenser admired Young and served him.

In the first two lines Morrell reveals his sympathy for the fallen figure, but the last two show that despite this he maintains his original position, that Thomalin will not climb because he is afraid.

It would indeed be a mistake to equate Morrell with the Renaissance figure of the aspiring mind. He is not Tamburlaine or Faustus. He is worldly, to be sure, but he is not corrupt. His argument, however flawed, is not mere sophistry. Even Thomalin admits that the hills have born great and humble men. One of these, in fact, is Algrind himself, who is always spoken of in the *Calender* in terms of his wisdom and humility. And he himself dwelt on a hill. It should be clear, then, that we are not to accept Thomalin's evaluation of the hills as the final word, for what we are given in "July" is not a single pattern of behavior associated with the hills but several patterns: the saints, Algrind, the corrupt Roman or Romanist Anglican clergy, and somewhere between the holy and the profane, Morrell. The hills thus represent a continuum of moral possibilities rather than a single and certain immorality.[12] Moreover, although we have only Morrell's word for it, the same can be said of the plains (we should recall how in the previous eclogue Colin perverts Thomalin's low estate through anger, fear, and obsession). The moral vision of the *Calender* is considerably less simplistic than an opposition of corrupt and ambitious hill-dwellers versus healthy and humble plains-dwellers. We may follow E.K. into his equation of Morrell with "proude and ambitious Pastours," but if we do we must follow

12. Robert Durr, however, *ELH*, 24 (1957), 284, follows E.K.'s lead and attributes a moralistic symbolism to the opposition of hills and dales and sheep and goats. While it is obvious that the hills represent aspiration and the plains the mean estate, it is doubtful that a clear-cut moral opposition is involved. The *Calender* affords several instances in which hills are not associated with evil. In "January" Colin takes his sheep to a hill to let them revive after being pent up in winter. In "February" Thenot speaks of learning "a tale of Truth" from Tityrus while "keeping his sheepe on the hills of Kent." In "June" Colin, while refusing to "presume to *Parnasse* hyll," itself a rationalization and fault in judgment, later says he wishes "my gentle shepheards, which your flocks do feede, / Whether on hylls, or dales, or other where" to bear witness to Rosalind's treachery. Finally, in "August" a shepherd falls in love on a hill. In light of this evidence, extreme caution is desirable in ascribing intrinsic moral failing to the hills.

As far as the sheep and the goats are concerned, one must be equally cautious in giving E.K.'s gloss much weight: "By Gotes in scrypture be represented the wicked and reprobate, whose pastour also must needes be such." There is, of course, in Theocritus' fifth idyll, a literary precedent for a contest between goatherd and shepherd that does not involve a moral contest of vices and virtues. Moreover, in the *Calender* itself goats are mentioned on two other occasions without apparent disapprobation. In "May" the Gate is not wicked or reprobate; and in "October" Piers, certainly not reprobate as a shepherd, offers Cuddie a goat. Finally, if goats are as intrinsically wicked as E.K. (and Durr) contend, Thomalin is certainly inconsistent in asking Morrell and his goats to come down to the plain.

him into his contradiction, when he is forced to admit the truths of both emblems, Thomalin's "In medio virtus" and Morrell's "In summo foelicitas":

> By thys poesye Thomalin confirmeth that . . . he taketh occasion to praise the meane and lowly state, as that wherein is safetie without feare, and quiet without danger, according to the saying of olde Philosophers, that vertue dwelleth in the middest, being enuironed with two contrary vices: whereto Morrell replieth with continuance of the same Philosophers opinion, that albeit all bountye dwelleth in mediocritie, yet perfect felicitye dwelleth in supremacie. For they say, and most true it is, that happinesse is placed in the highest degree.

In "July" then, Spenser is concerned with dramatizing a conflict of pastoral perspectives, neither of which is without merit. One is the risky "overture" and the other the more secure "couverture." In addition, Morrell chooses the hills not merely through self-interest but in the interest of his goats' welfare, just as the shepherd Thomalin chooses the dales for his sheep's welfare: some need Malampode and some do not. Equally relevant is that a natural fact and order are involved here: goats are generally raised on the higher levels and sheep on the lower. I do not think that Spenser is trying to persuade us that goats are bad and should become sheep: sheep are sheep and goats are goats, and there are good and bad goatherds just as there are good and bad shepherds. Insofar as Morrell's high places and ambition involve danger, they are not repudiated in the *Calender;* man has a choice, he may take the risk or avoid it. But insofar as ambition leads to self-seeking, a perversion of the shepherd's or goatherd's calling, the good man has no choice. It is significant that on this most crucial aspect of the debate on ambition Morrell and Thomalin at least partially agree.

If we are to understand "July" fully, we must realize that it is in part a companion piece to "June." Both, though in obviously different ways, deal with the issue of man's ambition and its relation to the traditional pastoral ethic of the tried estate. In "June," we find the philosopher of the tried estate, Hobbinol, encouraging his antagonist of sorts, Colin, to climb the Parnassian hill, while Colin refuses in what is both a parody of Thomalin's more extreme version of the low estate and at the same time a statement of its limitations. In "July" we are given a less sophisticated and complex presentation of the issue, but the message is much the same: if there are limitations to deviation from the Mantuanesque pastoral ethic, there are also limitations to that ethic itself. Even the pastoral world must have its saints and its Algrind, men who, in the martyrdom that the cautious Thomalin fears, have managed to synthesize in themselves humility of soul with the aspiration of their mission.

"September"

"September" contains the most open and vehement satire in the *Calender,* directed at both the English and Roman churches, which mirror each other in their exploitation of sheep, covetousness, idleness, ignorance, and overweening ambition. Earlier commentators, thinking Spenser a Puritan or at least strongly Puritanical, were willing to assume that Diggon Davie, the voice of this satire, was Spenser's mouthpiece; later critics, finding the ecclesiastical satire the focus of the eclogue, have generally followed suit.[13] For those, however, who have felt that the eclogue focusses on the flaw behind Diggon's move to "forrein costes," the main voice to be heard is Hobbinol's, the voice of classical moderation.[14] Although Hobbinol, in this eclogue as in "June," does voice one of the classic themes of pastoral, this theme is not the central theme of "September" or of the *Calender.*

13. Until the early 1940's, attempts at specific historical identification of Diggon Davie were not very convincing. Early efforts, not surprisingly, predicated their conclusions on the assumption that Diggon, like Spenser, was a Puritan. Alexander Grosart, for example, in his *Complete Works of Edmund Spenser,* I (London, 1882–84), 25–28, suggested Jan Vander Noodt, whose *Theatre of Worldlings* is a detailed account of many of the ecclesiastical abuses outlined in "September." The same Puritan bias is apparent in James Jackson Higginson's contention, *Spenser's "Shepheard's Calender" in Relation to Contemporary Affairs* (New York, 1912), pp. 188–197, that Diggon represents a Puritan clergyman absent from his living because of a trip to London, probably Richard Greenham, a prominent nonconformist divine. A turning-point seems to have been marked by W. L. Renwick, who noted in his edition of the *Calender* (London, 1930), p. 210, that the identification itself is not enormously important. What is important, he observes, is that "Spenser presents, and sympathetically, a cleric, strongly Protestant, and an apologist for the rank and file of English clergy." Diggon Davie, suggests Renwick, was probably not a convinced Puritan like Greenham; in fact, Spenser himself was probably "less involved in Puritan ideas than some people imagine." Renwick, however, cannot resist a scholar's stab-guess and suggests a certain Harrison, vicar of Radwinter. By far the most plausible identification, suggested by both Viola Hulbert, "Diggon Davie," *Journal of English and Germanic Philology* (*JEGP*), 41 (1942), 349–367, and Paul McLane, *Spenser's "Shepheardes Calender,"* pp. 216–234, is Richard Davis, Bishop of St. David's in Wales, which has both name and dialect going for it. McLane, in addition, is able to establish, quite convincingly, why Davis would have had reason to complain. In the identification of Diggon with Davis, a reformer but no Puritan, the transformation of Spenser's own image in this century is interestingly reflected.

14. Almost universally, earlier commentators assumed Diggon's satire to be the central thrust of the "September" eclogue. Herbert Cory, for example, *Edmund*

This pastoral perspective has its own limitations, and Hobbinol himself is made to appear not a little naive. The dialogue in "September" between pastoral perspectives works along the same lines as in the other moral eclogues: an ambivalence emerges from the confrontation of two limited perspectives. Hobbinol's pastoral ideal, while hardly unreligious, nonetheless tends to have a greater awareness of the secular, the world which man must adjust to as well as mold. Diggon's ideal, on the other hand, insists on the constant, unwavering vigilance of the good shepherd; it is an ideal of reform, the remolding of a corrupt world. "September" is thus a major statement in the *Calender* of the dual truth and limitations of the ethic of *otium*. The confrontation of the now austere Diggon Davie with Hobbinol is, fundamentally, a confrontation of the two principal pastoral perspectives in the *Shepheardes Calender*.

"September" opens with the conventional pastoral situation of the grieving shepherd bewailing the contrast between past contentment

---

Spenser: A Critical Study (Berkeley, 1917), pp. 29–30, claims that "the uncouth accents of the wanderer certainly voice Spenser's own beliefs"; and W. L. Renwick in his edition of the *Calender*, p. 210, maintains that Diggon "may represent Richard Greenham, but he utters Spenser's own views." More recently, this position has been restated by A. C. Hamilton, *ELH*, 23 (1956), 180. However, H. S. V. Jones, *A Spenser Handbook*, pp. 50–52, and Hallett Smith, *Elizabethan Poetry*, pp. 46–48, have both thought Hobbinol to voice the main theme of "September," moderation. According to Jones, "September's" criticism of restless ambition offers "the most persuasive statement of the philosophy of moderation"; and it is Hobbinol who supplies the remedy for such ambition ("content who lives with tryed state") and for Diggon Davie's reaction to the vices he finds himself surrounded by ("thilke same rule were too straight"). Jones concludes that "the philosophy of the tried estate . . . serves for the climax of the moral eclogues . . . We may conclude, then, that in the opinions of Harvey we may find a principle of unity for the *Shepheardes Calender* as a whole." Hallett Smith agrees with Jones, but he alters Jones's observation to fit his own contention that the *Calender* embodies "a pastoral idea." Smith notes, correctly, that the philosophy of moderation is hardly the distinctive property of Gabriel Harvey. The really significant point, then, "is that it is the central doctrine of pastoral. The *Calender* is organized as pastoral." My only disagreement with this is that, while the *Calender* is most certainly "organized as pastoral," it is not organized according to a single idea that can be said to be *the* pastoral idea but according to a dramatic conflict of pastoral ideas. For Robert Durr, *ELH*, 24 (1957), 285–286, the central moral lesson of "September" is Hobbinol's. Diggon, through sinful *amor sui,* sought the world and its riches; by ignoring the tried estate, he ignores God's order and has thus "laid himself open to all the wild desires flesh is heir to." William Nicolet, however, "Edmund Spenser's *Shepheardes Calender,*" pp. 216–226, suggests a different approach, observing that while Hobbinol's eagerness to conform to the demands of the time is inadequate, so too is Diggon's foolhardy indignation; but unfortunately, Nicolet, with this partial understanding of the possible ambivalence in the debate, returns to the old clear-cut distinctions, labelling Hobbinol a "bad" shepherd.

and present misery. Having dwelt in foreign lands for nine months, Diggon "dempt there much to haue eeked my store," but what he found in "forrein costes" was only a vile caricature of his ambition and desire for riches, there being "no being for those, that truely mene, / But for such, as of guile maken gayne." Diggon, in distinguishing between his simple desire to "eeke his store" and the guileful avarice of the "forrein" shepherds, does not consider his fault to be the search for gain per se. Diggon's new position is not an unselective repudiation of earthly goods, or a totally ascetic denial of "store." Rather, as Hobbinol says, his error was not in seeking gain but in seeking for "vnknown gayne." That is, he simply did not know what he was getting into:

> Ah fon, now by thy losse art taught,
> That seeldome chaunge the better brought.
> Content who liues with tryed state,
> Neede feare no chaunge of frowning fate:
> But who will seeke for vnknowne gayne,
> Oft liues by losse, and leaues with payne.

(68-73)

To interpret Hobbinol as meaning that Diggon's ambition is alien to the pastoral moral order is to fail to take into account that this is the same Hobbinol who urged Colin to climb Parnassus. Hobbinol is a pragmatist, perhaps too much so, and his comments to Diggon reveal not a moralistic disdain for riches (which, after all, Hobbinol urged Colin to seek) but a disapproval of an unwise and impractical way of pursuing them. His argument is quite simple: if one is reasonably content, as Diggon was before his adventure, then one is impractical to risk an already proved situation (the "tryed state"); but if, as was Colin's case, the present situation is unrewarding then it is impractical to keep on the same track. The Hobbinol of "June" and the Hobbinol of "September" are not contradictory.

Hobbinol's pastoral ideal of contentment is closer to the more practical one of the Arcadian pastoralists than it is to the more idealistic one of the Christian pastoralists. The ideal of contentment Hobbinol puts forth has only a verbal similarity to Thenot's contentment, an austere and stoic acceptance of divine providence. None of the representatives of austere contentment would be capable of advising Diggon to speak less openly of the abuses he has seen, lest it offend; but this of course is what Hobbinol does. Hobbinol's "philosophy of moderation" for all its merits at times seems to consist of simply moving with the punches. For example, after Diggon has attacked the vices of the foreign lands he ventured to, Hobbinol interrupts and asks him to speak more plainly:

Diggon, I praye thee speake not so dirke.
Such myster saying me seemeth to mirke.

(102-103)

But when Diggon begins to speak more plainly, when it becomes quite clear that he is attacking an established and powerful social institution, Hobbinol at once reverses himself:

Nowe Diggon, I see thou speakest to plaine:
Better it were, a little to feyne,
And cleanly couer, that cannot be cured.
Such il, as is forced, mought nedes be endured.

(136-139)

Hobbinol's practical ideal of pastoral contentment can apparently brook evil "if it be forced," but his phrase "mought nedes be endured" can only be thought an ironic parallel to Thenot's phrases of endurance. Hobbinol's endurance is political and practical, while Thenot's and Piers's is quite the opposite: Piers is untouched by Palinode's contention (similar to Hobbinol's) that his frankness, his intransigent unwillingness to endure human weakness, may destroy the whole institution of the Church.

If Hobbinol's practical contentment verges on blind acceptance of evil, it has also blinded him to evil. As in "June," Hobbinol's pastoral paradise is to some extent artificial and cloistered; it is a paradise only because he himself is blind to its limitations: he does not know, or at least he cannot accept the fact, that Eden has fallen, that there are wolves in the world. When Diggon informs Hobbinol that sheep "wander at will, and stray at pleasure" so that many "bene of rauenous Wolues yrent," Hobbinol replies naively:

Fye on thee Diggon, and all thy foule leasing,
Well is knowne that sith the Saxon king,
Neuer was Woolfe seene many nor some,
Nor in all Kent, nor in Christendome.

(150-153)

Hobbinol's blindness to wolves, if not to foxes, thus sets him apart from Thenot and Piers. Thenot and Piers are both aware of wolves, and from that awareness arises their ideal of the pastoral life so different from Hobbinol's. The naive and cloistered, though rational, Hobbinol must learn from the wild-eyed, irrational, and sometimes incoherent Diggon Davie that wolves "with sheepes clothing doen hem disguise." Hobbinol naively suggests, "or priue or pert yf any bene, / We han great Bandogs will teare their skinne," and Diggon replies with the lesson of Piers:

> But not good Dogges hem needeth to chace,
> But heedy shepheards to discerne their face.
> For all their craft is in their countenaunce,
> They bene so graue and full of mayntenaunce.

(166-169)

Piers's lesson in the fable of the Fox and the Kid and Diggon's lesson here are the same: instinct is not enough; one must know, perceive. That is the central point of Diggon's tale of Roffy.

The specific situation referred to in Diggon's tale has never been satisfactorily explained, although it is generally agreed that, as F. M. Padelford suggested, the episode is based on some sort of trouble between Bishop Young and an aggressive Roman Catholic, possibly Thomas Watson.[15] But its general point is clear: if Roffy, who is "wise, and as Argus eyed" is tricked, how much greater the risk for Hobbinol, who is totally blind to wolves. This exemplum further illustrates the limitations of Hobbinol's ideal. His flaw, like Diggon's when he went out to seek his fortune, is ignorance. Ironically and significantly, the one led by ambition, the other by the "tryed state," share the same flaw.

If I have focussed entirely on the limitations of Hobbinol's pastoral perspective, it is not because that perspective is without merit, but because it is the negative aspect of that ideal on which "September" primarily focusses. "September" provides a needed qualification of Hobbinol's ideal as it is seen in "June." Even in "September," however, this ideal is not meritless, for Hobbinol's awareness of practicality is a valuable counter to Diggon's wild-eyed and unrestrained protests. When Hobbinol asks Diggon "how mought we Diggon, hem be-hold," Diggon replies with typical impracticality and intransigence, much in the style of Piers:

> How, but with heede and watchfulnesse,
> Forstallen hem of their wilinesse?

15. F. M. Padelford, "Spenser and the Puritan Propaganda," *Modern Philology* (*MP*), 11 (1913), 100.

For thy with shepheard wittes not playe,
Or sleepe, as some doen, all the long day:
But euer liggen in watch and ward,
From soddein force theyr flocks for to gard.

(230-235)

Such austerity needs a practical awareness of human limitations, and
that is what Hobbinol provides:

Ah Diggon, thilke same rule were too straight,
All the cold season to wach and waite.
We bene of fleshe, men as other bee,
Why should we be bound to such miseree?
What euer thing lacketh chaungeable rest,
Mought needes decay, when it is at best.

(236-241)

Hobbinol, therefore, is not *the* spokesman of the *Calender's* ethic.
He is a spokesman for one of the contending ethics. His ethic, the
practical ideal of contentment, like the austere ideal of Diggon and
Piers, has its weaknesses and its strengths. Its value can be seen in
"June," where Hobbinol's exhortations to Colin contain an indis-
putable common sense. Its weaknesses are seen here when Hobbinol
must himself suddenly confront the evils of the world and the limitations of his own vision.

Characteristic of the *Calender,* therefore, is "September's" patterning of perspectives according to what I have called ethical ambivalence: the incompleteness of ideals, the necessity for one ideal and
one man to counter and balance another. Hobbinol's practical ideal
affords an important counter to Diggon Davie's wild-eyed impractical
ideal. With his new knowledge, Diggon runs the risk of new ignorance; like Piers in "May," he lacks full knowledge of the practical
risks involved in his correction of disorder. But the September eclogue
is also an important qualification of Hobbinol's practical ideal of
contentment. In "June," it may *seem* that Hobbinol's ideal of compromise and moderation could suffice to recapture the earthly paradise.
In "September," this is obviously not true. When Hobbinol first pro-
nounces his ethic, moralizing that Diggon was impractical and mistaken in leaving the "tryed state" for "vnknowne gayne," he appears
to have the same possession of the full truth that he seemed to have
in "June." As the dialogue progresses, however, we become increasingly aware of the inadequacy of this ideal to the world Diggon
describes. Diggon has fallen, but he has returned with a knowledge

of evil that Hobbinol, in his cloistered innocence, has not yet perceived. The ironic fact is that, while Hobbinol's ethic can pinpoint the source of Diggon's woes (abandonment of the contented life), it is not sufficient to cure them. It is diagnostic but not therapeutic. Hobbinol's version of the pastoral ethic tells Diggon much about what he should not have done, but it is much less useful in telling him what he should now do. In the face of his new knowledge of wolves, the Hobbinol ethic seems suddenly disoriented and incomplete. It is, therefore, thoroughly inaccurate to make Hobbinol the sole spokesman of the *Calender's* ethic. The September eclogue, in fact, provides us with the most direct confrontation of a legitimate form of the Arcadian pastoral ethic, Hobbinol's, with a legitimate form of the Mantuanesque austere and wintry ethic, Diggon's, and in so doing this eclogue, perhaps more than any other, interprets for us the dual limitation and strength of these two contending forms of conventional pastoral wisdom.

"October"

Because it deals with poetry and the poet, "October," probably more than any other eclogue in the *Calender,* has tempted readers to extract from it a single point of view, one that would contain Spenser's own conception of poetry.[16] E.K. certainly has played no small part in this temptation, observing that "in Cuddie is set out the perfecte paterne of a Poet" and that "the Author herof" has elsewhere discoursed at great length on poetical matters in his book called the "English Poete." Inevitably, critics have attempted to discover in the October eclogue this lost treatise. The problem, however, is that while E.K. maintains that it is Cuddie who is "the perfecte paterne of a Poete,"[17] it is Piers whose poetics many critics have

16. A survey of the attempts to identify either Piers's or Cuddie's views with Spenser's and even to equate Spenser with Piers and Cuddie can be found in the Variorum Edition, VII, pt. 1, pp. 366–378. Typical of the nature of this commentary are the remarks of C. H. Herford in his edition of the *Calender,* p. xlv, that "in the *October* Spenser has given direct expression to his poetic ideals," and of E. de Selincourt in his edition of the *Poetical Works,* pp. xvi–xvii, who claims that Piers and Cuddie "prefigure two conflicting elements in the poet's own nature; the practical . . . and the ideal."

17. What is probably intended by this description is exactly what it says, that Cuddie is the perfect image or the perfect likeness of a poet, not that he is "the paterne of a perfecte Poete." This misreading has caused needless confusion, and it has obscured the fact that much of what Cuddie says, though no doubt partially true, is sometimes downright nonsense and is often comic in its typicality— the constant railing against the audience of the time, the belief that Piers, the

felt most akin to Spenser's. Consequently, critics have been hard-pressed to determine whether Spenser's views are Piers's or Cuddie's, or whether they are perhaps a combination of both. Regardless of the stance taken, the result has invariably been to impose a single central thesis on the eclogue: one character is given the whole truth, or if characters share the truth, there is still one single truth. This, I believe, distorts the eclogue. "October," like the other moral eclogues, consists of dramatic conflict of pastoral perspectives. The central or focal issue is now the function and nature of poetry rather than age versus youth or participation versus withdrawal, but, in a general sense, the problems of the shepherd-as-poet resemble the problems of shepherds in the other moral eclogues. The shepherd-poet must accommodate himself to the natural year and world, he must survive; yet at the same time he must not fail his eternal mission. The problem confronting the poet, then, is another manifestation of the general problem confronting all shepherds in the *Calender:* how and to what extent can a man participate in the world and yet preserve himself and his eternal responsibility from being tainted? What is the ideal balance between the self and the other, between this world and the next? More specifically, "October" is fundamentally a dramatic confrontation of a practicing Renaissance poet and his practical needs both material and poetic, with an inherited, idealistic, and in part inadequate poetic. The confrontation here, as elsewhere in the moral eclogues, is dramatic and ambivalent with two perspectives of partial if not equal legitimacy.[18]

The debate for October occurs between Piers, the exponent of Renaissance poetic and moral idealism, and Cuddie, the poet who must deal with material reality as well as the ideal. From this debate no real resolution emerges: as Piers tosses out to Cuddie one by one his noble commonplaces, their inadequacy, at least for Cuddie, be-

---

mere aficionado (or critic, or the poet of a past generation—the principle is the same), does not really understand the present state of poetry and the poet, and so forth and so on.

18. The balance in the debate is, in fact, Spenser's most important deviation from Mantuan's fifth eclogue as well as Alexander Barclay's imitation of it. In both of these, the poet's antagonist, the miserly rich man, is made to appear a selfish and materialistic fool. "October's" more balanced debate between the realist and the idealist, to oversimplify the confrontation, is much more akin to Boccaccio's thirteenth eclogue, "Laurea." Though the poet in this eclogue espouses a Piers-like position, denying the value of perishable worldly goods, arguments of the practical merchant, Stilbon, are not altogether invalid. "October" seems simply to shuffle the arguments.

comes increasingly obvious; at the same time, it is equally obvious
that Cuddie is inadequate for these ideals. The debate is divided
into three parts, the first taking up the rewards of poetry, the second
its proper subjects and inspirations, the third (an extension of the
second) the Colin-exemplum and the relationship of love to poetry.
The eclogue opens with the conventional elegiac contrast between
the happy past and the sad present. Piers recalls to his silent, unsing-
ing friend, how

> Whilome thou wont the shepheards laddes to leade,
> In rymes, in ridles, and in bydding base:
> Now they in thee, and thou in sleepe art dead.

(4-6)

Cuddie's situation parallels Colin's. Both have, in a general sense,
abandoned public song for lack of gain: Colin, for failing to gain
Rosalind; Cuddie, for failing to gain some material reward that will
enable him to survive the natural year:

> *Piers,* I haue pyped erst so long with payne,
> That all mine Oten reedes bene rent and wore:
> And my poore Muse hath spent her spared store,
> Yet little good hath got, and much lesse gayne.
> Such pleasaunce makes the Grasshopper so poore,
> And ligge so layd, when Winter doth her straine.
>
> The dapper ditties, that I wont deuise,
> To feede youthes fancie, and the flocking fry,
> Delighten much: what I the bett for thy?
> They han the pleasure, I a sclender prise.
> I beate the bush, the byrds to them doe flye:
> What good thereof to Cuddie can arise?

(7-18)

Cuddie's knowledge of the material needs of man need not suggest
that he is guilty of sinful self-love. Self-love in the *Calender* is not
of necessity sinful any more than it is in Christianity's "love thy
neighbor as thy self." The problem is to strike a balance, and both
Cuddie and Piers, not Cuddie alone, in their earlier appearance in
the *Calender* as well as here, have failed to do that. Cuddie's argument
is an extension of his argument in "February," just as Piers's is an
extension of his argument in "May." In his earlier appearance, Cuddie
was acutely aware of man's need to accommodate himself to the natural demands of the year and himself. Unlike the conventional *senex*-
figure Thenot, he realized the importance of participation, procreation,

and simple survival. In "October" we find Cuddie once again framing his complaint in terms of the natural year: winter comes, and the grasshopper-poet must survive. Cuddie's perspective, therefore, is really still the same; only the framework—now the question of man's rewards here on earth—has changed. His vision is certainly incomplete and carried to Roman extreme could of course lead to sinful self-love. But Cuddie is not a Roman, though aware of the material world and its demands; it is a matter of degree, and we must observe that distinction. To Cuddie's thoroughly legitimate fear that he will be mastered by the year, Piers proposes an Orphic idealism: the poet himself can master the year, and triumph through lasting fame:

> *Cuddie*, the prayse is better, then the price,
> The glory eke much greater then the gayne:
> O what an honor is it, to restraine
> The lust of lawlesse youth with good aduice:
> Or pricke them forth with pleasaunce of thy vaine,
> Whereto thou list their trayned willes entice.
>
> Soon as thou gynst to sette they notes in frame,
> O how the rurall routes to thee doe cleaue:
> Seemeth thou dost their soule of sence bereaue,
> All as the shepheard, that did fetch his dame
> From *Plutoes* balefull bower withouten leaue:
> His musicks might the hellish hound did tame.
>
> (19-30)

A noble idealism, to be sure, with its awareness of the poet's public and social mission, but it is blind to the personal needs of the poet in real life. For Cuddie, Piers's conventional and idealistic poetic evades the question, how does he survive:

> So praysen babes the Peacoks spotten traine,
> And wondren at bright *Argus* blazing eye:
> But who rewards him ere the more for thy?
> Or feedes him once the fuller by a graine?
> Sike prayse is smoke, that sheddeth in the skye,
> Sike words bene wynd, and wasten soone in vayne.
>
> (31-36)

Praise does not feed, and man must eat. The first stage of the debate thus ends in a standstill.

Piers, getting nowhere with his idealistic appeal to the Orphic triumph of the poet over nature, turns now to what he considers more practical alternatives, though these alternatives are as conventional as his Orphic idealism. He suggests that Cuddie try other genres and find his practical reward in the patronage of the aristocracy; he should imitate Virgil and abandon "the base and viler clowne. . . / And singe of bloody Mars, of wars, of giusts." For Cuddie, however, Piers's slogans are unrealistic, they are out of touch with the world as it is. Since his reply is probably the most important speech in the eclogue, I will quote it in its entirety.

> Indeede the Romish *Tityrus,* I heare,
> Through his *Mecoenas* left his Oaten reede,
> Whereon he earst had taught his flock to feede,
> And laboured lands to yield the timely eare,
> And eft did sing of warres and deadly drede,
> So as the Heauens did quake his verse to here.
> But ah *Mecoenas* is yclad in claye,
> And great *Augustus* long ygoe is dead:
> And all the worthies liggen wrapt in leade,
> That matter made for Poets on to play:
> For euer, who in derring doe were dreade,
> The loftie verse of hem was loued aye.
>
> But after vertue gan for age to stoupe,
> And might manhode brought a bedde of ease:
> The vaunting Poets found nought worth a pease,
> To put in preace emong the learned troupe.
> Tho gan the streames of flowing wittes to cease,
> And sonnebright honour pend in shamefull coupe.
>
> And if that any buddes of Poesie,
> Yet of the old stocke gan to shoote agayne:
> Of it mens follies mote be forst to fayne,
> And rolle with rest in rymes of rybaudrye:
> Or as it sprong, it wither must agayne:
> Lulled the shepheards . . .
>
> (55-78)

Ironically, Cuddie's complaint is predicated on the same assumptions as Piers's in "May":

> The time was once, and may againe retorne,
> . . . . . .
> When shepheards had none inheritaunce,
> . . . . . .
> But tract of time, and long prosperitie:
> That nource of vice, this of insolencie,
> Tom Piper makes vs better melodies.
>
> (103-119)

For the poet Cuddie as well as Piers the ecclesiastical critic, Rome has fallen. For Piers in "May," it was the Rome of primitive Christianity, an idealized age of duty; for Cuddie in "October," it is the Rome of Augustus. Cuddie predicates his objections on Piers's own theme, the loss of the golden age: man has degenerated from the virtuous pattern of the remote past, corrupted by "a bedde of ease" and "long prosperitie." For Cuddie, Maecenas and the great heroes that gave impetus to the great epics, as for Piers the great and noble shepherds, are "yclad in claye." Cuddie has thus appropriated the wintry themes of Piers in "May" to undermine Piers's argument in "October." The age Piers refers to is gone. Piers's ideals are out of touch with life as it is, and in terms of Cuddie's practical vision, it is life, the present, that must inspire.

Cuddie's revelation for a moment sets the incredulous Piers back: "O pierlesse Poesye, where is then thy place?" But Piers, amusingly, returns to his bag of commonplaces and offers the obvious last alternative: if life does not inspire, then it must be heaven that will inspire: "Then make thee winges of thine aspyring wit, / And, whence thou camst, flye backe to heauen apace." Cuddie again replies in practical terms: he is himself too limited "so high to sore, and make so large a flight." Such a flight were fit for Colin, but even Colin, the chosen poet, is "with loue so ill bedight" that he, too, cannot "such famous flight to scanne." At this point we enter the third and final stage of the debate, the relationship of love to poetic inspiration. Piers, still unwilling to view life as it is, refuses to believe Cuddie's information; he is a "fon" (as Cuddie was to Thenot) to believe that love would restrain Colin's flight:

Ah fon, for loue does teach him climbe so hie,
And lyftes him vp out of the loathsome myre:
Such immortall mirrhor, as he doth admire,
Would rayse ones mynd aboue the starry skie.
And cause a caytiue corage to aspire,
For lofty loue doth loath a lowly eye.

(91-96)

But Colin's love is no longer "lofty loue"; it is a mortal obsession, which rather than freeing him for heaven binds him to earth and death. Again, as in Piers's other counsel, his ideals are traditional and conventional, out of touch with the world, in this case Colin, as he now is.

Cuddie replies that love, instead of spurring Colin on, actually inhibits him:

> All otherwise the state of Poet stands,
> For lordly loue is such a Tyranne fell:
> That where he rules, all power he doth expell.
> The vaunted verse a vacant head demaundes,
> Ne wont with crabbed care the Muses dwell:
> Unwisely weaues, that takes two webbes in hand.
>
> (97-102)

But of course this, too, has its limitations as truth. For love did at one time spur Colin on to poetry, as "August" itself testifies. Once again, neither interpretation is totally valid. Nor is Cuddie's contention that wine, not love, is suitable inspiration for poetry entirely acceptable: his belief that wine will stimulate him to "reare the Muse on stately stage, / And teache her tread aloft in buskin fine" is only a naive material substitute for genuine inspiration. He himself merely echoes inadequate Bacchic platitudes; and amusingly, his courage wanes almost at once:

> But ah my corage cooles ere it be warme,
> For thy, content vs in thys humble shade:
> Where no such troublous tydes han vs assayde,
> Here we our slender pipes may safely charme.
>
> (115-118)

Here is another side of the aspiration issue of "July": Cuddie contents himself with the lesser ambitions of the "humble shade" because his "corage cooles," not because of positive moral reasons. We thus again return to the matter of decorum: love can inspire, it can inhibit; man must have ideals but he must also survive; some shepherds' skills are more suitable to the "humble shade," others' to the more lofty and ambitious calling. One can see in "October," therefore, that the same flexible ethical principle of decorum operates in it as in the other eclogues. The single, rigid ethical standard is not a part of the world and events of the *Calender.*

"October's" debate ends in a standstill. None of the questions introduced is finally resolved. But the whole thrust and intent of the eclogue was not to resolve them, but to expose and explore them. To attribute to either disputant a single Spenserian truth is to miss the mark entirely. It is also to ignore the comedy of human limitations in this confrontation. Piers's persistent unwillingness to see his ideals in terms of real life lends comedy to the debate. Offering one commonplace alternative after another, he is finally and amusingly driven to the ultimate retreat of heaven. It is the comedy of the innocent mystified by the sudden disorientation of his secure commonplaces. The portrayal of Cuddie is no less comic, for he is indeed "the perfecte paterne of a Poete," who in all ages complains of the neglect of and contempt for his calling, once so highly esteemed, now in disrepute. We have, somehow, heard Cuddie's complaints many times before, and will no doubt hear them many times again. There is, no doubt, a bit of comic self-posturing in his complaints. Certainly we are meant to be amused by the last image he presents us with:

> Thou kenst not *Percie* how the ryme should rage.
> O if my temples were distained with wine,
> And girt in girlonds of wild Yuie twine,
> How I could reare the Muse on stately stage,
> And teache her tread aloft in buskin fine,
> With queint *Bellona* in her equipage.

> (109-114)

Fine-sounding language, a lofty pose: "But ah my corage cooles ere it be warme, / For thy, content vs in thys humble shade," and the pose crumbles. "October," then, for all its concern with the serious questions of poetry and its function, is at the same time a comic portrayal of the manner in which men pursue and at the same time evade the answers to these questions. Like the debate between age and youth in "February," "October" amuses us with the typicality of human limitations and frailty, with characters and situation well known to us. Always behind the *Calender's* sober disputations, with their serious debate of undeniably serious issues, is a comedy of men and manners. In the *Calender*, the tragedy of human limitations is counterpointed and balanced by this human comedy.

The dialogue between Piers and Cuddie is essentially a confrontation between conventional, idealistic Renaissance poetic theory and the practical necessities of the practicing poet and the year.[19] Just

19. This reading of "October" diverges considerably from what are probably the two most influential modern readings, A. C. Hamilton, *ELH*, 23 (1956), 180–181, and Robert Durr, *ELH*, 24 (1957), 287–289. According to Hamilton, "October" is another stage in Colin's repudiation of pastoral life for "the truly dedicated life . . . that of the heroic poet whose high calling is to serve the Queen by inspiring her people to all virtuous actions." Hamilton reaches this conclusion through what strikes me as being an illogical ascription to Colin of Piers's argument, "O what an honor is it, to restraine / The lust of lawless youth with good aduice."

as we discovered in "May" that Piers's idealism is inadequate for life in the real world, it is also inadequate here, and perhaps more so: in both eclogues, he is fundamentally unaware of the practical limitations of man as well as the demands of the year. The Cuddie of "October," like the Cuddie of "February," is more aware of practical necessity; in both eclogues he is aware that man does participate in the year, cannot withdraw from it, and must make some sort of practical accommodation to it. Both perspectives have obvious limitations: withdrawal to celestial ideals will not enable one to survive the demands of real life; survival will not entail eternal life. The October eclogue is principally a drama of pastoral perspectives, not a treatise on the "English Poete." Like its fellow moral debates, it is an exploration of ideas and problems through a continual cross-reference of pastoral perspectives, each pointing to the limitations of the other, in which no solution emerges as final.

LOVE IN THE *Calender:* THE TRAGIC AND COMIC PERSPECTIVES

In his portrayal of love, as in the moral debates, Spenser is less concerned with reaching a definitive judgment than he is with posing several possibilities and perspectives and with suggesting the continuing discrimination of differences and values such complexity requires.

Hamilton accepts as total truth Piers's contention that Colin is inspired by a love that "lyftes him up out of the loathsome myre"—while Piers's statement tells us little about Colin but a great deal about Piers, whose ideals about what should be have blinded him to what is.

Robert Durr argues that "October's" Cuddie is the same complaining "fon" of "February"; a child of the world who knows nothing but material values. Piers, in contrast, is Spenser's spokesman, voicing Spenser's idea of the poet as "divinely gifted priest": "Enlightened by the Holy Ghost, in his noblest function he teaches *sapientia.*" Cuddie, measured by this rigid standard, becomes "a lesser Colin Clout . . . ruined by *cupiditas.*" Cuddie has ignored the "inevitable" conclusion: "the poet is God's priest, his song inspired by Him, and therefore great poetry must be fundamentally divine . . . It is perverse for the poet to push for the petty price of the world's regard; he is to do his Father's work and at His knee find his reward." Durr, however, has distorted Piers's argument by his own diminishing of the lower genres in order to establish divine poetry and divine inspiration as *the* valid mode of poetic expression. He ignores the fact that Piers does in fact urge Cuddie to seek the world's regard, its praise, and that Piers exhorts Cuddie to religious poetry only after he has exhausted all other alternatives. Moreover, Piers does not, as Durr claims, consider epic poetry "of dubious value"; and even Piers will permit Cuddie to sing "when the stubborne stroke of stronger stounds, / Has somewhat slackt the tenor of thy string: / Of loue and lustihead," and that "lustihead" certainly refers to something other than divine love.

To this end there is, as Guarini will later say of his own *Il Pastor Fido*, "a mixture . . . of tragic and comic characters," a counterpoising of comic and tragic perspectives and experience.[20] Colin's tragic love for Rosalind is of course the central love of the *Calender*, and were it the only love we might well be tempted to conclude with the Mantuanesque Thenot in "February" that "All that is lent to loue, wyll be lost." But counterpointing and qualifying Colin's tragic experience are the comic experiences of Thomalin in "March" and Perigot in "August": both comic love-stricken shepherds ape and exaggerate the love and rhetoric of the nobler character, Thomalin's gestures become mock-epic, Perigot's mock-tragic. The two comic eclogues make it clear that the *Calender* does not adopt the antieroticism of Mantuanesque pastoral; for in these eclogues, love is portrayed and accepted as a natural, amusing part of human experience, a mixture of pleasure and pain that is the nature of the animal. As in the moral eclogues, then, the qualifying perspective of comedy tempers a too moralistic judgment and suggests that Colin's love is not simply a Mantuanesque exemplum of the dangers of submitting to the spiteful fiend.

The first question concerning Colin's role in the *Calender* is, does he fail in his dual role of shepherd and poet? As one of a long line of shepherd-poets like Sincero, who when cured of their love abandon the pastoral world for the higher mission of epic, Colin could be considered to share that promise of success. From this point of view, the pastoral world, despite its amorous therapy, is in part a temptation of the epic poet from his greater quest. Colin's various antipastoral gestures throughout the poem, such as his breaking his pipe in "January," are part of his development, necessary for his greater mission. From this point of view the values of the pastoral world are not the values whereby Colin should be measured, and his ultimate departure from the pastoral world represents triumph not defeat.[21] If, however, these are the values whereby Colin *should*

---

20. In the preface to the 1602 edition; see Appendix I of *A Critical Edition of Sir Richard Fanshawe's 1647 Translation of Giovanni Battista Guarini's "Il Pastor Fido,"* ed. Walter F. Staton, Jr., and William E. Simeone (London, 1964).

21. The ablest statement of this interpretation is by A. C. Hamilton, *ELH*, 23 (1956), 171–182. Since for Hamilton the central argument of the *Calender* is the rejection of the pastoral world of pleasurable ease for the truly dedicated life in the real world, Colin's progress in the *Calender* is fundamentally anti-pastoral rather than unpastoral: Colin instead of being unable to cope with the pastoral life is morally obliged to repudiate that life. His breaking his pastoral pipe in

be measured, then it would seem likely that Colin's renouncing the pastoral world is a moral and artistic failure. A second question then arises: if Colin does fail, how does he fail and why? From the Mantuanesque perspective of an antierotic shepherd like Piers of "February," the answer would seem obvious: it is his love for Rosalind that destroys him; love leads him to be a bad shepherd by involving him in the secular and nonpastoral world at the expense of his duties as shepherd. Colin's participation in romantic love becomes an excessive participation in the merely natural; having allied himself to the merely natural, inevitably he must succumb to the winter of the natural year, as he would seem to do in "December."[22] In essence, the fundamental question is whether Colin should be viewed as modeled on a figure like Sincero of Renaissance classical pastoral, or whether he should be viewed as modeled on a figure like Amyntas of Mantuanesque pastoral.

To answer these questions, we must address ourselves to that unavoidable bugaboo of *Calender* criticism, the relationship of Colin to Spenser. If we accept an equation of Colin with Spenser, Colin's career in the pastoral world must be seen as ultimately successful. Colin's departure from the pastoral world becomes Spenser's first step in his *imitatio Virgilis:* Colin, like Spenser, is abandoning the pastoral world for the higher mission of epic. It may at first seem obvious that Spenser is Colin. E.K. notes that "this Poete secretly shadoweth himself under the name of Colin." But E.K. as usual is only partially correct. Whatever the similarities between the hero of the *Calender* and its author, Colin does not equal Spenser any more than Sincero equals Sannazaro or Daedalus equals Joyce. No doubt in all three instances biographical events are transformed into art—but that is the point: they are transformed. Colin's parting scene in "December," for example, is obviously fictional: Spenser was not

---

"January," his inability to participate in Hobbinol's pastoral paradise in "June," and his parting in "December" thus constitute a series of rejections, real and symbolic, of pastoral life for the dedicated life of the heroic poet.

22. Robert Allen Durr, *ELH*, 24 (1957), 269–295, concludes that Colin in committing himself to the life of the flesh fails to attain pastoral success and Christian salvation. For Durr, the *Calender* is organized around a conflict between the truly pastoral (repudiation of self and the world, *caritas*) and the unpastoral (selfulness, love of the world, *amor concupiscentiae*). Within this framework, Colin is the Mantuanesque unpastoral prototype of all those, who, like Cuddie in "February," Palinode in "May," Morrell in "July," and Diggon Davie in "September," are "enthralled . . . by the eternal woman who is the world."

at the time hoary and wrinkled, and he was not on the verge of dying. A literal equation of Colin and Spenser, then, is biographically unfounded. It is Immeritó, not Colin, who "equals" Spenser. Yet even if the equation of Spenser and Colin were biographically sound, Colin's antipastoral actions cannot possibly be equated with Spenser's rejection of pastoral poetry since, obviously, it is Spenser who is writing the pastoral *Calender*. Moreover, even Colin *qua* Colin does not reject pastoral poetry, since it is a pastoral elegy he sings in "November" and an autobiographical pastoral elegy in "December." In "June" Colin continues "pyping lowe in shade of lowly groue" (the images suggest pastoral), but he plays only for private satisfaction, "to please my selfe." Colin does not reject pastoral poetry so much as his public mission as pastoral poet. Finally, Colin does in fact remain part of the pastoral world, that is, he continues to keep his flock, until "December"; then he says "adieu" to his sheep, not because he is committed to a heroic poem, but simply because he is dying. Colin, therefore, does not equal Spenser, and his career in the *Calender* cannot be said to share in the future epic success of Spenser.

I think one is forced to conclude, then, that Colin does fail within the pastoral world. The problem still remains, of course, as to what is the nature of his failure and what our attitude to that failure should be. If we adopt a solely Mantuanesque perspective on Colin's love for Rosalind, we would have to conclude that Rosalind represents the life of lust, the triumph of passion over reason, which is alien to pastoral success. But to take such a perspective results in making Colin and Rosalind much more depraved than they actually are.[23]

23. Identifications of Rosalind, whether general or specific, have not generally assumed her depraved, though Robert Allen Durr, *ELH*, 24 (1957), 286, is an exception, claiming that Rosalind represents the temptation of the sinful world. From a literary point of view, attempts to supply Rosalind with a specific historical identity are of slight importance. Only an identification like Paul McLane's, *Spenser's "Shepheardes Calender": A Study in Elizabethan Allegory* (Notre Dame, Indiana, 1961), pp. 27–46, in which Rosalind is identified with Elizabeth, has potential literary importance, since Colin-Spenser's wooing of Rosalind becomes the attempt of the English people to woo their Queen from Alençon. One may, however, legitimately wonder why, if Colin does represent the English people wooing their queen, the English shepherds of the pastoral world lament this wooing as a self-destructive obsession.

General identifications of Rosalind have rarely been persuasive. It has been argued, for example, by "C.," "The Faerie Queen Unveiled, Letter III," *Notes and Queries* (*N&Q*), 3rd ser., 4 (1863), 101–103, that Rosalind is an anagram for "Rond-Elisa," or "Rondelais" and that, since the rondelais was a form common to pastoral poetry, Rosalind may actually represent Spenser's pastoral muse. One has only to turn to "January" to see that this is impossible: "Shepheards deuise she hateth as

It is of course true that Colin's love for Rosalind interferes to some extent with his pastoral responsibilities—that is a pastoral commonplace from Theocritus onward—and in "January," Colin himself laments that interference:

> Thou feeble flocke, whose fleece is rough and rent,
> Whose knees are weake through fast and euill fare:
> Mayst witnesse well by thy ill gouernement,
> Thy maysters mind is ouercome with care.
> Thou weake, I wanne: thou leane, I quite forlorne:
> With mourning pyne I, you with pyning mourne.
>
> (43-48)

But Colin's self-accusation here is less moral reprobation than it is a conventional pastoral assumption of correspondence between the mood of the master and the condition of his sheep. Moreover, the opening two stanzas of the January eclogue's framework, which provide an objective perspective on Colin's state, make it clear that Colin utters his complaint in the very act of discharging his duty as a shepherd (as he also does in "December"):

> A Shepeheards boye (no better doe him call)
> When Winters wastful spight was almost spent,
> All in a sunneshine day, as did befall,
> Led forth his flock, that had bene long ypent.
> So faynt they woxe, and feeble in the folde,
> That now vnnethes their feete could them uphold.
>
> All as the Sheepe, such was the shepeheards looke,
> For pale and wanne he was, (alas the while,)
> May seeme he lovd, or els some care he tooke:
> Well couth he tune his pipe, and frame his stile.

---

the snake." Thomas Keightly, "On the Life of Edmund Spenser," *Fraser's Magazine,* 60 (1859), 413, has put forth the perhaps more useful suggestion that Rosalind is an anagram for the Italian "rosa linda" or "beautiful rose," and that as such she represents "a purely ideal being like . . . Corinna, like Beatrice, Laura, and others." The common objection to this suggestion is that Rosalind is not at all idealized in the manner that Laura and Beatrice are, that she does not inspire Colin to a vision of Platonic beauty, and that Colin's love for her produces neurosis rather than vision. But in fairness to Keightly's suggestion, one might justifiably reply that the epithet means not Rosalind as she is to Colin but as she should be. Finally, it is not altogether inconceivable that when E.K. claims that the feigned name, "being wel ordered, wil bewray the very name of hys loue and mistresse," the ordering is a matter of translation rather than anagram. Whether the mistress' real name was Machabyas Chyld or someone else, her "true" name is "beautiful rose"—a fine and gracious compliment.

Tho to a hill his faynting flocke he ledde,
And thus him playnd, the while his shepe there fedde.

(1-12)

The fact that the flock is "feeble" and "faynt" is no reflection on the character of Colin. In the popular calendar, January is the last of the three winter months: "Nouember. December. and Ianyuere. and these iii monethes is the wynter."[24] It is the real winter, then, not Colin's bad shepherding that has forced his sheep to be "long ypent" and consequently weak and feeble. Now that winter is coming to an end and the weather is right ("All in a sunneshine day"), Colin, as any good shepherd would, is exercising his flock so that they can overcome the effects of being pent up during winter and be ready for spring. In the January eclogue, then—and this is true of the eclogues for June and December as well—there is no substantial evidence to indicate that Colin fails to discharge his obligations to his sheep. Colin is not one of Mantuan's predatory and purely natural shepherds, and yet in his refusal to discharge his obligation as chief poet of the pastoral world he certainly disqualifies himself from being a truly good shepherd. "There remains, then, the character . . . of a man who is not eminently good and just, yet whose misfortune is brought about not by vice or depravity, but by some error or frailty":[25] this much, I think, can be said of Colin. A man chosen among men in his mission as chief poet on the pastoral world, a man of great estate in that world, he fails through frailty not vice. Colin is not a bad shepherd, nor is he a good shepherd, but "a character between these two extremes." Colin's obsessive love for Rosalind is pathetic rather than sinful, and as a result he is not satirized or condemned. He engages our pity as a man who, however gifted in the order of poetry, cannot order his own life. The private romantic disorder of Colin no doubt functions as a psychological analogue to the social disorder in the pastoral world, but our feeling for Colin is, in the end, something quite different from our feeling for the disorderly and flock-devouring prelates. Colin is a figure of tragic paradox and contradiction, containing in himself the limitations of both sides of the debate between participation in and withdrawal from the natural world which pervades the moral eclogues. If he

24. Citations from *The Kalender of Shepherdes*, vol. III, are to the edition of H. Oskar Sommer (London, 1892).

25. Aristotle, *Poetics*, in *Criticism: The Major Texts*, ed. Walter Jackson Bate (New York, 1952), p. 27.

is aged, he is not wise but sterile. If he is young, he is not fertile but unwise. In contrast, Cuddie in "February" has a healthy involvement in the procreative spring of the natural year, and is bound to the year no more than his elder is; his is the normal aging into death. But Colin's participation in the year, like his withdrawal, is unhealthy. His life is thus telescoped as his spring becomes winter and a single year his life and death. He is the prototype not of one side of the moral oppositions in the *Calender* but of both, illustrating the danger and limitations of Cuddie's as well as Thenot's perspective. Colin's tragically wasteful and misplaced participation in and withdrawal from the natural world is reflected in his relationship to the wintry setting:

> Thou barrein ground, whome winters wrath hath wasted,
> Art made a myrrhour, to behold my plight:
> . . . . . .
> Such rage as winters, reigneth in my heart,
> My life bloud friesing with vnkindly cold:
> Such stormy stoures do breede my balefull smart,
> As if my yeare were wast, and woxen old.
> And yet alas, but now by spring begonne,
> And yet alas, yt is already donne.
>
> (19-30)

The genesis of Colin's tragedy and waste lies not in his participation in the coming spring and fertility of the natural year, as the Mantuanesque view would have it, but in his inability to participate in it successfully. He who by nature should be young has become instead the embodiment of winter and its "wastful spight," and has unnaturally identified himself psychologically with the destructive wintry principle of nature. The cycle of nature, with its alternating principles of spring and winter, is a cycle of at least potential order and balance, as in the "Mutability Cantos"; the destructive and creative principles are both part of natural order. Colin, however, in his misguided accommodation to the year, compares himself successively to the barren ground, the ruined flowers, and the leafless trees. Simile becomes metaphor, and Colin is transformed into a paradox of age-in-youth and youth-in-age, deprived of the advantages of both.

In "January" there is a tentative exploration of Colin's character as illustrating the limitations of the two contending perspectives in the *Calender:* his identification with the Thenot-like perspective of winter, that is, an acceptance of age, results in the destruction of his rightful youthfulness and in sterility not wisdom; his identification with the Cuddie-like perspective of spring and youth, illustrated in his obsessive love for Rosalind, leads not to procreation and fertility but to sterile frustration and stagnation. In the June eclogue, Colin makes his second and most important appearance in the *Calender;* for this eclogue, more than any other, defines for us Colin's moral relationship to the two contending forms of pastoral behavior. Because of its considerable importance, this eclogue requires fuller analysis than I will be giving the other eclogues in which Colin appears.

Colin's confrontation with Hobbinol in "June" is indebted to the confrontation of Tityrus and Meliboeus in Virgil's first eclogue, but Spenser has significantly altered the ways of life involved in the confrontation. In Virgil the confrontation is that between the private world of the pastoral retired life and the public world of the active life. In Spenser's eclogue, Hobbinol's way of life, that of the classical happy man of pastoral *otium,* corresponds to Tityrus' way of life fairly exactly. The difference between the two eclogues is that between Meliboeus and Colin. Meliboeus is a man whose obligations to the active life of the public world prevent him from remaining in Tityrus' pleasant retreat. Colin, on the other hand, not only cannot accept the retired life, but he also cannot accept the responsibility of the active life. Absorbed in his own private world, "pyping lowe in shade of lowly groue . . . to please my selfe, all be it ill," he has, through a distorted and stagnant version of pastoral *otium,* abandoned his public responsibilities as poet of the pastoral world. Private retreat and public participation are both alien to Colin. The confrontation in Virgil's first eclogue has been transformed in "June" to one between the classical man of reason and content and the man immobilized by his own passion.[26]

The June eclogue is, according to E.K., "wholly vowed to the complayning of Colins ill successe in his loue . . . And this is the whole Argument of this Aeglogue." This, however, is by no means

---

26. This confrontation is a common one in pastoral literature and can be found in a variety of forms from Theocritus' tenth idyll to Garcilaso's second eclogue. The routine advice offered by the sensible man to the passionate man consists of his advising him to get his mind off love and on to something more practical—weaving, mowing, hoeing. Another frequently recommended escape is song. The advice Hobbinol gives Colin in "June" belongs, therefore, as much to this pastoral tradition as it does to Virgil's first eclogue.

"the whole Argument"; for the June eclogue resembles the moral eclogues in that it is a confrontation of pastoral perspectives for the purpose of exploring their virtues and limitations. In its juxtaposition of the sensible man and the passionate man, "June" dramatizes the limitations of the wintry, Mantuanesque ethic, with its repudiation of aspiration and riches, and the limitations of Hobbinol's seemingly paradisiacal world of pastoral *otium*. As in the January eclogue, the limitations of both pastoral perspectives will be dramatized by Colin.

Within his apparent paradise of pastoral harmony, Hobbinol, the happy shepherd of classical moderation, seems perfectly adapted to the fertile temperateness of the June season:

> Lo *Collin,* here the place, whose pleasaunt syte
> From other shades hath weand my wandring mynde.
> Tell me, what wants me here, to worke delyte?
> The simple ayre, the gentle warbling wynde,
> So calme, so coole, as no where else I fynde:
> The grassye ground with daintye Daysies dight,
> The Bramble bush, where Byrds of euery kynde
> To the waters fall their tunes attemper right.
>
> (1-8)

Colin, however, blaming "angry Gods" and not himself, cannot participate in this seeming paradise:

> O happy *Hobbinoll,* I blesse thy state,
> That Paradise hast found, whych *Adam* lost.
> Here wander may thy flock early or late,
> Withouten dreade of Wolues to bene ytost:
> Thy louely layes here mayst thou freely boste.
> But I vnhappy man, whom cruell fate,
> And angry Gods pursue from coste to coste,
> Can nowhere fynd, to shroude my lucklesse pate.
>
> (9-16)

It would seem that Hobbinol has found through compromise the ancient paradise that Piers and Palinode could not find. But this is Colin's testimony. We have only to anticipate Hobbinol's awakening from naiveté in "September" to realize that his paradise is, in part, artificial and deluded. To be sure, Hobbinol does represent the standard classical pastoral ideal of *otium* and the contented life, but for the fallen world where wolves seize sheep, this ideal is incomplete. In "June," Hobbinol is *magister* of moderation, and as such he teaches an ideal that undoubtedly pervades the *Calender.* But Hobbinol's ideal and his life, like those of his fellow shepherds, are inevitably imperfect; for he too is fallen and of the year. He must learn in "September," when he himself becomes a student, what the protagonist of Marvell's "The Garden" learns: fallen man cannot recapture Eden.

As *magister* of moderation, Hobbinol has found a tentative and precarious compromise between the impossible austerity of Piers and the dangerous indulgence of Palinode in "May." Hobbinol is thus capable, without the irresponsibility of Palinode, of urging Colin to seek material prosperity, represented by the rich dales:

> Then if by me thou list aduised be,
> Forsake the soyle, that so doth thee bewitch:
> Leaue me those hilles, where harbrough nis to see,
> Nor holybush, nor brere, nor winding witche:
> And to the dales resort, where shepheards ritch,
> And fruictfull flocks bene euery where to see.
> Here no night Rauens lodge more black then pitche,
> Nor eluish ghosts, nor gastly owles doe flee.
>
> But frendly Faeries, met with many Graces,
> And lightfote Nymphes can chace the lingring night,
> With Hegdeguyes, and trimly trodden traces,
> Whilst systers nyne, which dwell on *Parnasse* hight,
> Doe make them musick, for their more delight:
> And *Pan* himselfe to kisse their christall faces,
> Will pype and daunce, when *Phoebe* shineth bright:
> Such pierlesse pleasures haue we in these places.
>
> (17-32)

The advice Hobbinol offers Colin appropriately carries out the themes of "May" and something of the paradisiacal description of "April." The first stanza of the quotation comments on the ethical conflict between the versions of paradise in "May," austere Mantuanesque and otiose Arcadian. The second stanza continues the ritualistic motif of dance and song found both in "May" and in "April." In Hobbinol's advice to Colin, therefore, we have two major aspects of what constituted worldly temptation for the Mantuanesque Piers: prosperity (the rich South) and the rites of spring (dance and song). The rites in "June," however, are like those of "April"; far from being a source of potential disorder, they symbolize the order that Colin as poet can and should attain for himself and, as we learn from

Hobbinol's next speech, impose on nature. Like Elisa, Colin too can become a source of order as an artist—in a sense Elisa's earthly representative, her Orpheus. Colin will, says Hobbinol, teach the birds to "frame to thy songe their cherefull cheriping"; Colin will be like the lark "whose Echo made the neyghbour groues to ring." Both descriptions portray Colin as he is later portrayed in *Colin Clout's Come Home Again,* as the Orphic voice that while participating in natural order masters and surpasses it. Instead of being controlled by nature, he himself should order nature. In this respect especially, Colin's mission resembles Elisa's. It is therefore appropriate that Hobbinol's speech specifically recalls the procession of the Muses in "April":

> I sawe *Calliope* wyth Muses moe,
> Soone as thy oaten pype began to sound,
> Theyr yuory Luyts and Tamburins forgoe:
> And from the fountaine, where they sat around,
> Renne after hastely thy siluer sound.
>
> (57-61)

Hobbinol's description of Colin's relationship to the Muses reinforces the comparison in "April" between Colin and Elisa. Once again, we are shown Colin in past tense when, possessed with the divine Orphic power of art, he too attracted the Muses led by Calliope, like Elisa, the focus of order and harmony.

The first stage of Colin's refutation of Hobbinol takes the form of a curious perversion of the Mantuanesque pastoral ethic with its demand for a mature withdrawal from youthful follies and unpastoral ambitions:

> And I, whylst youth, and course of carelesse yeeres
> Did let me walke withouten lincks of loue,
> In such delights did ioy amongst my peeres:
> But ryper age such pleasures doth reproue,
> My fancye eke from former follies moue
> To stayed steps: for time in passing weares
> (As garments doen, which wexen old aboue)
> And draweth newe delightes with hoary heares.
>
> Tho couth I sing of loue, and tune my pype
> Vnto my plaintiue pleas in verses made:
> Tho would I seeke for Queene apples vnrype,
> To giue my *Rosalind,* and in Sommer shade

Dight gaudy Girlonds, was my comen trade,
To crowne her golden locks, but yeeres more rype,
And losse of her, whose loue as lyfe I wayd,
Those weary wanton toyes away dyd wype.

(33-48)

"Youngth," says Thenot, "is a bubble blown vp with breath"; and
Piers, "For Younkers *Palinode* such follies fitte, / But we tway bene
men of elder witt." Colin's contention that "ryper age such pleasures
doth reproue" refers us to "May" and Piers's argument for "elder
witt" which it echoes. In Colin, however, the Mantuanesque ethic
is perverted into a rationalization for failure. Colin's is a parody
of this pastoral wisdom. Its ethic is not right for him: rather than
protecting him from winter, it submits him untimely to it. "Those
weary wanton toyes" that delighted Hobbinol (and even Thenot,
as we see in "November") were symptoms of sanity and balance,
not youthful follies. In "January," as we saw, Colin took upon himself
the psychology of age and winter. In "June" he has forced its "wisdom" upon his youth and talent. The source of Colin's disorder is
not youth, but the unnatural assumption of age by youth: Colin's
disorder is not that he is young but that he is old.

The second stage of Colin's rebuttal continues to distort not only
the austere Mantuanesque pastoral ethic but also Arcadian *otium* and
the private life of retirement. Hobbinol has claimed that Colin's songs
put the Muses to shame, and Colin replies:

Of Muses *Hobbinol*, I conne no skill:
For they bene daughters of the hyghest *Ioue*,
And holden scorne of homely shepheards quill.
For sith I heard, that *Pan* with *Phoebus* stroue,
Which him to much rebuke and Daunger droue:
I neuer lyst presume to *Parnasse* hyll,
But pyping lowe in shade of lowly groue,
I play to please my selfe, all be it ill.

(65-72)

Just as Colin's previous speech was a parody of Thenot's Mantuanesque wisdom and its rejection of the follies of youth for the
sobriety of age, here the conventional pastoral rejection of ambition
is a parody of Thomalin's rejection of aspiration in the next eclogue
("This reede is ryfe, that oftentime / great clymbers fall vnsoft")
and a parody of classical *otium* and the retired life. Traditional pas-

toral ideals have become an instrument whereby Colin can justify his neurotic withdrawal:

> Nought weigh I, who my song doth prayse or blame,
> Ne striue to winne renowne, or passe the rest:
> With shepheard sittes not, followe flying fame:
> But feede his flocke in fields, where falls hem best.
> I wote my rymes bene rough, and rudely drest:
> The fytter they, my carefull case to frame:
> Enough is me to paint out my vnrest,
> And poore my piteous plaints out in the same.
>
> (73-80)

Ironically both of the contending forms of pastoral vision in the *Calender* are perverted by Colin into a rationalization for abandoning his mission. Hobbinol's pastoral ideal of contented self-sufficiency is twisted into tormented self-indulgence, the low estate into stagnant passivity, *otium* into autoeroticism. If Colin is to fulfill his mission and quest, he must, as Hobbinol realizes, aspire "to *Parnasse* hyll."[27] The rigid ethic of Thenot and Thomalin, eschewing fame, is inadequate, as is the classical pastoral ethic of *otium* and self-sufficiency. Colin thus illustrates the dangerous seeds within these two different pastoral perspectives. Both when carried to an extreme lead to an abandonment of aspiration and quest. Neither *humilitas* nor *otium* is enough for the pastoral hero.

The final stage of Colin's rationalization very much resembles Cuddie's in "October": the present does not inspire, the inspiration of past days is lost and irretrievable. Tityrus-Chaucer, the "God of shepheards," is dead, "And all hys passing skil with him is fledde." Just as Cuddie imagines how he "could reare the Muse on stately stage" if his temples were "distaind with wine," so Colin imagines that

27. Hobbinol's encouraging Colin to leave the hills for the dales has led Robert Allen Durr, *ELH*, 24 (1957), 282–284, to conclude that the issue in "June" is that of "July," "*superbia* and worldly ambition versus *humilitas* and the contentment of the tried estate." However, it is Hobbinol who urges Colin to over-reach the Muses as he once did, and it is Colin, not Hobbinol, who replies in terms of Thomalin's *humilitas* and fear of aspiration's dangers: "I neuer lyst presume to *Parnasse* hyll." The moral issue involved in "June" is not whether Colin has or does not have worldly ambition, but that he has the wrong ambition, to please only himself if he cannot please Rosalind. Hobbinol is urging Colin to find contentment in *valid* ambition, the ambition to be a great poet. In "June," for Colin, *both* northern hills and the "lowly groue" run the invalid extremes, respectively, of false ambition (Rosalind) on the one hand and false avoidance of ambition (neurotic withdrawal into self, the abandonment of his mission and quest) on the other.

. . . if on me some little drops would flowe;
Of that the spring was in his learned hedde,
I soone would learne these woods, to wayle my woe,
And teache the trees, their trickling teares to shedde.

Then should my plaints, causd of discurtesee,
As messengers of all my painfull plight,
Flye to my loue, where euer that she bee,
And pierce her heart with poyny of worthy wight.

(93-100)

Mere rationalization; Colin chooses to ignore his own failure to order his own emotions and places the blame outside himself. The fault is not Rosalind's but Colin's; for Chaucer, too, as Colin notes unperceivingly, was caught up in the woes of love and yet he wrote. Chaucer was "the soueraigne head / Of shepheards all, that bene with loue ytake":

Well couth he wayle hys Woes, and lightly slake
The flames, which loue within his heart had bredd,
And tell vs mery tales, to keepe vs wake,
The while our sheepe about vs safely fedde.

(85-88)

Chaucer as artist and lover successfully fused the public and private aspects of his life: his poetry slaked the flames of love, while at the same time his "mery tales" fulfilled his public responsibility by keeping shepherds awake while their sheep grazed. As this portrayal of Chaucer assures us, love and the pastoral world, love and poetry, love and the fullfillment of mission need not be at odds. In contrast to Chaucer, Colin's private obsession totally dominates his role as poet. His Orphic voice, rather than ordering nature, would impose its own disorder on all nature. Colin perverts the poet's public responsibility as teacher into teaching nature to be an extension of himself: "I soone would learne these woods, to wayle my woe, / And teache the trees, their trickling teares to shedde." And with Chaucer's skills, he would take vengeance on Rosalind and Menalcas, exposing their villainy and treachery—a further perversion of poetry as teaching into poetry as vengeance. Colin thus distorts aesthetic orthodoxy as he does the moral orthodoxies of classical and Mantuanesque pastoral in an effort to justify his stagnation and selfishness. Self, of course, is not a value alien to the *Calender:* the world is fallen, and the self must survive within the natural year. But self must be balanced with public and social responsibility. Chaucer integrated private and social ends, love and duty, in his poetry; but Colin has failed to achieve this integration, and while Chaucer "lyeth wrapt in lead" and "all hys passing skil with him is fledde," his fame "doth dayly greater growe," Colin's emblem for "December" will be missing, "the meaning whereof is that all thinges perish and come to theyr last end, but workes of learned wits and monuments of Poetry abide for euer." June is mid-year, when as the Master Shepherd says, the sun is "hyest in his meridyornall":

> he may assende no hyeer in his stacyone his glemerrynge goldene beames rypeethe the corne and than is man xxxvi. He may assende no more for than hathe nature gyuen hym beauty and strength at the full / and repyd the sedes of vnderstondynge.[28]

June finds man and the sun ascending to their highest point. Colin, however, continues to descend, having reaped the seeds of his imperfect understanding. After June the sun descends. The emblem tells the tale, "Gia speme spenta." The rest is anticlimax.

Death surrounds Colin's final two appearances in the *Calender*, the death of Dido in "November" and his own death in "December." Colin's assuming his public role as poet in "November" is only apparently a resurgence: the topic he choses for his song is a reflection and comment on his own death. Colin's present "sleepe" that Thenot speaks of is both an analogue to the death of Dido and an anticipation of his own death and sleep in "December":

> *Colin* my deare, when shall it please thee sing,
> As thou were wont songs of some iouisaunce?
> Thy Muse to long slombreth in sorrowing,
> Lulled a sleepe through loues misgouernaunce.
> Now somewhat sing, whose endles souenaunce,
> Emong the shepeheards swaines may aye remaine.
>
> (1-6)

The theme of the triumph over time granted works of poetry (the "endles souenaunce," or remembrance, that will "aye remaine" among shepherds) of course refers back to "October," where Piers maintained that art enabled the poet to triumph over time and mortality. But of equal importance, it anticipates "December," where the same

28. *The Kalender of Shepherdes*, III, 11.

theme is introduced, as E.K.'s gloss for the lost emblem demonstrates. The invitation to the sleeping Colin thus reinforces the image of Colin as the lost hero who, in forfeiting his mission, has also forfeited the reward of the mission, gaining not "endles souenaunce" but merely death.

Also significant, in that it suggests once again the unnatural aging of Colin, is Colin's refusal to sing the "songs of some iouisaunce" requested by Thenot:

> *Thenot,* now nis the time of merimake.
> Nor *Pan* to herye, nor with loue to playe:
> Sike myrth in May is meetest for to make,
> Or summer shade vnder the cocked haye.
>
> . . . . . .
>
> Thilke sollein season sadder plight doth aske:
> And loatheth sike delightes, as thou doest prayse:
> The mornefull Muse in myrth now list ne maske,
> As shee was wont in youngth and sommer dayes.

(9-20)

Colin's refusal here is similar to that in "June," where he refused to sing in summer the same songs that now in winter he says were fit for summer. His refusal, while it is phrased in the totally orthodox doctrine of decorum, is nonetheless probably rooted less in the aging of the year than in his own aging. In his movement toward death, only sadness can now inspire Colin. Colin, ironically, is older than Thenot.

"November's" elegy for Dido is significant not only for what it is, a lament for the death of Dido, but also for what it tells us about Colin, his obsession with death, his nostalgia for and yet increasing alienation from the pastoral world. Amplifying the personal significance of the elegy for Colin is the fact that Dido is, in part, a foil to Rosalind. She is, in a sense, an image of Rosalind as Colin would have liked her to be:

> She while she was, (that was, a woful word to sayne)
> For beauties prayse and plesaunce had no pere:
> So well she couth the shepherds entertayne,
> With cakes and cracknells and such country chere.
> Ne would she scorne the simple shepheards swaine,
>   For she would cal hem often heame
>   And giue hem curds and clouted Creame.

O heauie herse,
Als *Colin cloute* she would not once disdayne.
O carefull verse.

(93-102)

We have only to recall the lines from "January" to see the implied comparison:

Shee deignes not my good will, but doth reproue,
And of my rurall musick holdeth scorne.
Shepheards deuise she hateth as the snake,
And laughes the songes, that *Colin Clout* doth make.

(63-66)

For Colin, the loss of Dido is emotionally charged with the loss of Rosalind. To be sure, the lament for the lost Dido does not deal primarily with Colin's own love, but we would be mistaken to think that his feelings for Rosalind and his sense of unjust deprivation do not carry over into his feeling for Dido.[29] The November elegy is an elegy not only for the lost Dido but also for the lost Rosalind.

The elegiac mood that characterizes "November," and indeed the *Calender's* overall movement from spring to winter, climaxes in "De-

---

29. With one exception, attempts to equate Dido with a specific historical person have had no great relevance to the literary interpretation of "November." It makes little difference to the literary structure of the *Calender* whether Dido is an illegitimate daughter of Leicester by Lady Sheffield, Ambrosia Sidney, sister of Philip, or Susan Watts. But if, as both Mary Paramenter, "Spenser['s] 'Twelve Aeglogues Proportional to the Twelve Monthes,' " *ELH*, 3 (1930), 214–216, and Paul McLane, *Spenser's "Shepheardes Calender,"* pp. 47–60, claim, Dido is actually Elizabeth, the structure of the work is very much involved. Both Parmenter and McLane believe that the elegy mourns the "death" of Elizabeth, who because of the Alençon negotiations was "dead" to Lobbin or Leicester. The chief problem presented by this interpretation is that criticism of Elizabeth's marriage plans would be inconsistent with the celebration of Dido's life: the elegy would be working at cross-purposes. Moreover, if Spenser were criticizing Elizabeth for becoming "dead" to Leicester and to England, why should Colin become joyous that she's gone? In effect, Elizabeth's involvement is the Alençon marriage negotiations becomes, somewhat absurdly, a way to celestial bliss. The shift to joy that is part of the conventions of the pastoral elegy thus renders absurd any effort to see the November eclogue as a criticism of Elizabeth's suicidal marriage negotiations.
There is, I think, a simpler explanation for the similar portrayal of Elisa and Dido: Dido is *like* Elisa, but she does not equal Elisa. In the April eclogue, Elisa is a goddess, or near it, when we meet her: unlike Dido, she escapes the taint of mortality, her birth is supernaturally virgin. She is more ideal and mythic than real. Dido is real and therefore mortal, and thus like other mortals she must die to ascend. What Spenser is doing in his portrayal of Elisa seems to me quite simple: he is drawing upon the associations he developed for his mythic and ideal Elisa to expand the significance of Dido's life and death. Elisa is the pattern on which Dido's life and character are based. The similarity between the two of them thus flatters and enhances Dido.

cember." The introductory portrait of Colin establishes at once the elegiac mood, the contrast of past and present, that will dominate the eclogue:

> The gentle shepheard satte beside a spring,
> All in the shadow of a bushye brere,
> That *Colin* hight, which wel could pype and singe,
> For he of *Tityrus* his songs did lere.
>> There as he satte in secreate shade alone,
>> Thus gan he make of loue his piteous mone.

(1-6)

Setting mirrors the mind, as the isolated Colin withdraws further into the dark shadows that by the end of the eclogue envelop him.

Alone in the desolation of the winter he embodies, Colin examines the contents and harvest of his life: spring and his innocent youth; summer and his love for Rosalind; autumn and his lost harvest; winter and his death.[30] The freedom of innocence, with its joys and limitations, characterizes Colin's youth. The instinctive joys of his "ioyfull spring," the joys of hunting and climbing trees, are countered by the danger of innocent blindness to evil and to the destructive, wintry principle of the year: "What wreaked I of wintrye ages waste, / Tho deemed I, my spring would euer laste." Colin's falling in love with Rosalind marks the termination of the freedom of spring for the bondage of summer (the bitterness with which he speaks of his love is not the bitterness of Spenser but that of the disillusioned and frustrated speaker):

> But ah such pryde at length was ill repayde,
> The shepheards God (perdie God was he none)
> My hurtlesse pleasaunce did me ill vpbraide,

---

30. For A. C. Hamilton, *ELH*, 23 (1956), 175 and 181, "December" culminates not with Colin's death but with his resurrection from the pastoral world into the life of the heroic poet. Colin's hanging up his pipe thereby becomes symbolic of his rejection of pastoral poetry. We should remember, however, that when Colin breaks his pipe in "January" he breaks it not because he is dissatisfied with the pastoral mode but because he has not won Rosalind. Correspondingly, in "June" Colin has withdrawn from the public pastoral world to sing to himself, to nurse his wounds, not because he is rejecting pastoral poetry, but because he still has not won Rosalind. And in "November" his refusal to sing "songs of ioussaunce" is hardly a rejection of pastoral poetry, since what follows is a pastoral elegy. Moreover, when Colin says of the "shepheards God" that "perdie God was he none," Colin is not rejecting the lesser, pagan Pan for the greater, Christian Pan, as Hamilton suggests; he is simply rejecting Cupid. The god, according to Colin, is called "Loue," and that would of course mean Cupid; E.K.'s note confirms the obvious, "Cupid, which is loue . . ."

My freedome lorne, my life he left to mone.
  Loue they him called, that gaue my checkmate,
  But better mought they haue behote him Hate.

(49-54)

At the same time that Colin is initiated into sexual maturity, he also learns the practical arts of manhood, how to make timber shelters for his sheep, baskets to catch fish with. He masters matters of intelligence and reason, gaining knowledge of the tides, the sound of birds, the power of herbs. But all his knowledge could not cure his "sore hart roote, / Whose ranckling wound as yet does rifelye bleede." Colin's failure, as I have suggested before, is a failure in integration. Neither the awakening of reason and intelligence nor his initiation into love is, categorically, a vice. Both are typical and necessary parts of man's summer. The failure is in balance and control: for all his knowledge, Colin cannot control his heart and emotions.

The procreative impulse in Colin, not because it is intrinsically evil and destructive but because it is unchecked by the restraint of reason, brings about his lost harvest of autumn: "Thus is my sommer worne away and wasted, / Thus is my haruest hastened all to rathe." In withdrawing himself from mankind (unlike any of the other, "normal" plaintive shepherd-lovers), he removes himself from the potential therapy offered by human society and fellowship. It is this neurotic withdrawal, accompanied by obsessive love, that defeats Colin, withdrawal from his fellow men and withdrawal from his social mission as poet; and that is what is suggested by the following stanza:

And I, that whilome wont to frame my pype,
Vnto the shifting of the shepheards foote:
Sike follies nowe haue gathered as too ripe,
And cast hem out, as rotten and vnsoote.
  The loser Lasse I cast to please nomore,
  One if I please, enough is me therefore.

(115-120)

The complication posed by this stanza is in the identity of "loser Lasse" and "one." The "loser Lasse" may be "the lightfooted shepherd-girls to whose dances he [Colin] had played," as C. H. Herford suggests, or possibly Rosalind.[31] Herford's suggestion fits in nicely

---

31. *The Shepheards Calender*, p. 192 (Notes).

with the preceding lines. If, however, we accept the identification as Rosalind, we would have to be careful not to interpret the lines as meaning that Colin has broken the bonds; that is inaccurate. The introductory stanza, after all, states that "thus gan he make of loue his piteous mone"; and when Colin bids adieu to Rosalind, he still speaks of himself as "*her* Colin." More crucial is the identity of "one." Herford suggests that by "one" is meant Rosalind. This is possible, but it seems to me more likely that Colin means himself. The line echoes the solitary autoeroticism of Colin's rationalization in "June," where he says, "But pyping lowe in shade of lowly groue, / I play to please my selfe, all be it ill." Indeed, the entire passage seems to repeat the Mantuanesque rationalization of "June":

> But ryper age such pleasures doth reproue,
> My fancye eke from former follies moue
> To stayed steps . . .
>
>   . . . . . .
>
> And losse of her, whose loue as lyfe I wayd
> Those weary wanton toyes away dyd wype.
>
> (36-49)

"Sike follies" as Colin speaks of in "December" are the same symptoms of sanity and creativity that they were in "June," and they represent a legitimate part of his development as a poet. Even Thenot, the epitome of aged wisdom, did not consider Colin's songs follies "rotten and vnsoote." The whole passage would seem, then, to be a continuation of Colin's distortion of aged Mantuanesque wisdom to rationalize his withdrawal from his mission and his failure: rejecting the follies of his youth, he will no longer pipe for dancing shepherds, though that was part of his mission in the pastoral world; he will please only "one," himself. Colin thus resembles the solitary Briar, who living solitary, solitary dies.

His and the natural year ending, Colin is left old and solitary in the darkness of the dying day:

> The carefull cold hath nypt my rugged rynde,
> And in my face deepe furrowes eld hath pight:
> My head besprent with hoary frost I fynd,
> And by myne eie the Crow his clawe dooth wright.
>   Delight is layd abedde, and pleasure past,
>   No sonne now shines, cloudes han all ouercast.
>
> (133-138)

Colin, destroyed by the winter within him, has become the image of December:

> Than cometh December full of colde with froste / and nowe with great wynds and stormy weders that a man may nat laboure nor noughte do. The sonne is than at the lowest that it may descend. Than the trees and the erthe is hyd in snowe. For than begynneth mannes here to wax whyte and gray / and his body croked and feble / and then he leseth his perfyte vnderstandynge . . . and if he lyue anymore it is by gode gydynge in his youth.[32]

"Such rage as winters, reigneth in my heart, / My life bloud friesing with vnkindly cold: / Such stormy stoures do breede my balefull smart," he said in "January." Now, in "December," Colin is defeated totally by the wintry disorder within. We have thus witnessed the aging of Colin, unnaturally telescoped, from the winter within to and including the winter without, from an unnatural psychological aging to an actual physical aging. The aging is real not metaphorical. Colin observes that his hair is white with "hoary frost" and that his face is wrinkled with crow's-feet, "deep furrowes old"; and I see no reason not to accept his observation at face value. The survey of his life, after all, does encompass the events of a full life according to the symbolic condensing of life into a year found in the *Kalender of Shepherdes;* and when Colin says his "yeare drawes to his latter terme," he is speaking of the year of his life very much as it is expressed in the *Kalender:*

> This must ye rekene for euery moneth syxe yere. or ellys it may be vnderstonde by the foure quarters and seasons of the yere. So deuydyde man into foure partyes as to youthe / strengthe. wysdome / and age. he to be. xviii. yere. younge. eyghttene yere stronge. xviii. In wysdome and the. foureth eyghttene yere to go the full of the age of lxxii.[33]

The death Colin speaks of, then, is the real death of man at the end of his year:

> Now leaue ye shepheards boyes your merry glee,
> My Muse is hoarse and weary of thys stounde:
> Here will I hang my pype vpon this tree,
> Was neuer pype of reede did better sounde.
> 　Winter is come, that blowes the bitter blaste,
> 　And after Winter dreerie death does hast.

(139-144)

32. *The Kalender of Shepherdes,* III, 12.
33. *The Kalender of Shepherdes,* III, 10.

"Was neuer pype of reede did better sounde," but that is past tense; Colin has only to commit his final act of withdrawal:

Adieu delights, that lulled me asleepe,
Adieu my deare, whose loue I bought so deare:
Adieu my little Lambes and loued sheepe,
Adieu ye Woodes that oft my witnesse were:
Adieu good *Hobbinol*, that was so true,
Tell *Rosalind*, her *Colin* bids her adieu

(151-156)

Now himself an image of the year, his face furrowed, his head covered with "hoary frost," Colin has succumbed to the time he was to vanquish. Dido will go to "the fields ay fresh, the grasse ay greene"; she will triumph over time and winter in eternal spring, her emblem "La Mort n'y mord." Colin's emblem, however, is missing, the meaning whereof is "that all thinges perish and come to theyr last end, but workes of learned wits and monuments of Poetry abide for euer." And the omission, while perhaps accidental, seems symbolic.[34]

The conclusion seems to be unmistakable, Colin does fail within

---

34. Numerous attempts have been made to supply the missing emblem. W. L. Renwick, "December Emblem of the *Shepheardes Calender*," *Modern Language Review* (*MLR*), 14 (1922), 415–416, has suggested that the omission can be explained on the grounds that the November emblem was intended for "December" as well, since in both eclogues Spenser is imitating Marot. However, although the two are similar in their theme of triumph over death and time, E.K.'s explanation suggests that the emblem carried additional import. Allan H. Gilbert, "The Emblem for 'December' in the *Shepheardes Calender*," *Modern Language Notes* (*MLN*), 63 (1948), 181–182, has suggested that the motto, *Merce con mercede*, isolated at the end of the *Calender*, is the missing emblem, meaning that the goods of this world perish but not the poet's reward or fame. This is possible, but it is equally possible if not more so that this motto was intended to speak for the *Calender* as a whole since it follows Immeritó's parting stanza:

Loe I haue made a Calender for euery yeare,
That steele in strength, and time in durance shall outweare:
And if I marked well the starres reuolution,
It shall continewe till the worlds dissolution.

The theme in this passage is the same as that of the missing emblem and the motto, and it is not impossible that the motto serves a dual function, although it hardly makes sense to print "Colins Embleme" and let nothing follow it. J. Hughes, finally, has restored the missing emblem as "Vivitur ingenio, caetera mortis erunt," and this restoration has been accepted by the editors of the Variorum Edition (VII, pt. 1, p. 426). Hughes's suggestion fits, but even so we cannot be certain of its accuracy or that the omission was not intentional. From all these suggestions, in fact, only one constant emerges: each of the suggested emblems contains the promise offered Colin should he fulfill his public and social mission as poet; but they represent the promise, not the realization, of a triumph over time, and that is their function.

the pastoral world, in terms of both his art and life. But his failure is a result not of the intrinsic nature of love but of his peculiarly abnormal and obsessive love. Of all the lovers in Spenser's pastoral world only Colin withdraws from that world: Cuddie, Thomalin, and Perigot, with their more normal passion, exist within the world, experiencing the usual pain and pleasure of love. To make Colin the pattern or type for these other shepherd-lovers is mistaken. Colin represents a distortion of the principle of spring in which they are more or less normally involved. Colin's distortion of love no more entails rejection of love per se than does the fact that in Colin's behavior we find a distortion of both the principal contending pastoral perspectives in the *Shepheardes Calender*. Arcadian *otium* and Mantuanesque *humilitas* both are perverted into a rationalization for stagnation, for abandonment of the quest. Indeed, the central figure of the *Calender,* rather than justifying or exemplifying either of the contending pastoral perspectives, dramatizes the potential weakness and incompleteness of them both. Colin, judged incomplete by the values of either Arcadian or Mantuanesque pastoral, himself testifies to the incompleteness of the very values by which he is measured.

That Colin's obsessive love leads to the tragedy of his self-destruction must not lead us to attribute to the *Calender* the antierotic attitude of Mantuanesque pastoral; for, as we have seen, Colin's relationship to love is not typical but abnormal and obsessive. And while his life is admittedly an illustration of the potential dangers of love, it is not an exemplum for the repudiation of love. Merely because love can be taken to extremes no more postulates rejection of it than of the Mantuanesque or the Arcadian perspectives, both of which can also be taken to extremes, as the moral debates and the career of Colin illustrate. But in addition to these qualifications of the tragic perspective, there is another, and a very important one, the perspective of comedy.

One of the most prevalent misconceptions of pastoral is, as I have suggested before, that it is simply a celebration of the virtues of innocence. To some extent this is undeniably true. Pastoral characteristically both looks back to a golden age of untroubled innocence and looks ahead to a new golden age of the return of innocence; the pastoral world is often a retreat from the world of passions, military or amorous. Virgil's Meliboeus desires to withdraw to Tityrus' otiose retreat, Dante's Tityrus and Meliboeus have withdrawn from the political hostilities of Florence, Sannazaro's Sincero has retired from Naples to Arcadia for reasons both political and amorous. Arcadia, then, provides potential protection and therapy. Nonetheless, the innocence of Arcadia makes it peculiarly vulnerable to experience. The same innocence that may signify the uncorrupted mind may also blind the mind to its potential corruption. (In the *Shepheardes Calender* Hobbinol exemplifies this mixed blessing.) Innocence can also be baffled by love, with either tragic or comic results. The confrontation of innocence with love may lead, as with Sincero or Albanio, to a situation in which the love-sick victim sees life from a perspective so distorted that he withdraws from reality through death or madness. On the other hand, this confrontation may lead to normal human absurdity, a normal but comic exaggeration and distortion of human experience. Consider, for example, the experience of the young rustic in Theocritus' twentieth idyll. The city girl's refusal of his petitions evokes in the rustic an exaggerated hostility which, comically, totally reverses his original perception of the desired object: Eunica becomes "a filthy drab" caviling at "a well-favoured fellow like me." Like most shepherds of comic amorous pastoral, this one ponders his merits with a delightfully innocent lack of awareness of the comedy behind his preening and mirror-gazing:

> Tell me true, master Shepherds; see you not here a proper man, or hath some power taken and transmewed him? Marry, 'twas a sweet piece of ivy bloomed ere now on this tree, and a sweet piece of beauty put fringe to this lip; the hair o' these temples lay lush as the parsley . . . these eyes were beamy as the Grey-eyed Lady's, this mouth trim as a cream-cheese . . . And there's not a lass in the uplands but says I am good to look to, not one but kisses me, neither.[35]

He ends with a curse, that Cypris cause Eunica to "lie lone and sleep sole for the rest of her days." We recognize at once, of course, the age-old comedy of the rejected male animal, his sexuality frustrated by an unwilling female. What would be a potential tragedy for a Sincero or a Colin becomes here simply the comedy of man as a sexual and thinking animal, neither function entirely realizing its purpose.

It is within this traditional comic framework of rustic love that the experiences of Thomalin in "March" and Perigot in "August"

35. *The Greek Bucolic Poets*, p. 241.

fall. Their relationship to love is a comic foil to, rather than a parallel to, Colin's tragic love. Their exaggerated response to love participates in the comic absurdity and contradictions of more or less normal experience; it is part of the human comedy of Spenser's pastoral world. However painful their love is, with all its agony, their disease is not incurable, and their lives, unlike Colin's, will not be wasted. These two eclogues provide us with comic parodies of Colin's tragic love, "March" parodying Colin through mock-epic exaggeration, "August" through mock-tragic exaggeration.

The March eclogue is a comic portrayal of man's initiation and perennial re-initiation into the sexual rites of spring. March, according to the popular calendar, is the second month of spring, when man begins to participate in nature's revival.[36] We therefore meet Willye and Thomalin, "two shepheards boyes," on a spring day, appropriately discussing the revival of nature. The introductory dialogue, in which Willye and Thomalin talk at comic cross-purposes, neither able to grasp the other's point, provides a fitting framework for the two shepherds' comic misperception of love. For Willye, winter is the time of sorrow, spring the time of joy; it's all quite simple, and now that spring is here he cannot understand Thomalin's dour restraint: "Thomalin, why sytten we soe, / As weren ouerwent with woe, / Vpon so fayre a morow?" Thomalin, completely mistaking Willye's intent, construes Willye's remark to be a warning, since for Thomalin April is indeed the cruelest month:

> Sicker Willye, thou warnest well:
> For Winters wrath beginnes to quell,
>   And pleasant spring appeareth.
>
> (7-9)

Willye misses the point entirely, and continues to provide Thomalin with his conventional and prettified picture of the rebirth of nature. The hawthorne begins to "vtter his tender head," and

> *Flora* now calleth forth eche flower,
> And bids make ready *Maias* bowre,
>   That newe is vpryst from bedde.
> Tho shall we sporten in delight,

36. "Than comethe. Marche in the whiche the laborer sowith the erthe and planted trees and edyfye howses. the chylde in these vj. yere waxeth bygge to lerne doctryne. and syens" (*Kalender of Shepherdes*, III, 11).

100

> And learn with Lettice to wexe light,
>   That scornfully lookes askaunce,
> Tho will we little Loue awake,
> That nowe sleepeth in *Lethe* lake,
>   And pray him leaden our daunce.

(16-24)

This is no matter of Hell and harlots, as E.K. suggests, but rather the comic naiveté of one who expects to realize his idealized conception of love as a rose without thorns. (Lettice, of course, is Willye's comic, naturalistic parody of the Petrarchan mistress: she scorns only later to consent.) Too much can easily be made of this speech, as E.K.'s antierotic glosses to "Flora" and "Lethe" indicate, implying that Willye manifests an irresponsible evasion of his role as shepherd by putting sex and the things of the mortal world before eternal spring.[37] Flora, according to E.K., was the goddess of flowers, "but indede (as saith Tacitus) a famous harlot, which with the abuse of her body hauing gotten great riches, made the people of Rome her heyre: who in remembraunce of so great beneficence, appointed a yearely feste for the memoriall of her." Willye's Flora is thus a pagan harlot presiding over an outrageously sinful Mayday festival, and so for E.K. it is appropriate that Lethe "is a lake in hell, which the Poetes call the lake of forgetfulness. . . So that by loue sleeping in Lethe lake, he meaneth he was almost forgotten and out of knowledge, by reason of winters hardnesse, when all pleasures as it were,

---

37. Robert Allen Durr, *ELH*, 24 (1957), 277–278, relies heavily on E.K.'s glosses and on the emblems for "March." He quotes with approval E.K.'s narrow and antierotic gloss on the "Embleme," that "hereby is meant, that all the delights of Loue, wherein wanton youth walloweth, be but follye mixt with bitternesse, and sorrow sawced with repentaunce." But he ignores the fact that E.K.'s gloss has overlooked the lovelorn Thomalin's less rigid emblem: "Of Hony and of Gaule in loue there is store: / The Honye is much, but the Gaule is more." Even for the lovesick Thomalin, there is much honey in love, though the honey is less than the gall just as spring is less than winter in the natural year that frames the *Calender*. Moreover, Willye's emblem ("To be wise and eke to loue, /Is graunted scarce to God aboue") is probably not meant to be as rigidly antierotic as E.K.'s interpretation of it would have us think. To be sure, Willye pities Thomalin's plight, but his role throughout the poem has hardly been one of discouraging Thomalin in love, quite the contrary. His emblem can be read, then, not as simply antierotic—which, after all, seems contradictory to his character—but as containing two opposite but complementary meanings: the lover cannot be wise, but the wise man also cannot love—or in terms of "February," Cuddie cannot be Thenot, but neither can Thenot be Cuddie. Neither lover nor wise man is complete in himself. Such a synthesis is granted to God alone, and not by a very wide margin. Moreover, we should remember that Willye's emblem reads "to be wise and eke to loue," not "to loue and eke be wise."

sleepe and weare oute of mynde." E.K.'s moralized mythology is simply not relevant here. To be sure, the images of Flora and Lethe suggest the theme to be developed that there's a lot more to "little Loue" than Willye realizes; but they do not moralize ironically on Willye's eroticism. The allusions, and the speech as a whole, are to be understood in terms of the limited vision and experience of the character who makes them. The point developed later in the eclogue and to some extent here is not that "little Loue" is a big sin, but that "little Loue" is considerably bigger than Willye thinks. This, of course, is what Thomalin will teach Willye. But at the same time, as we will see, the mock-heroic portrayal of Thomalin's exaggerated perception of and participation in love will show us the other side of the coin, that "little Loue" while not as little as Willye thinks is not so big as Thomalin, with his equally limited and distorted perception of Cupid, thinks. "March" is a mock-epic comedy of rustic and youthful initiation into the rites of spring, not a Mantuanesque moralization on the hellish fiend.[38]

Up to this point Willye and Thomalin have been talking at comic cross-purposes; but the unbelieving Thomalin suddenly gets Willye's message, and in utter astonishment bursts out with:

> Willye, I wene thou bee assott:
> For lustie Loue still sleepeth not,
>   But is abroad at his game.
>
> (25–27)

It is not "little Loue," but "lustie Loue"; and he is a predator "abroad at his game," not a dance leader. Willye, in open-eyed disbelief, responds with a rapid-fire series of questions:

> How kenst thou, that he is awoke?
> Or hast thy selfe his slomber broke?
>   Or made preuie to the same?
>
> (28-30)

The childishly comic exaggeration we have seen in the shepherds' response to each other and in their perspective on love carries over

---

38. Hallett Smith, *Elizabethan Poetry*, pp. 48–49, has noted, corroborating this interpretation, that the verse form is that of Chaucer's *Sir Thopas*, and that the eclogue is comic, with Thomalin functioning as a mock-heroic counterpart to Sir Thopas. Lea Spitzer, "Spenser, *Shepheardes Calender*, March ll. 61–114, and The Variorum Edition," *SP*, 47 (1950), 494–505, sees the poem as a description of puberty. D. C. Allen, "Three Poems on Eros," *CL*, 8 (1956), 177–193, and Robert Durr, *ELH*, 24 (1957), 277–278, stress the moral elements.

into Thomalin's refusal to reply: he would tell Willye how he came to meet Cupid, but he fears his sheep would stray. Willye replies that he will keep "a double eye" on their flocks while Thomalin tells his story; but Thomalin still refuses, fearing his sheep may stray nonetheless. Thomalin recounts how three days ago, oppressed by love-sorrow, he happened to fall asleep, and awakened to find a ewe who had hurt her leg by falling into a dell. One might gather that Thomalin's experience has simply made him a trifle over-solicitous about being a good shepherd, but suddenly he does an about-face:

> Mought her necke bene ioynted attones,
>   She shoulde haue neede no more spell.
> Thelf was so wanton and so wood,
> (But now I trowe can better good)
>   She mought ne gang on the greene.

> (53-57)

From this we see at once, Thomalin's concern is not that of the good shepherd, but a comic parody of the Mantuanesque perpetual vigil. His excessive caution, like his petulant reaction to the ewe's injury, is part of the childish exaggeration characteristic of him. Thomalin has carried his newly learned lesson of duty to comic excess: he is so carried away with his fear that his sheep will stray that he has hardly a moment to talk. One excess (sleeping on the job because of "sorrowe") has been exchanged for another (an eternally nervous Mantuanesque vigil). In terms of pastoral responsibility as well as love, Thomalin shows himself childishly incapable of perceiving and coming to grips with reality without distorting it. The framework to his tale of Cupid thus effectively dramatizes Thomalin's growing pains in terms of pastoral responsibility as well as love and sex.

Thomalin tells his tale with the comic, literal-minded earnestness of a mind still too naive, innocent, and young to comprehend the experience it has been involved in. Typical of the boasting between one man and another, the events he narrates to Willye are exaggerated and blown up out of all proportion to what really happened. Hearing a "busie bustling" in a thick bush, this self-styled brave hunter moved in close on his prey, not knowing if it be "faerie, feend, or snake." This stalking episode is a mock-heroic parody of the characteristic need of a boy becoming a man to confirm his masculinity and courage in deeds that (at least in the telling) are epic. The tale of Cupid is thus a comic and mock-epic re-enactment of youth's initiations into the rites of love and manhood, while at the same time the heroic exaggeration in which the tale is told itself reveals something of the psychology of the character involved in those rites:

Tho peeping close into the thicke,
Might see the mouing of some quicke,
  Whose shape appeared not:
But were it faerie, feend, or snake,
My courage earnd it to awake,
  And manfully thereat shotte.

(73-78)

The terribly earnest hunter, discharging the manly duties of Mars, is suddenly and comically confronted with Venus' "naked swayne, / With spotted winges like Peacocks trayne" dwelling incongrously among the English bushes. The battle that ensues is every bit as much a mock-epic battle as Fielding's in *Tom Jones,* ludicrously involving the mythic Cupid and a country bumpkin who is a kind of Braggadocchio, mock-hero, *miles gloriosus:*

[I] shott at him with might and maine,
  As thicke, as it had hayled.
So long I shott, that al was spent:
Tho pumie stones I hastly hent,
  And threwe: but nought availed:
He was so wimble, and so wight,
From bough to bough he lepped light,
  And oft the pumies latched.
Therewith affrayd I ranne away:
But he, that earst seemd but to playe,
  A shaft in earnest snatched,
And hit me running in the heele.

(86-97)

The comedy here emerges from the ludicrous ineffectuality of Thomalin's battle strategy, from Homeric arrows to frantic Ovidian stones.[39] His ineffectual and naively incongrous battle plans are a comic analogue to his inability to *perceive* his enemy: he simply fails to grasp the nature of the beast he is fighting with. The limited and childlike perceptions of the hero comically undermine the gran-

---

39. The pumice stones, as A. E. Friedman, "The Diana-Aceton Episode in Ovid's *Metamorphoses* and the *Faerie Queene*," *CL,* 18 (1966), 292–293, indicates in his discussion of the bower to which Belphoebe leads Timias (*FQ,* III. v. 39), are not native to England and in all probability have a literary source; he suggests *Metamorphoses* III. 158.

deur of his physical pretensions: Thomalin has a child's mind and experience with a hero's ambitions.

The strange creature "that earst seemed but to playe" shoots this English Achilles in the heel, giving him a wound he knows not how to cease. Neither in the stalking, nor in battle, nor in wounded defeated has Thomalin come to grips with his antagonist. Nor is Willye more learned. He can confirm that "perdie with loue thou diddest fight" from something he heard his father say once about how he encountered Love one day entangled in a fowling net—but it is locker-room knowledge, and nothing more. Willye, like Thomalin, is part of "March's" comedy of man's perennial mystification by the rites of love.

The August eclogue is divided into two parts, the light-hearted singing-contest between Perigot and Willye and the weighty sestina of Colin. The eclogue is thus structured around two versions of pastoral love. Perigot's mock-tragic experience of love is contrasted with Colin's genuinely tragic love in much the same way that in "March" Thomalin's mock-heroic experience is, by implication, contrasted with the more serious and devastating experience of the *Calender's* hero. Perigot's love is characterized by inflated gestures and exaggerated responses. Like the young and naive Bucaeus in Theocritus' tenth idyll, his youthful and rustic innocence precludes a sensible perception of himself and his experiences. His exaggerated responses to love, his clumsy imitation of the hero's lofty passion, and his inability to see himself as others see him make him a sitting duck for the irony of the detached, "sensible" Willye.[40]

"August" opens with the introductory sparring conventional in the pastoral singing-contest. Willye is egging on his rival, teasing him about the physical excuses he will make to avoid the contest:

Tell me *Perigot,* what shalbe the game,
Wherefore with myne thou dare thy musick matche?
Or bene thy Bagpypes renne farre out of frame?
Or hath the Crampe thy ioynts benomd with ache?

(1-4)

Perigot's excuse, though, is nothing so mock-serious and imaginary, nothing so physical and down-to-earth as stiff joints or an out-of-tune

---

40. The confrontation of sensible man and passionate man in "August" is a comic counterpart to the serious confrontation of "June."

bagpipe—at least to his mind. He replies to Willye, sighing with deadly seriousness: "Ah *Willye*, when the hart is ill assayde, / How can Bagpipe, or ioynts be wellapayd?" If we take Perigot as seriously as he takes himself, we may very well conclude, with some of our modern critics, that he is in the clutches of Satan. The light mockery of Willye's beside-the-mark questions, however, suggests that this is not the case. Willye's mockery is part of the alternation of utter earnestness and light mockery, of parody and tragedy that informs the entire structure of the eclogue. The Willye-Perigot episode is a parody of Colin's tragedy; its motifs are, as we will see, similar, but in terms of man's sanity and fruitfulness, quite unlike. The first of these motifs is that of the agonizing lover. The second is that of the lover-poet whose love now interferes with the song-making in which he once excelled:

> What the foule euill hath thee so bestadde?
> Whilom thou was peregall to the best,
> And wont to make the jolly shepheards gladde
> With pyping and dauncing, didst passe the rest.
>
> (7-10)

Perigot replies that he has learned "a newe daunce":

> Loue hath misled both my younglings, and mee:
> I pyne for payne, and they my payne to see.
>
> (17-18)

To this weighty pronouncement (an echo of Colin's in "January"), Willye replies:

> Perdie and wellawaye; ill may they thriue:
> Neuer knewe I louers sheepe in good plight.
> But and if in rymes with me thou dare striue,
> Such fond fantsies shall soone be put to flight.
>
> (19-22)

The sentiment of the first two lines might at first seem to be identical with Thenot's in February," but it is much more matter-of-fact and much less homiletic and moralistic than Thenot's. Instead of pursuing a long diatribe, Willye drops the matter and turns abruptly to what interested him in the first place, the contest. Willye is not endowing Perigot's lovesickness with cosmic and catastrophic moral importance. He is sufficiently aware of the commonness and naturalness of Perigot's exaggeratedly lofty agonies to treat them rather lightly and mat-ter-of-factly, sufficiently lightly in fact to poke fun at Perigot in their roundelay. It would be a mistake to confuse Willye's inability to take Perigot's lovesickness as seriously as Perigot himself does with antieroticism. His light cynicism, as we will see in the roundelay, acts as a foil to Perigot's naiveté, but the opposition of the two charac-ters is hardly that of sinful eroticism versus wise antieroticism.

The singing-contest is a sort of Petrarchan pastourelle, a rustic parody of Petrarchan love. Perigot's narrative is as conventional as his own experience of love. On a holy eve a shepherd spies "the bouncing Bellibone" tripping over the dale. Bellibone has the usual features of her type: she wears a gray frock, a green kirtle, and a chaplet of violets. Her eye pierces the soul of the shepherd, and the wound (as with Thomalin in "March") "ranckleth ay more and more." The shepherd-lover cannot put his love from his thought, and he thus resigns himself to death.

The very conventionality, in theme and situation, of the roundelay accounts for its structural and thematic importance as a foil to Colin's sestina. The lover's "death" here is not the tragic death of Colin. His wounds are, like Thomalin's, simply too normal and common-place to be taken with the moral seriousness with which we view Colin's. The experience of the shepherd in the song may or not be Perigot's; we cannot be sure about this. But the simple fact that Perigot takes on the role of the hapless shepherd would suggest that he and the shepherd are at least similar if not identical in their love-sickness. The similarity or identity of the love experience in the roundelay with Perigot's contradicts any effort to impose the tragic waste of Colin's experience on Perigot, for Perigot himself (once the roundelay is finished) calls it a "mery thing," whereas Colin's is "sadde":

Now say it [a verse made by Colin] Cuddie, as thou
   art a ladde:
With mery thing its good to medle sadde.

(143-144)

These seem to me extremely important lines, for if Perigot himself finally finds his own experience—or at least an experience like it—a "mery thing," we can probably be sure that the emphasis in "August" depends on a contrast of seemingly similar experiences, one sufficiently normal (however painful) to be treated in a merry and light-hearted fashion, the other tragically destructive and therefore to be treated in a "sadde" or serious fashion. The point to be made is similar to that in "March": Colin's experience is a tragic distortion of normal, natural human experience, whether it be youthful love or aged wisdom. Further evidence of contrast lies in the fact that in "June" Colin's discarding the "wanton toyes" of poetry represented not wisdom but a waste of talent, for such "wanton toyes" were symptoms of sanity; they were, potentially, a creative outlet for passion which, while satisfying his personal needs, also satisfied his social mission as poet of the pastoral world. Such poems were, again potentially, healthy symptoms of psychological and social integration—though the sestina shows indications of the disintegration affecting Colin. Perigot and Colin, therefore, however similar the outline of their career in love, are foils not parallels to each other. Perigot may claim that he cannot sing because of lovesickness, but Perigot *does* sing, while Colin pipes only to himself alone in lowly dales. Perigot's wounds are normal and curable; Colin's are not. Perigot's "death" is normal, he will revive; Colin's life has been abnormally telescoped, passing from youth to age in a single year, and his life gives no sign of revival.

Such an interpretation, based on the contrast of comic normality and tragic abnormality, has the virtue of not only being more in line with the contrast found in the other eclogues, but also of preserving the obvious tonal contrast between the singing-contest and the sestina that would be obscured by reducing the eclogue to a heavy-handed moralization. It also accounts for the pervasive parody and mockery in the roundelay. The roundelay is structured around a simple alternation between Perigot's lines and Willye's. Perigot provides the narrative lines, and they are characterized by a serious mien so lofty and exaggerated, and at the same time so conventional, that they parody themselves. Willye's lines fall into two alternating categories, which for brevity I will call A-lines and B-lines. His A-lines are all variations on the formula of "hey hoe," which prefaces an echo of a word or idea contained in Perigot's previous line. The bouncy lightness of these doggerel lines inevitably undermines the exaggerated seriousness of Perigot's lines preceding them. Willye's B-lines are for the most part a mock-earnest extension of an idea, image, or sentiment found in Perigot's preceding lines. The B-lines burlesque the conventional seriousness of Perigot's poetry, sometimes by outright mockery, but more frequently by carrying Perigot's lofty seriousness one step further to absurdity. The structure of the roundelay, then, is a clever interplay between the seriousness of Perigot's lines and the irony and mock-seriousness of Willye's. In order to see how this structure works, we must look at one or two passages in some detail:

> Per. A chapelet on her head she wore,
> Wil.   hey ho chapelet,
> Per. Of sweete Violets therein was store,
> Wil.   she sweeter than the Violet.

(69-72)

In this passage, Willye's last line takes advantage of the commonplace that inevitably develops in this kind of poetry: if Bellibone has a chaplet of sweet violets, then it necessarily follows that she is sweeter than violets. Willye supplies the same sort of ironic comment in the following passage:

> Per. She roude at me with glauncing eye,
> Wil.   as cleare as the christall glasse:
> Per. All as the Sunnye beame so bright,
> Wil.   hey ho the Sunne beame,
> Per. Glaunceth from *Phoebus* face forthright,
> Wil.   so loue into thy hart did streame:
> Per. Or as the thonder cleaues the cloudes,
> Wil.   hey ho the Thonder,
> Per. Wherein the lightsome leuin shroudes,
> Wil.   so cleaues thy soule a sonder.
> Per. Or as Dame *Cynthias* siluer raye
> Wil.   hey ho the Moonelight,
> Per. Vpon the glyttering waue doth playe:
> Wil.   such play is a pitteous plight.
> Per. The glaunce into my heart did glide,
> Wil.   hey ho the glyder,
> Per. Therewith my soule was sharply gryde,
> Wil.   such woundes soone wexen wider.
> Per. Hasting to raunch the arrow out,
> Wil.   hey ho Perigot,
> Per. I left the head in my hart roote:
> Wil.   it was a desperate shot.
> Per. There it ranckleth ay more and more,
> Wil.   hey ho the arrowe,

Per. Ne can I find salue for my sore:
Wil.   loue is a curelesse sorrowe.

(79-104)

There is something of a rustic Don Alfonso in Willye. He knows the clichés of love and the conventions of love poetry sufficiently well to understand that neither is all that it pretends to be. Willye completes Perigot's high-flown similes with tongue-in-cheek irony. If she has an eye, it will of course be as clear as crystal glass. If the glance from her eye is like a sunbeam, so is love like a sunbeam streaming into the lover's heart. Willye is familiar with love's astronomy, the cosmic analogies of the lover and love. The wounds of course "soone wexen wider," and it was of course "a desperate shot," for love is always, most earnestly, "a curelesse sorrowe." The irony of Willye's lines thus depends on the alternation of coy lightness and ironic sobriety.

Thus, neither the tone nor the pervasive irony within the singing-contest justifies an equation of Perigot's experience in love with Colin's. As in "March," we have a comedy of normal excess and exaggeration. In "March," the comedy of normal love is blown up to mock-heroic proportions; in "August," to mock-tragic proportions. Though the pain of love in "March" and "August" is similar to Colin's experience in the plaintive eclogues, the similarity is a matter of comic and tragic polarity. We are not to take Perigot as seriously as he seems to take himself, or Spenser's carefully planned irony, his portrayal of the comic aspect of normal human experience, degenerate into gibberish.

Colin's sestina treats seriously and elegiacally the same themes the singing-contest treats comically and mock-tragically. Whether the song was written before Colin's renunciation of his public role, or after, is not made clear. Regardless, it reflects the same tragically self-destructive obsession found in the Colin of "January." The sestina is little more than an elaborate invocation to nature to wail Colin's woes. Colin, quite unlike Perigot, renounces human society for the forest:

Resort of people doth my greefs augment,
    The walled townes do work my greater woe:
    The forest wide is fitter to resound
    The hollow Echo of my carefull cryes.

(157-160)

Like a hermit, Colin retires to the forest to waste away to death:

> Here will I dwell apart
> In gastfull groue therefore, till my last sleepe
> Doe close mine eyes: so shall I not augment
> With sight of such a chaunge my restlesse woe.
>
> . . . . . .
>
> Thus all the night in plaints, the day in woe
> I vowed haue to wayst, till safe and sound
> She home returne . . .
>
> (169-181)

The sentiment here and its expression are both considerably more weighty and tragic than the rest of the August eclogue. Moreover, there is nothing in Perigot's lovesickness to suggest that he wills destruction upon himself. He is simply the victim of love's dart, not the victim of a death urge. Furthermore, such talent as he has he is still using; he has not abandoned his public role as poet and he has not neurotically retreated into himself. With Perigot, there is no tragic waste as there is with Colin. The function of the sestina here is similar to that of the lay of Elisa in "April," a testimony to Colin's great talent and mission that he has abandoned. The very fact that it is Cuddie and not Colin who rehearses the sestina for the shepherds itself testifies to the waste and failure surrounding Colin. The August eclogue, therefore, is more a series of contrasts than parallels. It is, fundamentally, a contrast between the comedy of normal human experience and its natural disorders and the tragedy of human waste and unnatural disorder.

Portrayal of love in the *Shepheardes Calender* is not uniform, and to formulate a philosophy of love for the *Calender* strictly according to either the antierotic philosophy of Thenot or the proerotic philosophy of Cuddie can only mistake the dramatic complexity of the *Calender*. Throughout the *Calender*, Spenser is making distinctions— distinctions between the love of Colin and the love of Cuddie and the apparently joyous lovers of "April," distinctions between the tragedy of Colin's unnatural deviation from normal love and the comedy of love. Love can destroy, it can create; it can cause pain, it can cause joy. Love is not all of a piece; nor is the *Calender*. The *Calender*'s vision of love, like its vision of morality proper, is not confined by the rigid limits of Mantuanesque moralization; it does not view all of life with the sober eye of the inflexible moralist. The influence of pseudo-Chaucer and the moralistic "Ploughman's Tale" is often noted, but the influence of Chaucerain comedy is noted all too infrequently. The *Shepheardes Calender* presents us with versions of pastoral and varieties of pastoral experience. Spenser is aware of the diversity and paradoxes of experience, and the *Calender* is constructed not as an exposition of a single, sure perspective, but as an exploration of perspectives. It is a use of pastoral to explore pastoral and, beyond that, the uncertain and tangential truths of all our visions of certitude.

THE GOLDEN AGE AND THE RESOLUTION OF PERSPECTIVES

One of the central animating forces behind pastoral is the longing for the golden age—an age symbolized and brought forth by a messianic figure, whose presence brings a resolving harmony to the conflict and disorder of the real world.[41] Winter passes, and eternal spring is restored; nature makes a gift of herself; wars cease, and the order of peace returns along with the virgin goddess of justice, Astraea. The world Elisa presides over in "April"—like Virgil's golden-age eclogue, the fourth in the series—is the golden age of Spenser's pastoral world. In it are resolved the conflicts plaguing the iron-age world of the *Calender*, both within the mind and within society: Venus and Diana, love and chastity, are reconciled, as are the red rose and the white. To the winter of the iron age, Elisa brings paradisiacal spring. To its injustices and conflicts, she brings and embodies justice and peace, as Elizabeth I, virgin, is transformed into Astraea, Virgo.[42]

41. The best brief account of the golden age and the Renaissance is by Harry Levin, "The Golden Age and the Renaissance," in *Literary Views: Critical and Historical Essays*, ed. Carroll Camden (Chicago, 1964), pp. 1–14. The most thorough studies are Profesor Levin's recent book, *The Myth of the Golden Age in the Renaissance* (Bloomington, Ind., 1969) and Elizabeth Armstrong's *Ronsard and the Age of Gold* (Cambridge, Eng., 1968). Also valuable to a study of the golden age are the following: A. O. Lovejoy and G. Boas, *A Documentary History of Primitivism and Related Ideas* (Baltimore, 1935), I, especially 291–303; E. Lipsker, *Der Mythos vom goldenen Zeitalter in den Schäferdichtungen Italiens, Spaniens und Frankreichs zur Zeit der Renaissance* (Berlin, 1933); P. Meissner, "Das Goldene Zeitalter in der Englischen Renaissance," *Anglia*, 59 (1935), 351–367; E. Graf, "Ad aureae aetatis fabulam symbola," *Leipziger Studien zur classichen Philologie*, 8 (1885), 3–84; A. Bartlett Giamatti, *The Early Paradise and the Renaissance Epic* (Princeton, 1966), especially pp. 15–33; and my own "Imitation and Metamorphosis: The Golden-Age Eclogue in Spenser, Milton, and Marvell," *PMLA*, 84 (1969), 1559–70.

42. This association of Elizabeth with the goddess of justice is by no means

The significance of the April eclogue depends in part upon the contrast between the framework and the lay, a contrast between two "chosen" people, one chosen to order life as queen, the other chosen to order life as artist and poet. The two features of order and harmony represented by Colin and Elisa, the ordering of art and the ordering of life, are interrelated. Indeed Elisa, as the messiah who, unlike Colin, realizes her mission, is celebrated in terms of traditional images of artistic order and expression; she becomes one of the Graces, by tradition associated with the Muses and artistic inspiration. The first stanza of the lay's invocation establishes at once the complementary order of life and art:

> Ye dayntye Nymphs, that in this blessed Brooke
>   doe bathe your brest,
> For sake your watry bowres, and hether looke,
>   at my request:
> And eke you Virgins, that on *Parnasse* dwell,
> Whence floweth *Helicon* the learned well,
>   Helpe me to blaze
>   Her worthy praise,
> Which in her sexe doth all excell.

(37-45)

In the next stanza of the invocation, Spenser establishes more specifically the connection, in terms of artistic order, between the virgin Muses and "the flowre of Virgins":

> Of fayre *Elisa* be your siluer song,
>   that blessed wight:
> The flowre of Virgins, may shee florish long,
>   in princely plight.
> For shee is *Syrinx* daughter without spotte,
> Which *Pan* the shepheards God of her begot:
>   So sprong her grace
>   Of heauenly race,
> No mortall blemishe may her blotte.

(46-54)

It is commonplace, of course, for the messianic figure to come of lofty parentage. If we follow E.K. and the historical commentators here, the noble parents are, somewhat extravagantly, Pan as Henry

---

unique; see Frances A. Yates, "Queen Elizabeth as Astrea," *Journal of the Warburg and Courtauld Institute* (*JWCI*), 10 (1947), 27–82.

VIII and Syrinx as Ann Boleyn. But that is not the central meaning of the genealogy. The genealogy makes better poetic logic if we see it as a continuation of the interrelated themes of art and virginity, already suggested by the nine virgin Muses. As E.K. explains the Pan-Syrinx myth:

> Syrinx is the name of a Nymphe of Arcadie, whome when Pan being in loue pursued, she flying from him, of the Gods was turned into a reede. So that Pan catching at the Reedes in stede of the Damosell and puffing hard (for he was almost out of wind) with hys breath made the Reedes to pype.

As the "child" of Pan and Syrinx, Elisa is, quite simply, Song; more particularly, pastoral song. Unless we grasp this, Elisa's ultimate ascension to heaven as one of the dancing Graces and her being begotten without spot and "mortall blemishe" make little sense. By having Elisa represent Song and consequently harmony, and by having her represent the divine artist as well as the divinely anointed ruler, Spenser portrays the order of art and the order of the ruler and the body politic as corresponding extensions of divine order, and as corresponding aspects of the new order of the golden age.

In her role as queen as well as artist, Elisa—like the son of Pollio in Virgil's fourth eclogue, or the child of Catherine de Medici in Marot's fourth eclogue—has been divinely appointed to rule and perfect her earthly kingdom, to reform its old errors into a new order:

> See, where she sits vpon the grassie greene,
>   (O seemely sight)
> Yclad in Scarlot like a mayden Queene,
>   And Ermines white.
> Vpon her head a Cremosin coronet,
> With Damaske roses and Daffadillies set:
>   Bayleaues betweene,
>   And Primroses greene
> Embellish the sweete Violet.
>
> Tell me, haue ye seene her angelick face,
>   Like *Phoebe* fayre?
> Her heauenly haueour, her princely grace
>   can you well compare?
> The Redde rose medled with the White yfere,
> In either cheeke depeincten liuely chere.
>   Her modest eye,

Her Maiestie,
Where haue you seene the like, but there?

(55-71)

The golden-age messiah, according to convention, reconciles conflicts, ends wars, and brings about the return of peace. This, of course, is true of Elisa, who as ruler has united the dissident factions of York and Lancaster. Like the son of Pollio, Elisa embodies in herself and creates within her empire the social and political order of the golden age. But Spenser goes beyond Virgil and the conventional golden-age pastoral on this point. For not only is the above passage a description of Elisa as social and political order, but it also suggests by analogy a continuation of the allegory of Elisa as Song, Elisa as divine art, possessing the power of the artist as well as the ruler to reorder and perfect life into one harmonious and golden whole.

The world of the golden-age eclogue is a world of spring. The messiah stimulates nature to newer and greater fertility; he is the center of the natural abundance that his presence has wrought, and nature in appreciation offers him gifts from her bounty. The same is true of Elisa, though in Spenser's poem the situation is slightly altered, for Elisa has become a virgin goddess of spring, the "flowre of Virgins" (an image suggesting both her virginity and her fertility), presiding over the April rites of spring. The inhabitants of her world celebrate her by decking her with the flowers, the greenery, and the husbandry she has brought forth. The gifts offered Elisa reflect her multiple roles as presider over the golden age. In her role as goddess of eternal spring and fertility, Colin appropriately offers her a lamb, and invokes the "shepheards daughters" to offer Elisa carnations and sops in wine ("worne of Paramoures"); and as goddess of art, Colin offers Elisa his own song of praise. As goddess of spring, Elisa is also the goddess of love; she is therefore adorned with the flower offerings of young lovers. Moreover, inasmuch as Elisa is the virgin goddess of love as well as Virgo ruling the Red Rose and the White, it is significant that the colors red and white are also the traditional colors of love; and that, as C. H. Herford points out, the "cremosin coronet" is in all probability an allusion to the common medieval description of Venus as crowned with a garland of red roses.[43] It is significant, too, that both of the emblems describing Elisa, Thenot's *"O quam te memorem virgo?"* and Hobbinol's *"O*

43. *The Shepheardes Calender*, p. 117 (Notes).

dea certe," derive from Aeneas' speech to Venus in the *Aeneid* (I. 327–328). Elisa, though herself virgin "like *Phoebe* fayre," is goddess of love and procreation as well as goddess of chastity and virginity. In herself she reconciles the warring polarities of the *Calender*'s iron age—Diana and Venus, chastity and love—as does that later version of Elizabeth, Britomart.

One of Spenser's transformations of the golden-age motif of the return of the virtues is the conflation of Elisa with Virgo, embodiment of justice. The return-of-the-virtues motif undergoes a further transformation in the poem. Analogous to the return of the virtues in the conventional golden-age eclogue is the return of the Muses, their return signaling the rebirth of art, a new golden age of art under Elisa comparable to the new golden age of virtue in Virgil. The representatives of art, the Muses, respond to Elisa's presence in the same way that the representatives of nature and virtue have done in "April" as well as in the golden-age tradition as a whole:

> I see *Calliope* speede her to the place,
>   where my Goddesse shines:
> And after her the other Muses trace,
>   with their Violines.
> Bene they not Bay braunches, which they doe beare,
> All for *Elisa* in her hand to weare?
>   So sweetely they play,
>   And sing all the way,
> That it a heauen is to heare.

(100-108)

In that she is symbolic of a new golden age of Song and art, the Muses offer Elisa bay branches, a sign, as E.K. notes, of both poets and rulers:

> Bay branches) be the signe of honor and victory, and therfore of myghty Conquerors worn in theyr triumphes, and eke of famous Poets, as saith Petrarch in hys Sonets.
>   Arbor vittoriosa triomphale,
>   Honor d' Imperadori & di Poëti, &c.

In the image of Elisa receiving bay branches, once more are symbolized the order of art and the order (heroic triumph) of the ruler ordering life: both meanings are contained within the image of the bay branches. So, too, in the image of the Graces. Their arrival to offer a dance continues the theme of music and dance—art—as order and social harmony; for not only were the Graces Venus' hand-maidens, and co-dwellers on Olympus with the Muses, not only were they thought to favor poetry, but they were also symbolic of the principles of social order and the peaceful relations of man. As E.K. notes, the three virgin sisters are called

> Charities, that is thanks, whome the Poetes feyned to be the Goddesses of al bountie and comeliness, which therefore (as sayth Theodontius) they make three, to wete, that men first ought to be gracious and bountiful to other freely, then to receiue benefits at other mens hands curteously, and thirdly to require them thankfully: which are three sundry Actions in liberalitye.

The Graces, like Elisa, therefore, embody the ordering principles both of art and society. It is perfectly natural that Elisa should join them as a fourth Grace:

> Wants not a fourth grace, to make the daunce euen?
> Let that rowme to my Lady be yeuen:
>   She shalbe a grace,
>   To fyll the fourth place,
> And reigne with the rest in heauen.
>
> (113-117)

Just as Pollio's son will be seen among heroes and gods, and be one of them, so Elisa as Song is seen among, and is one of, the Graces.[44]

Elisa, like the conventional golden-age messiah, is a figure of peace; fittingly she is crowned by Chloris, personification of spring, with a crown of olive branches as queen of peace.[45] This is the climax of April's rites:

> *Chloris,* that is the chiefest Nymph of al,
> Of Oliue braunches beares a Coronall:
>   Oliues bene for peace,
>   When wars doe surcease:
> Such for a Princesse bene principall.
>
> (122-126)

---

44. The relation of music and dance to order is, of course, an ancient common-place, though especially prominent in the Renaissance, as E. M. W. Tillyard, *The Elizabethan World Picture* (London, 1943), pp. 94–99, has shown in his chapter on "The Cosmic Dance." Tillyard's example, Sir John Davies' *Orchestra,* also ends with Elizabeth presiding over a dance.

45. Cf. Marot, "Eglogue IV," l. 47: "Ja le Laurier te prepare couronne."

Spenser's April eclogue is thus part of the tradition of the golden-age eclogue used by Virgil, Calpurnius, Marot, and others. Most of the motifs are there, but transformed. There is, in the first place, the standard opposition of golden-age order versus iron-age disorder, a contrast of Colin-disorder in the framework and Elisa-order in the lay. Moreover, Elisa, like Virgil's child, leads the new pastoral golden age in which all the conflicts of the iron-age world are resolved within a new harmony. Also, like the conventional golden-age messiah, she is of lofty parentage, she receives the gifts from the new abundance of nature, she dwells among gods, she presides over a world of spring, and she signals the surcease of wars and the return of peace and justice. But the conventional motifs are transformed, partly because of the setting, that is, the rites of spring, and partly because of the allegory. Spenser has taken the golden-age eclogue's theme of the world remade, and made it into an allegory of the transforming power of Song, art—an allegory, too, of the interrelation of social and artistic order, and an allegory of the new age of song. According to these ends, Spenser transforms the conventions. Virgo, instead of being a separate figure from the messiah, is one with Elisa, virgin. The noble genealogy of the child is less historical than allegorical. The child's dwelling among and becoming one of the gods is symbolic, not merely flattering. The figure of Elisa, therefore, is more important on a symbolic than on an historical level. Elisa is certainly more than Elizabeth I. On a purely practical level of patronage, at most incidental to the artistic significance of the work, the eclogue for April can be read as a flattering celebration of Elizabeth I. However, if my interpretation is right, that Elisa signals a new golden age of song, a return of the Muses, then—if one demands an historical reading—the praise of Elisa is a praise of not only Elizabeth I but also Edmund Spenser, himself "the new Poete," in his *Calender* auguring that new age.

On poetic and artistic grounds, however, Elisa is Elisa, not allegorically "equaling" Elizabeth I but including and subsuming Elizabeth. Elizabeth is best seen as one of the types patterned on the ideal archetype represented by Elisa. Spenser employs characteristics of the historical Elizabeth to define and amplify, to give depth to, the characterization and meaning of Elisa, just as in much the same way he employs characteristics of Mary of Scotland to give depth to the characterization and meaning of Duessa. The historical Elizabeth is, artistically, put at the poetic service of the figure who, in a double sense, compliments her. Perhaps in total contradiction of the mode of composition, the poetic result is that Elisa is the ideal pattern on which Elizabeth is molded, not vice-versa. It is Elisa's multiple symbolism of modes of order, not the flattery of Elizabeth, that makes "April" relevant to the *Calender;* for Elisa, embodying Venus' animating and ordering power of love, represents the idealized synthesis of all the conflicts and oppositions of the natural, fallen world of the *Calender*'s iron age. Unlike any other figure in the *Calender,* Elisa is complete in herself; for she, whom "no mortall blemishe may . . . blotte," is eternal spring and April everlasting, untouched by the wintry limitations of the fallen world. She is a goddess, in the world but not of it. It would be false, therefore, to see in Elisa the ethical pattern for the Thenots and Cuddies of Spenser's pastoral world; their world is not the same. Elisa is the Arcadian ideal hoped for by fallen, iron-age man, but she is not the practical pattern a shepherd must or can follow. For in Elisa all the conflicts and oppositions pervading the iron-age world are mythically reconciled. Representing and reconciling in herself both heroic (the ruler) and pastoral (the shepherds' goddess), the high places and the low, love and virginity, art and life, she is above all a symbol of the perfect harmony and synthesis which is the ideal, the golden age, of Spenser's pastoral world of questions and doubts. She is its mythology.

2. The Unity and Design of the Shepheardes Calender

In discussing the unity of the *Shepheardes Calender,* the shadow of E.K. is somehow always with us. Those who have thought the *Calender* unified, as well as those who have not,[1] have largely abided by E.K.'s declaration:

> These xij. Aeclogues euery where answering to the seasons of the twelue monthes may be well deuided into three formes or ranckes. For eyther they be Plaintiue, as the first, the sixth, the eleuenth, and the twelfth, or recreatiue, such as al those be, which conceiue matter of loue, or commendation of special personages, or Moral: which for the most part be mixed with some Satyrical bitternesse, namely the second of reuerence dewe to old age, the fift of coloured deceipt, the seuenth and ninth of dissolute shepheards and pastours, the tenth of contempt of Poetrie and pleasaunt wits. And to this diuision may euery thing herein be reasonably applyed: a few onely except, whose speciall purpose and meaning I am not priuie to.

Obviously, however, dividing into parts is not the same thing as unifying into a whole. E.K.'s categories reveal more of the diversity than the unity of the *Calender;* their significance is to some extent more academic than artistic.

1. Virtually all recent interpretations of the *Calender* have relied on E.K.'s tripartite division: Hallett Smith, *Elizabethan Poetry* (Cambridge, Mass., 1952), pp. 31–51; Harry Berger, Jr., "The Prospect of the Imagination: Spenser and the Limits of Poetry," *Studies in English Literature* (*SEL*), 1 (1961), 110–112; A. C. Hamilton, "The Argument of Spenser's *Shepheardes Calender*," *ELH*, 23 (1956), 171–182; and Paul E. McLane, *Spenser's "Shepheardes Calender": A Study in Elizabethan Allegory* (Notre Dame, 1961), pp. 314–323.

Where, then, is the unity of the *Calender* to be discovered—assuming that it is unified? The forces that bring any complex work of art into a convincing unity are generally multiple, and this is certainly true of the *Calender*. Certain literal factors are involved: the *Calender* begins and ends in winter; Colin's love affair occupies the first, middle, and last eclogues of the work. However, the two major sources of unity in the *Calender* seem to me to be, first, the patterning of pastoral perspectives, and second, the serial development of seasonal themes. The first of these consists as we saw in the previous chapter, of a continual confrontation and cross-referencing of the Arcadian and Mantuanesque pastoral visions and of tragic and comic versions of pastoral experience. In the moral eclogues there is a recurring confrontation of classical and Mantuanesque pastoral perspectives, and a contrast of comic or seriocomic experience in the framework with the tragic experience of the exemplum; and in the recreative and plaintive eclogues, there is a contrast of tragic and comic relationship to pastoral love. All are part of the overall concern of the *Calender* to explore the values and limitations of various forms of pastoral experience and moral vision.

The most obvious, and perhaps in fact the most necessary, factor in the unity of the *Calendar* is the framework of the calendar and the year. Yet, surprisingly, this has been almost entirely ignored except for its general meaning.[2] E.K. contends that the eclogues "euery where

2. For A. C. Hamilton, *ELH*, 23 (1956), 174–177, the *Calender*'s winter-summer-winter sequence goes back to the ritual origins of pastoral. The ritual motif in the *Calender* is Colin's "quest for himself and the poem's major theme is the effort to 'find' himself." Hamilton adds that the association of the calendar with the Nativity adds a life-death-life sequence, a death in nature that is opposed to the life from death that the final two eclogues, with their "full Christian assurance of man's resurrection out of Nature," supply. The calendar framework thus involves the mutable world of the Fall and simultaneously the question of how man deals with and can transcend the year's time and his own mortality. For Robert Allen Durr, "Spenser's Calendar of Christian Time," *ELH*, 24 (1957), 290–292, the year also represents mutability. The *Calender* begins in the season of Christ's birth rather than in the season of nature's rebirth in order to declare that "man cannot, like the other creatures, live his life in accordance with the seasonal round; the consequence is grinding change and eventual death." According to S. K. Heninger, Jr., "The Implications of Form for *The Shepheardes Calender*," *Studies in the Renaissance* (*SRen*), 9 (1962), 317, "the calendar form, by its derivation from the Pythagorean tetrad, implied a synthesis of all disparate factors into a single well-ordered unity. One of each radical kind was to be incorporated into an all-inclusive whole. This accounts for the careful variety with which Spenser infused his literary microcosm . . . He crammed the greatest possible multeity into the unity of his calendar." The only full-scale attempt to relate the eclogues of the *Calender* to the months and their associations is the pioneering but generally unconvincing

answer to the seasons of the twelue months"; but most readers, while agreeing with Pope that the device of the year is "very beautiful," have also unfortunately agreed with him, in what has been for two centuries the basic criticism of the framework, that "the year has not that variety in it to furnish every month with a particular description, as it may every season."[3] To some extent, there is undeniably truth to Pope's criticism. The August eclogue, for example, is related to the year-structure by seasonal more than monthly motifs, since the heat and the harvest are characteristics of months other than August. But this fact does not invalidate Spenser's structure, which is, like the year itself, both a seasonal and a monthly structure. Moreover, the relevance of the seasonal structure becomes much clearer if we understand what associations the sixteenth century had for the months, as we find them demonstrated in the *Kalender of Shepherdes* and in Spenser's own "Mutability Cantos." But before examining the specific relationship of each eclogue to its month and the seasonal structure of the *Calender,* a few words are necessary on the general meaning behind the *Calender's* year.

Mutability is central to the meaning of the year framework. The world of nature is fallen and, as man's sole guide, untrustworthy. There is however, another aspect of mutability, an ultimate order residing under the appearance of disorder. The constant change seen in the alternation of the seasons from winter to summer and back to winter again is an orderly change. There is an orderly balance

---

attempt of Mary Parmenter, "Spenser['s] 'Twelve Aeglogues Proportional to the Twelve Monthes,'" *ELH*, 3 (1930), 190–217. On the use of temporal material in other of Spenser's works, see especially Sherman Hawkins, "Mutabilitie and the Cycle of the Months," in *Form and Convention in the Poetry of Edmund Spenser,* ed. William Nelson (New York, 1961), pp. 76–102; A. Kent Hieatt, *Short Time's Endless Monument: The Symbolism of Numbers in Edmund Spenser's "Epithalamion"* (New York, 1960), and "The Daughters of Horus: Order in the Stanzas of *Epithalamion,*" in *Form and Convention in the Poetry of Edmund Spenser,* ed. William Nelson (New York, 1961), pp. 103–121; Alastair Fowler, *Spenser and the Numbers of Time* (New York, 1964). Certain of Hawkins' remarks on the year in the Mutability Cantos hold for the *Calender* as well: "the laws of proportion and restraint are for Spenser and Milton as natural as the generative power itself" (p. 94); "in Spenser's calendar, April and May are balanced by August and September: seedtime and harvest represent the poles on which the Spenserian system turns" (p. 94); "in the circle of Spenser's calendar, with its counterpoint of labors and virtues, we see the eternal purpose incarnate in time" (p. 96).

3. "A Discourse on Pastoral Poetry," in *The Poems of Alexander Pope* (London, 1961), I, *Pastoral Poetry and An Essay on Criticism,* 32.

in nature's interaction of the procreative principle of spring and summer with the destructive principle of autumn and winter. The natural year itself, therefore, contains a complementing of seemingly conflicting principles: the procreative (the planting) and the destructive (the harvest). To the extent that man must, as part of the natural world, participate in that world, he too is involved in an attempt to strike a corresponding balance between the dual aspects of his own nature: he is both a creature within nature, who must procreate, survive, and ultimately die, and he is a living soul to whom is offered the triumph of eternity. Correspondingly, the *Calender* is, as we have seen in previous chapters, organized around a recurring juxtaposition of the perspectives of winter (withdrawal, chastity, asceticism, self-denial, age) and the perspectives of spring (participation, love, indulgence, self-assertion, youth). The natural year in the *Calender*, then, represents the mutable world that man must adapt to and yet ultimately triumph over, and it symbolizes in its own precarious balance of winter and spring the balance-in-opposition necessary for man and pastoral society within the natural world. With this in mind, I would like now to embark on the relations of individual eclogues to the year-structure.

The eclogues of the *Calender* fall into two continuous groups linked by an overlapping, transitional group consisting of the eclogues for May, June, and July. The themes of the first group of eclogues, those from "January" to "June," emerge from the seasonal pattern of the contest of winter and spring and from spring's triumph over winter; they are concerned especially with the question of man's participation in the natural year, the moral conflict between man's eternal responsibilities and his natural desire to participate in spring, the conflict of age-winter and youth-spring. The central three eclogues of the *Calender* mark a transition from a concern with man's multifold relationship to spring, literal and metaphoric, to an examination of ambition, the rewards of harvest, and the final harvest of man himself—themes which are the concern of the second half of the *Calender*. The general thrust of the *Calender's* movement—and it *is* general—is from what and how man sows to what and how he reaps.

"January"

January, by the new calendar the first month of the year and by the old calendar the next-to-last month, is, according to the *Kalender of Shepherdes*, the last month of the winter season: "Than comethe, Nouember. December. and Ianyuere. and these iii. monethes is the wynter."[4] As the month just previous to the beginning of spring, it is fitting that Colin "When Winters wastful spight was almost spent, / All in a sunneshine day, as did befall, / Led forth his flock, that had bene long ypent." The natural setting of the eclogue agrees with the winter season: the trees are leafless and covered with icicles, the ground is barren, the flock is faint and feeble from being "long ypent." The wasteful setting is, of course, mirror to the mind of the hero. But Colin's embodiment of January's winter is a tragic paradox, as he himself recognizes:

> Such rage as winters, reigneth in my heart,
> My life bloud friesing with vnkindly cold:
> Such stormy stoures do breede my balefull smart,
> As if my yeare were wast, and woxen old.
> And yet alas, but now my spring begonne,
> And yet alas, yt is already donne.
>
> (25-30)

Colin's seasonal paradox is, as I noted in my longer discussion of him, a psychological distortion of the wintry pastoral vision represented by age (its rejection, like Thenot's of sexuality and impulse) and the springlike pastoral vision represented by youth (its desire, like Cuddie's, for sexual fulfillment, its self-assertion). In Colin's mind, then, there is a suggestion of "February's" contest between the old man and the youth, both of whose representative principles are exaggerated by Colin not just in "January" but in all of his appearances in the *Calender*. Conveniently for Spenser's seasonal portrayal of Colin's tragic contradiction, the interpretations of January in terms of the traditional year of man's life are themselves contradictory, Janus-like. On the one hand, as we see in the *Kalender of Shepherdes*, January represents the first month of man's life, his youth:

> Take fyrst syxe yere for Ienyuere the which is of no vertue nor strengthe in that seasone nothynge on the erthe growith. So man after he is borne tyl he be syxe yere is without wytte strength or connynge & may do no thynge that profytethe.[5]

4. *The Kalender of Shepherdes*, ed. H. Oskar Sommer (London, 1892), III, 10.
5. *The Kalender of Shepherdes*, III, 10

Yet, on the other hand, January represents age and the end of man's life, as it does in the "Mutability Cantos":

> Then came old *Ianuary,* wrapped well
>   In many weeds to keep the cold away;
>   Yet did he quake and quiuer like to quell,
>   And blowe his nayles to warme them if he may:
>   For, they were numbd with holding all the day
>   An hatchet keene, with which he felled wood,
>   And from the trees did lop the needlesse spray:
>   Vpon an huge great Earth-pot steane he stood;
> From whose wide mouth, there flowed forth the Romane floud.

(VII. vii. 42)

January, then, represents both the old man and the youth; it reflects Colin's psychological contradiction and his preparing to die in the midst of his spring.

"February"

In the February eclogue, the seasonal conflict in Colin's mind between winter and spring, age and youth, takes on social form, the conflict of generations, the recurring debate between age and youth. But whereas the seasonal conflict within Colin is an unnatural conflict, the conflict of age and youth, as represented by Piers and Cuddie, is as much a part of nature's order as is the conflict between winter and spring traditionally associated with the month. The divided interpretation of the month's significance in terms of man's year is, as it was for the January eclogue, appropriate for Spenser's material. February is at once the last month of man's age and winter (according to the old calendar), and the second month of his youth and spring (according to the new calendar and the *Kalender of Shepherdes*). It is obviously the former that E.K. has in mind:

> It [the eclogue] conteyneth a discourse of old age, in the persone of *Thenot* an olde Shepheard, who for his crookednesse and vnlustinesse, is scorned of *Cuddie* an vnhappy Heardmans boye. The matter very well accordeth with the season of the moneth, the yeare now drouping, and as it were, drawing to his last age. For as in this time of yeare, so then in our bodies there is a dry and withering cold, which congealeth the crudled blood, and frieseth the wetherbeaten flesh, with stormes of Fortune, and hoare frosts of Care.

("Argument")

125

The Master Shepherd of the *Kalender*, however, has in mind the
association of February with youth:

> Than cometh Feueryere and the dayes begynneth to wexe in length
> and the sonne more hotter. than the erthe begynneth to wexe grene.
> So the other six. yere tyll he come to twelue the chylde begynneth to
> growe bygger and to serue and lerne such as is taught him.[6]

February, then, like January, represents both the old man and the
youth, and it is therefore an appropriate setting for the eclogue's
debate between age and youth. Also relevant to the eclogue's subject
is the fact that February is portrayed in the eclogue as a contest
between winter and spring. It is clear from Cuddie's opening remark
that winter and spring are still vying for supremacy: "Ah for pittie,
will rancke Winters range,/These bitter blasts neuer ginne tass-
wage?" Moreover, Cuddie portrays both himself and Thenot as representatives of the two contesting seasons. Of Thenot he remarks:

> No marueile *Thenot,* if thou can beare
> Cherefully the Winters wrathfull cheare:
> For Age and Winter accord full nie,
> This chill, that cold, this crooked, that wrye.
> And as the lowring Wether lookes downe,
> So semest thou like good fryday to frowne.
>
> (25-30)

His own youth he identifies with the flowering of spring, to which
Thenot is the destroying frost of winter: "But my flowring youth
is foe to frost." He also speaks of his years as green, and his sexuality
as "the budding branch" of spring that Thenot "wouldest cropp."
The description of February in the "Mutability Cantos" portrays the
dual age-youth, winter-spring associations for the month, while it
also depicts as the function of age the very pruning of the branch
that Cuddie resents:

> And lastly, came cold *February,* sitting
>   In an old wagon, for he could not ride;
>   Drawne of two fishes for the season fitting,
>   Which through the flood before did softly slyde
>   And swim away: yet had he by his side
>   His plough and harnesse fit to till the ground,
>   And tooles to prune the trees, before the pride

6. *The Kalender of Shepherdes,* III, 11.

126

Of hasting Prime did make them burgein round:
So past the twelue Months forth, and their dew places found.

(VII. vii. 43)

The Master Shepherd, as we have seen, also portrays February in terms of the pruning and teaching of youth and the incipient flourishing of nature: as the earth grows green, the child grows bigger and begins "to serue and lerne such as is taught him." February is associated not only with age's teaching of youth, however; it is also associated with youth's teaching of age, as is clear from the parade of the months is the *Kalender of Shepherdes:*

I am February the moost hardy
In my season the pure moder vyrgynall
Offred her sone in the temple truely
Makynge to god a present specyall
Of Ihesu cryst the kinge of kynges all.[7]

February is also the month, then, of Christ's teaching the elders in the temple. The various descriptions of the month make it clear that February is associated with the relationship of age and youth, winter and spring, and that the principal ideas associated with the month are the pruning of nature and its flowering, and the teaching not only of youth but also of age. The debate between Thenot and Cuddie, therefore, is an extension in human terms (the conflict of generations) of the contest that is going on in nature. The contesting between the two of them is not unnatural; it is not only expected, it is also necessary and desirable. Only when the two principles become exaggerated and distorted, as they do for the Oak and the Briar, and also for Colin, are they unnatural. The two opening eclogues, then, set up for the *Calender* three of the major forms that the conflict of spring and winter, youth and age, and the corresponding Mantuanesque and Arcadian pastoral visions, will take throughout the *Calender:* the psychological perversion of these principles in Colin, the social perversion of them in the tale of the Oak and the Briar (their destruction forshadows his), and the potential social balance in their natural form in the debate between Thenot and Cuddie.

"March"

March, the second month of spring, is, as we learn from the *Kalender of Shepherdes,* like February a month of learning and initiation

7. *The Kalender of Shepherdes,* III, 17.

into doctrine; it is also a time of planting and building, a time when man begins to participate in the revival of nature:

> Than comethe. Marche in the whiche the laborer sowith the erthe & planted trees and edyfye howses. the chylde in these vj. yere waxeth bygge to lerne doctryne. and syens and to be fayre and honest. for than he is xviii. yere.[8]

According to the "Mutability Cantos," too, March is a month fertility, a month for sowing the womb of nature:

> First, sturdy *March* with brows full sternly bent,
> And armed strongly, rode vpon a Ram,
> The same which ouer *Hellespontus* swam:
> Yet in his hand a spade he also hent,
> And in a bag all sorts of seeds ysame,
> Which on the earth he strowed as he went,
> And fild her womb with fruitfull hope of nourishment.
>
> (VII. vii. 32)

In the March eclogue, spring has obviously arrived: the hawthorn is beginning to bud, the grass begins to be refreshed, the swallow peeps out of her nest, and Flora calls forth each flower. Spring is not yet in its full flourishing ("the joyous time now nigheth fast, / That shall alegge this bitter blast, / And slake the winters sorowe"); that must wait until April. But whereas in "February" winter and spring were still contesting, in "March" there is no question: spring and Cupid have won. In this month of the Ram, dominated by Venus, when man sows the womb of nature, the subject of the eclogue is appropriately love, man's initiation and perennial re-initiation into the rites of spring.

Thematically the March eclogue considers issues which are substantially the same as those of "February"—the relationship of pastoral duty to youthful love, the dual nature of love as both destructive and procreative. But the issues are presented through a more boisterous comedy, one devoid of the potential tragic implications that lie behind the seriocomic dispute of the old man and the youth in "February." However much "February" is comic in its age-old conflict of generations, it remains at the same time a serious debate between two forms of knowledge and experience, its argument at once amusing and crucial. In contrast, "March" is a totally comic, mock-heroic

---

8. *The Kalender of Shepherdes*, III, 11.

portrayal of two young men bumbling their way into knowledge and experience. The two eclogues are, nonetheless, companion pieces. Willye's enthusiastic anticipation of spring and love is a counterpart to Cuddie's in "February," and Thomalin's comic fear of spring and love a counterpart to Thenot's Mantuanesque moralizing; and their entire discussion of spring and man's participation in it, in which they talk at comic cross-purposes, neither at first realizing his disagreement with the other, is a counterpart to the disagreement of Cuddie and Thenot. Moreover, the March eclogue's comedy of inexperience, its comic portrayal of the normal confusion of youth in spring, is a foil to the tragic confusion of Colin in "January," while Thomalin's exaggerated fear of taking an eye off his sheep is a parody of Thenot's Mantuanesque insistence on duty in "February."

"April"

April is the last month and culmination of spring and the rebirth of nature, a time of extraordinary natural abundance. April is the month, according to the Master Shepherd,

> that the erthe and the trees is couered in grene and flowers. and in euery part good is increasyth habundantly. than cometh the chylde to gader the swete flowers of hardyness.[9]

April is similarly portrayed in the "Mutability Cantos":

> Next came fresh *Aprill* full of lustyhed,
>   And wanton as a Kid whose horne new buds:
>   Vpon a Bull he rode, the same which led
>   *Europa* floting through th' *Argolick* fluds:
>   His hornes were gilden all with golden studs
>   And garnished with garlonds goodly dight
>   Of all the fairest flowres and freshest buds
>   Which th' earth brings forth, and wet he seem'd in sight
> With waucs, through which he waded for his loues delight.
>
> (VII. vii. 33)

The natural flourishing and order of April provide an appropriate context for "April's" themes of human flourishing and order, as embodied in Elisa, and human disorder, as manifested in Colin. The paradisiacal abundance of the season accords well with the function of Elisa, who as goddess of spring rules over a counterpart to the golden age. In "April" the rites of spring afford a setting for Elisa in her

9. *The Kalender of Shepherdes*, III, 11.

dual capacity as a personification of the flourishing of nature and as an embodiment of the eternal spring that holds perpetual triumph over the mutability of nature and which is the golden ideal of the pastoral world.

April is by tradition the month of showers. Its wetness is emphasized by Spenser in the "Mutability Cantos" as we saw, and so it is in the *Kalender of Shepherdes'* parade of months:

> Amonge all monthes I am lusty Apryll
> Freshe and holsom vnto eche creature
> And in my tyme the dulcet droppes dystyll
> Called crystall as poets put in scrypture
> Causynge all floures the longer to endure.[10]

In accordance with this traditional representation of April, Spenser has established a thematically significant pattern of water imagery, whereby he contrasts the sterility and disorder of Colin with the flourishing and order of Elisa. Three passages are involved. In the first, Thenot asks Hobbinol,

> Or bene thine eyes attempred to the yeare,
> Quenching the gasping furrowes thirst with rayne?
> Like April shoure, so stremes the trickling teares
> Adowne thy cheeke, to quenche thy thristye payne.

$$(5-8)$$

Hobbinol's tears, unlike those of April, cannot quench "the gasping furrowes thirst with rayne" or even his own "thristye payne." They are the sterile product of the disorder wrought by Colin, and are thus in direct contrast to the life-giving rains of Elisa's season.

In the second passage, Hobbinol describes Colin's method of composing the lay of Elisa:

> . . . then will I singe his laye
> Of fayre *Elisa,* Queene of shepheardes all:
> Which once he made, as by a spring he laye,
> And tuned it vnto the Waters fall.

$$(33-36)$$

Water here suggests both psychological and artistic order. Hobbinol's image of Colin's method of composition embodies the conception of the true poet, tuning his song to the water's fall, that is, responding to the order of nature, creating from it rather than being victimized

10. *The Kalender of Shepherdes*, III, 17.

by it. Similarly, Elisa is also associated with the waters of Helicon in the first stanza of the lay:

> Ye dayntye Nymphs, that in this blessed Brooke
> doe bathe your brest,
> For sake your watry bowres, and hether looke
> at my request:
> And eke you Virgins, that on *Parnasse* dwell,
> Whence floweth *Helicon* the learned well . . .

(37-42)

Colin's harmonious relationship to the waters of Helicon is past tense. Once, when he tuned his song to the water's fall, perceiving and expressing the universal music and order within nature, he like Elisa was associated with the order of Helicon's waters. Now, however, Colin and Elisa are no longer paired in terms of the waters of Helicon. Elisa is supreme goddess of order and creativity both artistic and natural, embodying still the joyous spirit of Helicon; while Colin, alienated from Helicon, produces now the uncreative disorder of Hobbinol's tears. The pattern of water imagery in the April eclogue, then, not only serves as a literal detail to relate the eclogue to the month but also reinforces one of the central contrasts, that between Colin and Elisa, upon which the eclogue is structured.

"May"

The debate in "May" between reforming and conservative factions of the Anglican Church, and between reason and impulse, occurs as in the preceding eclogues, within the context of spring. As in "February" and "March," the ecclesiastical and moral issues are introduced within the framework of man's involvement in the rites of spring, with Palinode desiring to join the rites, and Piers insisting on the shepherd's responsibility to remain apart from spring. The rites of spring and love that form the background for the eclogue's discussion link it to the previous eclogue, where the rites of spring provide the setting for the praise of Elisa. But whereas in "April" these rites represented the natural, social, poetic, and eternal order of the pastoral golden age, in "May" these rites represent, at least to Piers, the potential disorder of reason submitting to instinct.

The eclogue's use of the rites of spring and love is totally consonant with the associations for the month. For the Master Shepherd, May is the month of natural flourishing and games:

Than cometh Maye that is fayre & pleasaunt / than byrdes syngeth in the forest nyght and day the sonne shynethe hote. and as than is man moste ioly & pleasaunt and of delyuer strengthe & seketh playes & sportes for than is he therty yere.[11]

And in the parade of months in the *Kalender of Shepherdes,* May praises itself as the month of natural beauty and lovers aroused with "hote loue":

> Of all the monethes in the yere I am kynge
> Flourysshynge in beaute excellently
> For in my tyme in vertue is all thynge
> Feldes and medes spredde moost beauteously
> And byrdes syngeth with ryght swete armony
> Reioycynge louers with hote loue all endewed
> With fragraunt floures all about renewed.[12]

Similarly, in the "Mutability Cantos," Spenser celebrates the month for its joyous fertility of nature and the rites of Cupid:

> Then came faire *May,* the fayrest mayd on ground,
> Deckt all with dainties of her seasons pryde,
> And throwing flowres out of her lap around:
> Vpon two brethrens shoulders she did ride,
> The twinnes of *Leda;* which on eyther side
> Supported her like to their soueraine Queene.
> Lord! how all creatures laught, when her they spide,
> And leapt and daunc't as they had rauisht beene!
> And *Cupid* selfe about her fluttred all in greene.

(VII. vii. 34)

That Spenser conceived of May as a month of natural joy in the *Faerie Queene* does not of course necessitate the same conception in the *Shepheardes Calender.* But the later work, in combination with the traditional associations identified by the *Kalender of Shepherdes,* at least suggests the possibility that Palinode is not corrupt in feeling May to be an occasion for natural joy.

In addition to the motif of the rites of spring, the golden-age theme also relates "May" to "April." In "April" Spenser portrays the golden-age as ideal and myth. "May," however, deals with the golden age as it pertains to the practical realities of man's conduct in the fallen world. For Palinode, spring seems to signal the return of the golden age. For a moment in spring, all instinct is innocent, all plea-

---

11. *The Kalender of Shepherdes,* III, 11.
12. *The Kalender of Shepherdes,* III, 17–18.

sure harmless and harmonious with natural order. It is an old order, of course, a golden state of pagan *otium* not a Christian Eden. Palinode's ideal world resembles the Kid's, where the dual aspects of instinct, giving and self-gratification, are both innocently and harmoniously realized within the fallen world. Palinode confuses the spring rites of May with those of April, Lady Flora with Elisa. On the other hand, Piers, like Palinode, is intensely aware of winter and destruction, and he knows that spring, as well as winter, is part of the fallen world. In this respect, his wisdom goes beyond Palinode's. Piers's conception of the golden age is the antithesis of Palinode's; it is the Mantuanesque golden age of austere Christian duty, of almost complete denial of self and impulse:

> The time was once, and may againe retorne,
> (For ought may happen, that hath bene beforne)
> When shepheards had none inheritaunce,
> Ne of land, nor fee in sufferaunce:
> But what might arise of the bare sheepe,
> (Were it more or lesse) which they did keepe.
> Well ywis was it with shepheards thoe:
> Nought hauing, nought feared they to forgoe.
> For *Pan* himselfe was their inheritaunce,
> And little them serued for their mayntenaunce.
> The shepheards God so wel them guided,
> That of nought they were vnprouided,
> Butter enough, honye, milke, and whay,
> And their flockes fleeces, them to araye.
> But tract of time, and long prosperitie . . .
>
> (103-117)

Piers's is a golden ideal of behavior determined by and for the fallen world but an ideal that at the same time contradictorily ignores the limitations of fallen man within that world. It is a naive, impractical ethical golden age of primitive Christianity, where Pan himself provides shepherds providentially with "honye, milke, and whay." Neither the golden age of Palinode nor that of Piers is complete, one running the risk of corruption, the other making impossible demands on human nature. The golden-age theme thus has two functions within "May": the first, to define the limitations of the pastoral perspectives of the two antagonists; the second, to relate "May" to "April" as a companion eclogue in its exploration of the meanings of the golden-age pastoral ideal.

"June"

The paradisiacal temperateness of the natural setting in "June" functions as an analogue to the temperateness of Hobbinol's mind, the temperateness of classical *otium:*

> Lo *Collin,* here the place, whose pleasaunt syte
> From other shades hath weand my wandring mynde.
> Tell me, what wants me here, to worke delyte?
> The simple ayre, the gentle warbling wynde,
> So calme, so coole, as no where else I fynde:
> The grassye ground with daintye Daysies dight,
> The Bramble bush, where Byrds of euery kynde
> To the waters fall their tunes attemper right.
>
> (1-8)

But while the natural setting of the month characterizes the mind of Hobbinol, characterizing Colin's only by contrast, the meaning of the month in terms of man's year applies to Colin. According to the Master Shepherd,

> Than co[m]eth. Iune & tha[n] is the sone hyest i[n] his meri-dyornall he maye assende no hyeer in his stacyone his glemerrynge goldene beames rypeethe the corne and than is man xxxvi. he may assende nor more for than hathe nature gyuen hym beauty and strength at the full / and repyd the sedes of perfet vnderstondynge.[13]

June is mid-year, when man and the sun are at their highest point. For Colin, however, June is, like January and December, merely another month of his continuing descent. He has not reaped the harvest of his perfect understanding, but the harvest of his imperfect understanding, as his discussion with Hobbinol bears out. Colin's hope for the harvest that should be his in the coming months of harvest is lost. His emblem summarizes his hopeless plight: "Gia speme spenta."

Thematically, the June eclogue is a companion piece to "May" and "April" in that it continues the motif of the rites of spring; but the rites, rather than being a potential source of temptation as they are in "May," are like those of "April," the rites of the Muses' dance which symbolizes the harmony of the mind of the poet with nature. But at the same time that "June" looks back to the rites of spring that provide the context of the preceding eclogues, it also looks ahead to "July" and the remaining eclogues in the *Calender*

---

13. *The Kalender of Shepherdes,* III, 11.

in terms of the issues that dominate it—ambition, aspiration, and Colin's harvest, as Hobbinol urges Colin to climb the Parnassian hill. The June eclogue, therefore, is a pivotal eclogue between the two major groupings of eclogues in the *Calender,* appropriately so since June is both mid-year and the mid-point of the *Calender.*

An additional factor in making the June eclogue relevant to the structure of the *Calender* is its use of the golden-age motif. The golden-age ideal of "April" takes the form of myth not reality, an impossible eternal spring in a world framed by winter. In "May," when we return to the real world, neither Palinode nor Piers can recapture their golden age, the one of classical *otium,* the other of Mantuanesque pastoral duty. Both Palinode's and Pier's nostalgia for the golden age is rooted in their bitter knowledge that the world is fallen, but neither man's ideal can come to total grips with this awareness. Both Palinode and Piers are limited by their own myths. Hobbinol's paradise is an apparent ideal of compromise between materialism and moral fulfillment. "That Paradise hast found, whych Adam lost," says Colin, but he errs. Though Hobbinol seems to have recaptured his golden age, this secular, classical Eden is flawed; for Hobbinol must learn Palinode's lesson in September before the onset of winter. Neither Hobbinol, balancing in awkward and cloistered compromise the winter and summer virtues of Piers and Palinode, nor Colin, caught between their conflicting extremes, can complete within the individual self "April's" mythic integration of the dualities and polarities of the natural year.

"July"

The only specific connection between the July eclogue and the month occurs in Thomalin's second speech:

And now the Sonne hath reared vp
  his fyriefooted teme,
Making his way betweene the Cuppe,
  and golden Diademe:
The rampant Lyon hunts he fast,
  with Dogge of noysome breath,
Whose balefull barking bringes in hast
  pyne, plagues, and dreery death.
Agaynst his cruell scortching heate
  where hast thou couerture?

                                          (17-26)

E.K. explains Thomalin's zodiacal imagery: the meaning is "that in July the sonne is in Leo." The association of scorching heat with July is also developed in the "Mutability Cantos," with the addition of July's being a month of harvest:

> Then came *Iuly* boyling like to fire,
>   That all his garments he had cast away:
>   Vpon a Lyon raging yet with ire
>   He boldly rode and made him to obay:
>   It was the beast that whylome did forray
>   The Nemaean forrest, till th' Amphytrionide
>   Him slew, and with his hide did him array;
>   Behinde his back a sithe, and by his side
> Vnder his belt he bore a sickle circling wide.
>
>   (VII. vii. 36)

The association of July with harvest is not developed within the eclogue, except metaphorically, though it is employed in the woodcut, where in the background a laborer is mowing the grass with a scythe. In the succeeding eclogues, the harvest is associated with man's ambition and what he reaps from this ambition, and that general implication may be relevant to the July eclogue. But the only specific and literal relationship of the eclogue to the month is in terms of its heat: the shepherd of "ouverture" risks the heat of the July sun and the shepherd of "couverture" prefers the lesser risk and heat of the shady dales. The month's heat, then, accords with the eclogue's central theme, ambition and its dangers, which theme links the eclogue to the previous one.

"July" continues the theme of man's relationship to the golden age which was explored in "May" and "June." The two contesting ideals of the golden age in "May" and "July" are roughly analogous; but whereas the framework for the two forms of golden age in "May" was the issue of man's participation in the natural world, in "July" the framework is the issue of ambition and what man reaps from ambition. Morrell, like Palinode, while aware that the world has fallen, would nonetheless like to act as though it had not:

> Whilome there vsed shepheards all
>   to feede theyr flocks at will,
> Till by his foly one did fall,
>   that all the rest did spill.

And sithens shepheardes bene foresayed
   from places of delight:
For thy I weene thou be affrayd,
   to clime this hilles height.

(65-72)

Just as there was once for Palinode a golden age in which man could indulge his instincts with impunity and without fear, so too Morrell looks back to a golden age when shepherds could feed their flocks on the hills as well as the plains without fear and danger. But with the fall of one, Morrell's hills, like Piers's childlike instincts, now involve risk, both personal and moral; and Morrell, like Palinode, urges his more otherworldly companion to run that risk.

Thomalin's conception of the golden age is the Mantuanesque golden age of Christian moral and pastoral duty, an age of pastoral simplicity with few needs, no ambition, and no pomp and circumstance:

Such one he was, (as I haue heard
   old Algrind often sayne)
That whilome was the first shepheard,
   and liued with little gayne:
As meeke he was, as meeke mought be,
   simple, as simple sheep . . .

(125-130)

Whilome all these were lowe, and lief,
   and loued their flocks to feede,
They neuer strouen to be chiefe,
   and simple was theyr weede.
But now . . .

(165-169)

Thomalin's Mantuanesque primitive age of Christian pastoral duty is obviously a counterpart to Piers's in "May." Like Piers, Thomalin would impose a rigid and austere ethic on shepherds. Puritanical like Piers and unworldly, he looks back nostalgically to an age when men lived according to his ideals.

May, June, and July are, according to the popular calendar, the summer months: "Than comethe sommer. as. May. Iune. and. Iuly," says the Master Shepherd. They form a natural transition between the two major groupings of eclogues in the *Calender,* the first based

137

primarily on the issues of spring and man's relationship to nature and impulse, the second based on ambition and the rewards of harvest. The transitional eclogues are linked by their use of the golden-age theme, which was introduced appropriately in "April," which is the culmination of spring according to the popular calendar. The three summer eclogues develop this theme according to man's relationship to the real, rather than ideal, world. "May" considers this theme within the context of the invitation to participate in the rites of spring-summer that characterizes the eclogues of the first group; "July" considers it within the context of the theme of rewards and ambition that characterizes the second. "June," as the pivotal eclogue of the series and the *Calender* as a whole, considers the theme from both perspectives, the rites of spring and man's aspiration.

"August"

Heat, the harvest, and just rewards are the major associations for the month of August. As we learn from the *Kalender of Shepherds*, August is the first of the months of autumn and a month of harvest:

> Thanne cometh. Autonne. as August. September and October. that all these fruytis waxeth rype and be gaderyde and howsyd.[14]

Of August specifically the Master Shepherd says:

> After that / than cometh August. Than we geder in our corne / and also the fruytes of the erthe. And than dothe man his dilygens to gader for to fynde hymselfe withall i[n] the tyme that he may nouther gete nor wyn than that vj / yere is xlviij.[15]

In the parade of months, the month's extreme heat is mentioned along with the harvest:

> I am named the hote moneth of August
> For redolent heet of Phebus bryghtnesse
> In my tyme eche man ought for to haue lust
> To laboure in haruest with grete bysynes
> To repe and shefe eschewynge ydlenesse
> And ryse erly with perfyte dylygence
> Thankynge our lorde of his good prouydence.[16]

And finally, in the "Mutability Cantos" Spenser relates the theme of harvest to the question of justice and rewards by means of the

---

14. *The Kalender of Shepherdes*, III, 10.
15. *The Kalender of Shepherdes*, III, 11.
16. *The Kalender of Shepherdes*, III, 18.

month's zodiac sign, Virgo-Astraea:

> The sixt was *August,* being rich arrayd
>   In garment all of gold downe to the ground:
>   Yet rode he not, but led a louely Mayd
>   Forth by the lilly hand, the which was cround
>   With eares of corne, and full her hand was found;
>   That was the righteous Virgin, which of old
>   Liv'd here on earth, and plenty made abound;
>   But, after Wrong was lov'd and Iustice solde,
> She left th' vnrighteous world and was to heauen extold.
>
> (VII. vii. 37)

There is little explicit development of the relationship of "August" to the month. Brief mention of the heat is made by Willye when he asks Perigot to retire from the heat: "But for the Sunnebeame so sore doth vs beate, / Were not better, to shunne the scortching heate?" And there is one reference to the season's harvest: "Tell me, such a cup hast thou euer sene? / Well mought it beseme any haruest Queene." Although this is the only literal reference to the seasonal harvest, the theme of the harvest, or the theme of rewards and the prize, is central to the eclogue, in terms of both love and poetry. For both Perigot and Colin the rewards of love are slight; ironically, both are unfruitful in their love during the season of harvest. Perigot's unfruitfulness, however, is natural, and he continues to produce poetry with a public function during harvest while Colin does not; Colin's poetry must be rehearsed by Cuddie. Colin dwells in "wastefull woodes," which suggests not only the desolateness of the woods but also a wasting of himself. Correspondingly, Colin claims "the daye in woe / I vowed haue to wayst," and that too suggests the tragic waste that jars with the hoped-for harvest of the season.

The theme of the rewards of poetry is developed in "August" in a light, "recreative" manner which anticipates the serious "moral" development of the same theme in the third of the autumn months, October, when Cuddie, who disposes the rewards of poetry here, will complain his own lack of rewards. Appropriate for the season, Perigot's song in the singing-contest wins for him a harvest cup. While this is the only specific detail that links the singing-contest to the season, granted the association of the month with harvest and rewards, August is perhaps as good a place as any for a singing-contest. "July," after all, has already developed the theme of ambition, competition, and the pursuit of rewards; and the singing-contest develops these themes in a light, comic fashion. Though the least tightly integrated into the seasonal framework of all the eclogues, "August" does develop the theme of the harvest in terms of the rewards of love and the production and rewards of poetry, both of which will be picked up in the October eclogue to which it is in part a companion piece.

"September"

The relationship of "September" to the year-structure of the *Calender* depends largely on the relationship of its theme of rewards and justice to the popular association of the month with the harvest. According to the Master Shepherd, September, as the second month of autumn, is a month of harvest, when man makes provision for the oncoming winter:

> Than comes september that vynes be made and the fruytes of trees be gadered / And thanne there withall he dothe fressheley begynne to garnysshe his house and makes prouysyon on nedefull thynges for to lyue in winter which draweth very nere and than is man in his moste joyful and coragyous estate prosperous in wysdome purposynge to gether and kepe as myche as shulde be suffysyent for hym in his olde age / when he may geder no more.[17]

The theme of *copia*, plenty, is also the basis of September's self-introduction in the *Kalender of Shepherdes:*

> Who can my name perfytely remembre
> With the commodytees of my season
> Ought of ryght to call me septembre
> Plenteous of goodes by all maner reason
> As wheet / rye / otes / benes / fytches / and peason
> Of which fruyte eche man ought to haue in store
> To lyue dyrectly / and thanks our lorde therfore.[18]

September, moreover, as the month of Libra, suggests appropriately both the balances of justice and the right distribution of rewards. That Spenser was aware of and used these popular associations of the month is clear from his description of September in the procession of the months in the "Mutability Cantos":

> Next his, *September* marched eeke on foote;
>   Yet was he heauy laden with the spoyle

17. *The Kalender of Shepherdes*, III, 11.
18. *The Kalender of Shepherdes*, III, 18.

Of haruests riches, which he made his boot,
And him enricht with bounty of the soyle:
In his one hand, as fit for haruests toyle,
He held a knife-hook; and in th' other hand
A pair of waights, with which he did assoyle
Both more and lesse, where it in doubt did stand,
And equall gaue to each as Iustice duly scann'd.

(VII. vii. 38)

September, then, is the month of harvest and rewards, the month in which a man reaps what he has sown. The themes of harvest-rewards and Libra-justice are both obviously relevant to the September eclogue.

In "September," the days are becoming shorter ("the dirke night doth hast"), the leaves fall, and Diggon Davie and Hobbinol retire to shelter not from the scorching heat of July and August but from the "blustring blast" of autumn and oncoming winter:

Diggon, I am so stiffe, and so stanck,
That vneth may I stand any more:
And nowe the Westerne wind bloweth sore,
That nowe is his chiefe souereigntee,
Beating the withered leafe from the tree.
Sitte we downe here vnder the hill:
Tho may we talke, and tellen our fill,
And make a mocke at the blustring blast.

(47-54)

E.K.'s gloss interprets the harvest imagery. The description, he says, is applied to "the tyme of the yeare, which is thend of haruest, which they call the fall of the leafe: at which tyme the Westerne wynde beareth most swaye." The literal suggestion of the harvest, by the reference to the fall of the leaf and the blowing of the western wind, is of course important. But, the primary relationship of "September" to the natural year is not literal but thematic. Once we have discovered September's traditional associations, their thematic relevance to the eclogue for the month becomes quite clear. Diggon Davie, through his lack of wisdom, has wasted his seed, as it were, and thus wrecked his harvest. In his quest for *copia*, he has nothing but waste and "decaye." In this month of plenty, his sheep manifest waste and fruitlessness:

My sheepe bene wasted, (wae is me therefore)
The iolly shepheard that was of yore,

Is nowe nor iollye, nor shephehearde more.
In forrein costes, men sayd, was plentye . . .

(25-28)

The reward of ignorance, deception, and self-deception is the loss
of harvest, and for the shepherd this means the loss of sheep. The
same theme is of course relevant to Roffy, who through a similar
though not identical blindness, might also have lost his entire flock
to the wolf. Diggon, however, has come to wisdom too late, and
his harvest and reward are waste and decay:

Nought easeth the care, that doth me forhaile.
What shall I doe? what way shall I wend,
My piteous plight and losse to amend?
Ah good Hobbinol, mought I thee praye,
Of ayde or counsell in my decaye.

(242-247)

Diggon's harvest is ironic and paradoxical: he has attained the wisdom
of the month but not its "prouysyon." His is the paradox of "Inopem
me copia fecit." In a month when man is "in his moste ioyful and
coragyous estate," Diggon has only frantic and questioning despair,
"What shall I doe?" The answer comes in the simplest of terms:
"I will thee comfort," says Hobbinol.

The theme of rewards and justice is especially relevant to the satire
on the injustice of English and Roman clergymen. Their harvest is
a false abundance, one in which shepherds feed on their own flock.
Their corruption makes them run the risk, as Diggon says, of destroying their flock, just as his was destroyed. Granted that September
is the month of abundance and justice, the month of Libra, it is
especially fitting that the September eclogue should contain the bitter-
est attack on ecclesiastical corruption and undeserved wealth found
in the *Calender*.

The September eclogue, therefore, though its literal seasonal details
are few, is thus successfully integrated into the *Calender*'s year-structure through the seasonal themes of rewards, justice, and the harvest.
The seasonal events and the ethical perspectives of this eclogue form
a series of characteristically Spenserian analogues, one commenting
on the other: the lost harvest of Diggon Davie; the potentially lost
harvest of Roffy and Hobbinol; the false and unjust harvest of the
corrupt clergy. "September's" serious treatment of the rewards of
ambition thereby looks back to "August's" light, "recreative" treat-

ment of the rewards of poetry, while at the same time it anticipates
the rewards theme in the next eclogue.

"October"

The literal seasonal details that relate the October eclogue to the
season are few. We learn from Piers's comment on "thys long lingring
Phoebus race" that the year is coming to an end, and there is a
suggestion of oncoming winter in Cuddie's comment on "the Gras-
hopper so poore, / [which] ligge so layd, when Winter doth her
straine"; but that is all. Once again, it is by determining the meaning
of the month that we understand the relevance of the eclogue to
the month. The Master Shepherd merely designates October as a
month of harvest: "And then cometh october that all is into the
forsayde house gadereth bothe Corne / and Also other maner
fruytes."[19] But in the parade of the months we learn that October
is especially the month of the wine harvest:

> Amonge the other October I hyght
> Frende vnto vynteners naturally
> And in my tyme Bachus is redy dyght
> All maner wyne to presse and claryfy . . .[20]

And in the "Mutability Cantos," Spenser, too, associates October with
the wine harvest:

> Then came *October* full of merry glee:
>   For, yet his noule was totty of the must,
>   Which he was treading in the wine-fats see,
>   And of the ioyous oyle, whose gentle gust
>   Made him so frollick and so full of lust.

(VII. vii. 39)

October's traditional association with wine makes it ideally appropriate
for the eclogue's discussion of poetic inspiration and poetry in general;
and it is this association that Cuddie draws upon in his concluding
speech:

> Who euer casts to compasse weightye prise,
> And thinks to throwe out thondring words of threate:
> Let powre in lauish cups and thriftie bitts of meate,
> For *Bacchus* fruite is frend to *Phoebus* wise.

19. *The Kalender of Shepherdes*, III, 11.
20. *The Kalender of Shepherdes*, III, 19.

And when with Wine the braine begins to sweate,
The nombers flowe as fast as spring doth ryse.

(103-108)

Moreover, as a month of harvest, October is the appropriate setting
for a discussion of the rewards of poetry and for the problem that
confronts Cuddie, the question of his survival in winter.

Thematically, October as a harvest month deals with the issue of
how and what man reaps that has dominated the three previous
eclogues. Its treatment of the relationship of poetry to love and of
the rewards of poetry is a counterpart to the lighter, "recreative"
treatment of the same themes in "August," which was also a harvest
month and in which Cuddie was also a participant. Moreover, in
both "September" and "October" there is fear of being overcome
by winter. Neither Diggon Davie, nor Cuddie, one deprived by the
folly of trusting in the unjust and untrustworthy, the other deprived
by the age, has the store with which to survive the winter; and both,
significantly, are helped in their poverty by their friends: Hobbinol
offers Diggon the comfort of his cottage, and Piers offers Cuddie
a kid "to store his farme." In both eclogues the generosity of a fellow
shepherd contrasts with the self-seeking stinginess of, on the one
hand, degenerate prelates, and on the other, the degenerate age. "September," of course, deals with the false ambition and the false harvest,
whereas "October" deals with true ambition and deserved but largely
unobtained rewards. The portrayal in "October" of the poor poet
receiving no material rewards extends the sense of injustice developed
in "September," where only the unjust live in wealth. Both eclogues,
develop the rewards theme of the harvest in terms of wealth and
perversions of what the true harvest of man's labors should be.

"November"

"November" contains the notoriously inaccurate zodiac sign that
has led numerous readers to conclude that not only "November"
but also the *Calender* as a whole is not related consistently to the
seasonal framework:

But nowe sadde Winter welked hath the day,
And *Phoebus* weary of his yerely taske,
Ystabled hath his steedes in lowly laye,
And taken vp his ynne in *Fishes* haske.

(13-16)

Whatever the meaning, intentional or unintentional, behind the sign, it in no way offers evidence for the contention, made by W. L. Renwick and others, that the calendar-framework is only an addition, inconsistently executed and of minor consequence. Curiously, E.K. repeats the error in his notes. Now this may mean that E.K. was assisted by Spenser in writing the notes, that Spenser himself was E.K., that E.K. was privy to some secret purpose involved in the seeming error, that the note is simply another of E.K.'s attempts to justify his author, or simply that E.K. also made a mistake. Regardless, there is a sufficient number of details relating the eclogue to the season to justify its presence in November. The fact that winter has "welked" or shortened the day would apply not to February, where the days are growing longer, but to November; and the withdrawal of Phoebus to his "lowly laye" suggests the beginning of winter rather than its end, which is what February would involve. E.K. reaches the same conclusion, for in his note to "In lowlye laye" he observes that this is "according to the season of the moneth November, when the sonne draweth low in the South toward his Tropick or returne." In addition, the conventional pathetic fallacy of the pastoral elegy is related to the November month. The lessening of light Colin mentions, for example, may be either a symbol of Dido's death or pathetic fallacy; but it certainly corresponds with the shortening of the day and the sun's light in winter: "The sonne of all the world is dimme and darke: / The earth now lacks her wonted light, / And all we dwell in deadly night." The seasonal basis behind the pathetic fallacy is found also in the later lines, "The faded lockes fall from the loftie oke" and "The mantled medowes mourne, / Theyr sondry colours tourne." Nature shows her grief for Dido's death through the seasonal details of the falling leaves, the changing of the leaves' colors, and the growing night of the month and season. Dido in fact becomes a personification of the death of nature in winter, just as Elisa was a personification of the rebirth of nature in spring. The sign of Pisces, then, may be an error or it may conceal some secret purpose, but it in no way substantiates the claim that the calendar framework is incompletely developed either in the November eclogue or in the *Calender* as a whole.

It is clear from the *Kalender of Shepherdes*, furthermore, that "November" takes advantage of the month's popular associations. According to the Master Shepherd,

Than comethe Nouember that the dayes be very shorte and the sonne
in maner gyueth no hete and the trees leseth thayr leuys / The feldes
that were grene loke hore and gray. than all maner of herbes be hydde
in the grounde. and than appereth no floures. And than wynter is come
that the man hathe vnderstandynge of age and hathe lost his kindely
hete and strengthe. his tethe begynne to rote and in his hede they
chatre / And then hathe he nomore hope of longe lyfe. But desyreth to
come to the lyfe everlastynge.[21]

Significantly, November introduces himself in the parade of the
months as the month of death:

> I Nouembre wyll not abyde behynde
> To shewe my kyndly worthynes and vre
> For in my tyme the blastes of the wynde
> Abareth lenes and shedeth theyr verdure
> Wherfore euery prudent creature
> Ought for to lyue ryght as they wolde dye
> For all thynge taketh ende naturally.[22]

"One bitter blast blewe all away," says Colin. The principal popular
associations for November are all in the eclogue: the short days,
the waning sun, the falling of the leaves, the changing of the colors
of the field from green to gray (Dido's hearse is related to the changing of colors, "the greene in gray is tinct"), the blasts of wind,
death and life everlasting.

One additional detail relates "November" to the serial structure
of the *Calender,* the theme of sleep. In "October", Piers, urging
Cuddie to pipe, remarks that:

> Whilome thou wont the shepheards laddes to leade,
> In rymes, in ridles, and in bydding base:
> Now they in thee, and thou in sleepe are dead.

$$(4\text{-}6)$$

In "November" Thenot says much the same thing to Colin:

> *Colin* my deare, when shall it please thee sing,
> As thou were wont songs of some iouisaunce?
> The Muse to long slombreth in sorrowing,
> Lulled a sleepe through loues misgouernaunce.

$$(1\text{-}4)$$

21. *The Kalender of Shepherdes,* III, 12.
22. *The Kalender of Shepherdes,* III, 19.

In both instances the image of poetic sleep accords with the sleep of nature in late autumn and winter; and in "November" the sleep of Colin's muse accords with Dido's sleep in death.

"November" thus continues to develop the harvest theme that has appeared in the preceding five eclogues. But whereas in the preceding eclogues, the theme was that of man's harvesting of nature, here (as in "December") the theme is that of nature's harvesting man. The harvest is now the harvest that is man's death. The questions that lie at the heart of the pastoral elegy—the meaning of aspiration, man's rewards in this world, the justice of life and death—are the same questions that have, from a different perspective, pervaded the preceding eclogues:

> Why doe we longer liue, (ah why liue we so long)
> Whose better dayes death hath shut vp in woe?
> The fayrest floure our gyrlond all emong,
> Is faded quite and into dust ygoe.
> Sing now ye shepheards daughters, sing no moe
>   The songs that *Colin* made in her prayse,
>   But into weeping turne your wanton layes,
>   O heauie herse,
>   Now is time to dye. Nay time was long ygoe,
>   O carefull verse.
>
> Whence is it, that the flouret of the field doth fade,
> And lyeth buryed long in Winters bale:
> Yet soone as spring his mantle hath displayd,
> It floureth fresh, as it should neuer fayle?
> But thing on earth that is of most availe,
>   As vertues braunch and beauties budde,
>   Reliuen not for any good.
>   O heauie herse,
> The braunch once dead, the budde eke needes must quaile,
>   O carefull verse.

(73-92)

These are the questions of Diggon Davie and Cuddie now framed by the ultimate perspective of death. In terms of man's relationship to the natural year, death seems the ultimate injustice: the good die, while the evil live, just as the deserving suffer poverty while the undeserving live in riches. And to this spectacle of injustice in the world, "November" supplies the same resolution as "Lycidas": "Fayre fieldes ay fresh, the grasse ay greene," the promised heaven of eternal spring.

"December"

December, according to the *Kalender of Shepherdes,* is the last month of man's life. It is the last month of Colin's life as he prepares for "dreerie death," having become himself an image of the wintry season:

> The carefull cold hath nypt my rugged rynde,
> And in my face deepe furrowes eld hath pight:
> My heat besprent with hoary frost I fynd,
> And by myne eie the Crow his clawe doth wright.
>
> (133-136)

Both Colin's and Dido's death are portrayed in terms of the death of nature in winter. But whereas Dido triumphs over nature and mutability, from winter emerging into eternal spring, realizing in her triumph the promise extended man, Colin fails.

The concluding two eclogues of Spencer's *Calender* complement each other. They are united by a common concern with death, man's being harvested by winter, and the promise of triumph over time, the year, and mortality; they are the natural culmination of the eclogues from "July" on. From the June eclogue to "December," the central themes of the eclogues have been man's ambitions and rewards. In the June, August, and December eclogues these themes are examined in terms of love and poetry. In the July, September, and October eclogues, these themes are examined in terms of man's ambitions within this life, his harvest of rewards on this earth. The last two eclogues in the *Calender*'s year appropriately continue these themes but consider, additionally, the harvesting of man by death and the promise of eternal rewards. The final focus on death and the eternal promise is of course integral to the elegiac temper of the *Calender,* with its repeated contrast between past and present, its recurring sense of loss, waste, and injustice, and its movement from what man sows and what he reaps, to his own being reaped by nature. Completing the elegiac movement of the *Calender*'s structure, the eclogues for November and December, one demonstrating the reward, the other the penalty of the promise extended man, provide the ultimate perspective of the *Calender*'s world, eternal April and final triumph over the year.

II. Andrew Marvell

3. The Christian Lyrics:
Pastoral and Anti-Pastoral

Within the fallen world of the *Shepheardes Calender* the tension between Arcadian and Christian pastoral perspectives is never fully resolved: while the desire for classical *otium* threatens to imperil man's Christian and spiritual nature, the commands of Christian and humanist spirituality continually threaten to deprive life of any intrinsic meaning. Except in "April," where the divine figure of Elisa reconciles the polarities of Spenser's pastoral world, the pastoral synthesis of pagan and Christian, nature and spirit, this life and the next remains an impossible, and indeed for the Mantuanesque shepherds an undesirable illusion. The best to be hoped for is a precarious balance of these polarities, Thenot restraining Cuddie's vitality, Cuddie compensating for Thenot's sterility. In the Christian pastorals of Andrew Marvell, however, the Spenserian antagonism of pastoral meanings is to a large extent resolved; the pagan pastoral world is subsumed within Christian boundaries.[1]

1. By "Christian pastorals" and "Christian lyrics," I mean poems that deal with topics like man's relationship to God, his salvation, his conversion, the after-life, the relationship of body and soul.

Harold E. Toliver, *Marvell's Ironic Vision* (New Haven, 1965), pp. 88–151, considers the pastorals as a unit consisting of two divisions: poems of pastoral success, in which a balance of the ideal and the real is attained; and poems of pastoral failure, in which this balance cannot be attained within the pastoral world. To some extent, the group of poems I designate as Christian pastorals corresponds to his poems of pastoral success: "The Garden," "Bermudas," "Clorinda and Damon," "The Mower Against Gardens," and to some extent "The Nymph Complaining for the Death of Her Faun" and "The Coronet." My classification

❦ The difference between the two pastoralists is perhaps most clearly reflected in their differing conception and portrayal of the natural world. In both Spenser and Marvell, nature is fallen; but the conclusions drawn from this assumption are almost entirely dissimilar. In the *Shepheardes Calender* is manifested one side of the Renaissance ambivalence toward nature, namely the fear that participation in the natural world may undermine man's superior rank in the hierarchy of existence by tempting him from the spiritual and rational to the merely natural. This fear of nature is, as I have suggested before, characteristic of Mantuanesque pastoral. In accordance with this fear, in Mantuanesque pastoral nature is rarely idealized: the natural setting—instead of being an Arcadian world of spring, flowers, and gentle breezes as it is in such classical pastoralists as Sannazaro, Guarini, and Tasso—is a world of floods, famine, tempest, and winter; such spring as there is becomes, as for Spenser's Piers and Thenot, a lure tempting man from the austerity and duty that knowledge of earth's winter imposes. The Arcadian ideal is the temptation of Mantuanesque pastoralists. Spenser, of course, by no means adheres altogether to the Mantuanesque tradition. His moral vision is considerably more subtle and flexible: he does accept the fact that man is a natural creature with natural needs which must be fulfilled if he is to survive. Man may not live by bread alone, but this does not mean he lives without bread. But as we have seen, this permissiveness is ambivalent. There remains a distrust of participation in nature, a fear that however necessary it is, it is also perilous. Clearly this is true of the participation of such worldlings as Cuddie and Palinode, but it is even true of such a shepherd of superior reason and responsibilty as Hobbinol. The world in which Hobbinol dwells in "June" is typical of the Arcadian happy paradise of the retired life, a "pleasant syte" of

---

is not intended to contradict his. Like any critical superstructure, mine is a mode of perceiving as well as of describing, and since my aim in this work is to describe forms of pastoral in Marvell, I prefer the terms "Christian pastorals" and in a later chapter "amorous pastorals."

I have excluded the amorous Mower poems from discussion as Christian pastorals because, unlike most recent critics, I believe their portrayal of pastoral love not Christian and mythic but psychological and witty; I think the poems best understood within the context of the tradition of amorous pastoral. I have also excluded "Thyrsis and Dorinda" from discussion here because, despite its interesting similarities to "Clorinda and Damon," it, too, seems to me to fall within the tradition of amorous pastoral and to be a witty treatment of the rustics' limited perception of abstract ideas.

"simple ayre" and "gentle warbling wynde": an Arcadian world of idealized nature, but also, as we learn in "September's" dialogue, a world vulnerable to the evil of the fox. The idealized relation to paradisiacal nature Hobbinol possesses, however pleasant and self-sufficient it seems in "June," is precariously vulnerable. As Hobbinol discovers from Diggon Davie, his Arcadian idealization has to a dangerous extent blinded him to evil and thus imperiled his soul.

Marvell's "The Garden" is the closest approximation in the pastorals to "June's" paradise of the retired life, and the difference between the two poems is emblematic of the difference between the pastoral vision of Spenser and Marvell. The idealized retired life within Arcadian nature, while it indisputably has some value, nonetheless is, within the context of the *Calender*'s wintry world, ultimately an illusion. In Spenser, the natural world and the spiritual world constitute a dualism, in Marvell a continuum. In "The Garden" nature becomes a vehicle for communing with God. Granted the proper motivation, one unlike Clorinda's, to participate in nature is to come closer to God. This use of nature is possible because nature, while fallen, still retains in it something of the divine image and "greenness"; and through meditation, man can attain a heightened awareness of divine presence.[2] Nature in Marvell's Christian pastorals, then, while it may be tempting if man adopts an improper perspective on it as Clorinda does, is fundamentally both a source of the supreme physical and psychological pleasures involved in the classical ideal of *otium*, and the spot for divine meditation. The retreat of the world--worn protagonist of "The Garden" is, as it is portrayed in the opening stanzas, a retreat like Hobbinol's, the Arcadian or classical retreat of the Horatian man to the happy life of *otium* and contemplation. But, what is not true of Hobbinol, this classical withdrawal into nature merges with and is transformed by Christian meditation. As a result, while the poem begins as a classical retreat into nature for contemplation, the poem concludes with a Christian meditation on the soul, on divinity, and on the Christian promise of immortality. The *otium* of the classical retired life in nature thus, rather than deceiving the soul, becomes the first stage in its greater, and Christian, enlightenment. Even in "Clorinda and Damon," where Clorinda offers the

2. On the seventeenth-century use of the physical garden as an emblem of meditation, see the highly informative work of Stanley Stewart, *The Enclosed Garden* (Madison, Wisc., 1966), especially pp. 111–128.

pagan temptation of a purely natural participation in nature, pagan pleasures are ultimately consecrated by Pan's words and by the converted, Christian perspective of the two lovers. In the Christian pastorals of Marvell, therefore, nature more clearly manifests divine presence and thus provides a meditative vehicle for the spiritual purification of man: the hand of the divine gardener and artist reaches out in the gardens of meditation.

The key word in dealing with Marvell's Christian pastorals is synthesis. Accordingly, "The Garden" cannot accurately be seen as a narrow exposition of a single philosophical tradition.[3] It is instead a synthesis of various philosophical traditions within a Christian framework. Frank Kermode has remarked that Marvell's use of Platonic light-symbolism is not "technical. . . but generalized."[4] This same generalizing-into-synthesis is characteristic of Marvell's handling of ideas as well as images. The neo-Platonic conception of the separation of the soul from Divine Intelligence, for example, is parallel

3. The customary critical approach to "The Garden" has, unfortunately, presupposed that the poem embodies a single philosophic tradition. Milton Klonsky, for example, "A Guide through the Garden," *Sewanee Review* (*SR*), 58 (1950), 16, writes that "The Garden" is "an arboretum where the seeds of neo-Platonic Ideas are brought to a metaphysical bloom"; and Maren-Sofie Røstvig, "Andrew Marvell's 'The Garden': A Hermetic Poem," *English Studies* (*ES*), 60 (1959), 75, sponsoring Hermetic ideas, concludes that "Hermetic ideas . . . carry the entire poem." For other points of view, see, M. C. Bradbrook and M. G. Lloyd Thomas, *Andrew Marvell* (Cambridge, 1940), pp. 59–64; Pierre Legouis, *Andrew Marvell*, 2nd ed. (Oxford, 1968), pp. 43–45; J. B. Leishman, *The Art of Marvell's Poetry*, 2nd ed. (London, 1968), pp. 292–318; William Empson, *Some Versions of Pastoral* (New York, 1960), pp. 113–139; Ruth Wallerstein, *Studies in Seventeenth-Century Poetic* (Madison, Wisc., 1950), pp. 319–335; Harold E. Toliver, *Marvell's Ironic Vision*, 138–151; Frank Kermode, "The Argument of Marvell's 'Garden,'" *Essays in Criticism* (*EIC*), 2 (1952), 225–241; Renato Poggioli, "The Pastoral of Self," *Daedalus*, 88 (1959), 686–699; Geoffrey Hartman, "Marvell, St. Paul, and the Body of Hope," *ELH*, 31 (1964), 175–194 (repr. in *Andrew Marvell*, ed. George deF. Lord [Englewood Cliffs, N.J., 1968], pp. 101–119); Anthony Hecht, "Shades of Keats and Marvell," *Hudson Review* (*HudR*), 15 (1962), 50–71; Lawrence Hyman, "Marvell's Garden," *ELH*, 25 (1958), 13–22; Harry Berger, Jr., "Marvell's 'Garden': Still Another Interpretation," *Modern Language Quarterly* (*MLQ*), 28 (1967), 285–304; Edward William Tayler, *Nature and Art in Renaissance Literature* (New York, 1964), pp. 166–168; Harold Wendell Smith, "Cowley, Marvell, and the Second Temple," *Scrutiny*, 19 (1953), 184–205. Two of the more convincing readings of "The Garden" are, in my opinion, Stanley Stewart's attempt, in *The Enclosed Garden*, pp. 152–183, to relate the poem to the Song of Songs and to the tradition of the *hortus conclusus* in seventeenth-century literature; and William Leigh Godshalk's attempt, in "Marvell's *Garden* and the Theologians," *SP*, 66 (1969), 639–653, to relate the poem to the background of contemporary Christian theology. Mr. Godshalk's reading came to my attention too late for me to make use of it, but we are in agreement on a number of essential points, most importantly the Christian significance of "this Dial new" of the final stanza.

4. Kermode, *EIC*, 2 (1952), 240.

to the orthodox Christian belief in the Fall of man.[5] Similarly, the Hermetic conception of the role of love in the Creation is, in its generalized statement, parallel to its orthodox Christian counterpart. Indeed, all of the really important ideas in "The Garden" are sufficiently generalized to be capable of assimilating their analogues in classical, neo-Platonic, Hermetic, and orthodox Christian thought: the withdrawal for repose and meditation whereby the soul prepares for its return to God; the progress of the soul (its descent, incarnation, and ascent); an activating force behind the Creation and the cycle of the soul's progress—perhaps the expansive nature of divine love or, here, "greenness"; stress on the spiritual as it pertains to (not repudiates) the material. In Marvell's poem, the ideas of a number of philosophic traditions are generalized to the point that they become analogous to one another, and through this analogical synthesis, Marvell illustrates and affirms a fundamental unity, an ultimate truth with prismatic emanations. "The Garden," then, is not a rigid embodiment of a single, esoteric system of ideas, but a free synthesis of related and analogous ideas within what we may loosely call the Christian tradition.

"The Garden" portrays the progress of a soul from the quest for the pagan paradise of pastoral *otium* and contemplation, to the quest for the lost Eden, and finally to the quest for God and the new Eden of Christian promise. Each quest coincides with a new awareness and illumination. The first of the speaker's illuminations has already occurred before he enters the garden. "Mistaken long," he sought "Fair quiet" and "Innocence thy Sister dear" in the "busie Companies of Men;" but now he has come to the new awareness that "Society is all but rude, / To this delicious Solitude."[6] "Delicious" is apt, for the conventional classical retreat pursued in the opening five stanzas, the first half of the poem, is primarily a contemplation and experience of the sensuous joys of the garden. This classical garden of pastoral *otium*, however, is ultimately subsumed within and becomes preparation for the fully Christian meditation of the mind in the final five stanzas. In the garden's paradise of pastoral *otium*, the senses are ultimately invoked to permit the mind a renewed and greater awareness of Christian man's relationship to God. The first half of the

5. See Wallerstein, *Studies*, p. 332.
6. Citations from Marvell are to *The Poems and Letters of Andrew Marvell,* ed. H. M. Margoliouth, 2nd ed. (Oxford, 1952).

poem, then, deals with the speaker's new classical awareness of the futile ambitions of social man and the value of the *otium* of the contemplative life; the second half deals with the increasingly Christian illumination of the mind in divine meditation.

Even within the classical pastoral retreat, however, are imbedded the seeds of an ultimate Christian conversion of the speaker to the fully Christian meditation of the concluding half of the poem. As Stanley Stewart has shown, the garden, as an emblem upon which the speaker meditates, contains the potential significance of the *hortus conclusus*. In stanza one, the "narrow verged Shade" of the man under the law, without Christ, contrasts with the shade of "all Flowers and all Trees" of man under grace; the same significance underlies the contrasts of the "incessant Labours" and "the Garlands of repose." Similarly, the plants are "sacred Plants" not only because Quiet and Innocence, who are found among them, are values so precious as to be worthy of worship, but also because "The trees (emblems of divine love and of its productive effects) represent the spiritual potentialities of man."[7] But such implications seem to me precisely that, implications—part of the gradual coming-to-awareness of the speaker in his perceptual and spiritual progress from a classical quest for retirement in the sensuous protectiveness of the garden to a fully Christian quest for union with the Gardener once he has perceived the symbolic truths contained in the garden. The speaker's classical orientation to the garden anticipates his ultimate Christian orientation in much the same way that, in the fourth stanza, Pan and Apollo imply and anticipate Christ:

> When we have run our Passions heat,
> Love hither makes his best retreat.
> The *Gods,* that mortal Beauty chase,
> Still in a Tree did end their race.
> *Apollo* hunted *Daphne* so,
> Only that She might Laurel grow.
> And *Pan* did after *Syrinx* speed,
> Not as a Nymph, but for a Reed.

Apollo and Pan were both traditionally interpreted as pagan types of Christ, though Marvell's witty conception of the relationship of type and antitype here is, as far as I know, unique with him. The pagan deities' amorous pursuit of mortal beauty for the making of

7. Stewart, *The Enclosed Garden,* p. 165.

laurel and a reed is analogous to the amorousness of Christian divinity as manifested in the amorous nature of the garden, but also, traditionally, in the Creation, the Incarnation, and the Crucifixion. Apollo and Pan as types of Christ are thus appropriately also amorous gardeners, their peculiar gardening imitating in a lesser and pagan way the divine gardening of "the skilful Gardner," God, and "the milder Sun [Son]" in the concluding stanza of the meditation. That Marvell intended us to regard Apollo and Pan as types of a far greater, and Christian, amorousness would seem to be abundantly clear from the word play of the third and fourth lines of the stanza: "The *Gods*, that mortal Beauty chase, / Still in a Tree did end their race." Involved in these lines is the tradition of Christ's Crucifixion signaling the end of the race of gods.[8] The Cross is the tree whereon their race was ended. In the Crucifixion the divine love for man, shadowed forth imperfectly by Apollo and Pan, finds its full and truer manifestation. The pagan shadowing forth of Christian truth, moreover, is analogous to the speaker's own experience: the experience of the classical man of retirement shadows forth imperfectly the experience of the fully Christian man in the second part of the poem.

Stanza five marks both the culmination and termination of the speaker's classical participation in the sensuous garden of pastoral *otium*, and at the same time it marks the conversion of the speaker to a fuller Christian perception of his relationship to the garden:

> What wond'rous Life in this I lead!
> Ripe Apples drop about my head;
> The Luscious Clusters of the Vine
> Upon my Mouth do crush their Wine;
> The Nectaren, and curious Peach,
> Into my hands themselves do reach;
> Stumbling on Melons, as I pass,
> Insnar'd with Flow'rs, I fall on Grass.

This portrayal of amorous nature, whatever its indebtedness to the Hermetic tradition, alludes to the pagan golden age, one of the more prominent characteristics of which is, as we see in Virgil, nature's free offering of herself to men:

> At tibi prima, puer, nullo munuscula cultu
> errantes hederas passim cum baccare tellus
> mixtaque ridenti colocasia fundent acantho.

8. See Klonsky, *SR*, 57 (1950), 21.

ipsae lacte domum referent distenta capellae
ubera, nec magnos metuent armenta leones;
ipsa tibi blandos fundent cunabula flores.

(IV. 18-24)

[Free-roaming ivy, foxgloves in every dell, and smiling acanthus
mingled with Egyptian lilies—these, little one, are the first modest
gifts that earth, unprompted by the hoe, will lavish on you. The goats,
unshepherded, will make for home with udders full of milk, and the
ox will not be frightened of the lion, for all his might. Your very
cradle will adorn itself with blossoms to caress you.]

The golden age represents the culmination of the pastoral desire for
otium, for a time when nature, instead of opposing man, loves and
protects him. But the golden age is also a new age, a rebirth, a
regeneration; and that association carries over into the Christian conversion of the meditator and his regeneration. What Stewart has to
say on the role of the *hortus conclusus* in stanza five is crucial to
this point: "the dense associations of this figure [the apple tree in
the garden which was in turn a type of the Cross] . . . taken together, meant Christ was the tree and its fruit also. He was the grapes
which crush themselves, and the tree was a winepress; he was the
fruit of the vine, and the liquor distilled through the Sacrifice. The
apples fall in Marvell's poem . . . and their falling is a reminder
that the Eucharist was freely given in an act of self-immolation."[9]
Christian meaning, then, is latent in the pagan imagery of stanza
five as it was in stanza four: whereas the pagan imagery of stanza
four figured forth Christ's sacrifice on the tree, the pagan imagery
of stanza five figures forth the effects of this sacrifice—the grace
freely offered man for his regeneration. The pagan world can only
take man so far; its golden age can promise complete physical and
psychological satisfaction in this life but it cannot prepare the soul
for its "longer flight" beyond this life to a new and greater paradise.
For that, Christ and grace are necessary.

Like the amorousness of nature, the speaker's falling on grass contains pagan and Christian meanings simultaneously. On the one hand,
the speaker's falling on grass is the climax of his sensuous experience
of the garden and of pastoral *otium:* his experience is an emblem
of that total repose of mind and body attained through a climactic
release of the senses in complete fulfillment. This ideal *otium* is as

9. Stewart, *The Enclosed Garden,* pp. 166–167. On the possible relationship
of Marvell's fruits to Eden, see Empson, *Some Versions,* p. 126.

far as retirement into a physical garden can take the speaker, this is as far as he can go without Christ; to go farther he must, as he does, retire into a garden of the mind, "A paradise within . . . happier far." Appropriately, therefore, the falling on grass contains the Christian implications necessary for this further journey. As Stewart informs us, the grass on which the speaker falls is the "bed of green" upon which the love of the Bride and Bridegroom is consummated, and the greenness of the bed is "the sign of regeneration made possible by the eclipse of the sun of the Law.[10] The amorousness of nature and the fall on grass suggest, then, the culmination and limitation of the classical retirement into a physical garden, but they also imply the Christian possibility of regeneration through, as Paul (Romans 5:15) calls it, the "free gift" of grace. It is precisely that regeneration, the renewal of man's spirit in Christ, suggested by the Eucharistic imagery of the fifth stanza, which is the subject of the stanzas that follow. The classical retreat into nature is, therefore, functional not terminal: the completion of the speaker's relationship to the garden in terms of classical *otium* is, from the Christian perspective, a means to a higher end.

From stanza six on, the speaker responds to the amorousness of God for man, demonstrated in the Cross and continually manifested in the Eucharist and in nature, with an amorous longing of his soul for God. In the withdrawal of the mind "into its happiness," creating "Far other Worlds, and other Seas; / Annihilating all that's made / To a green Thought in a green shade," the meditator creates and participates in a new garden, a "paradise within . . . happier far," a garden of "green Thought"—that is, I would think, hopeful

10. Stewart, *The Enclosed Garden,* p. 168; but see also the more general discussion on pages 94–96 on the relationship of greenness to divine love. But of course Marvell's "green" should not be restricted rigidly to one single significance. Frank Kermode, "Two Notes on Marvell," *N&Q,* 197 (1952), 137–138, has suggested what is no doubt the surface meaning of Marvell's greenness—freshness, innocence, vitality. Hope, too, is obviously relevant; see D. C. Allen, "Symbolic Color in the Literature of the English Renaissance," *Philological Quarterly* (*PQ*), 15 (1936), 81–92; Wallerstein, *Studies,* pp. 321–323; Hartman, "Marvell, St. Paul, and the Body of Hope," in *Andrew Marvell,* ed. George deF. Lord (Englewood Cliffs, N.J., 1968), p. 107. The association of greenness with hope, though in a secular not a religious sense, is made quite specific in "The Mower's Song":

My Mind was once the true survey
Of all these Medows fresh and gay;
And in the greenness of the Grass
Did see its Hopes as in a Glass.

thought permitted by the "green Shade" of Christ's grace.[11] Whereas Apollo and Pan in their physical love for man's body created with Daphne and Syrinx a physical greenness, Christ in His spiritual love for man creates with the meditator a spiritual greenness, a greenness of "thought." The spiritual garden of hope leads the soul to glide like a bird into the boughs of a tree—an imitation, as Stewart has shown, of Christ's climbing the tree, an *imitatio Christi* essential to the soul's profiting from grace.[12] The meditator, assisted by grace, thus imitates what the pagan gods, and his own earlier, limited experience in the physical garden could only foreshadow, as he too "Still in a Tree [does] end [his] race." His spiritual chase has gone as far as, in this world, it can. In a continual perceiving and reperceiving of the meaning of his experience in the garden, the speaker has progressed from a lesser and pagan understanding to a fuller and Christian understanding of the garden. In abandoning the busy world of men for the physical garden, the speaker enacts the first stage of his "annihilation" of the world, and progresses to a higher, Christian annihilation, a garden within himself auguring the total triumph of man's spirit over the world, a triumph possible only to Christian man.

In stanza five the speaker seemed almost to become one with the natural world; in stanza seven he desires, preparing "for longer flight," to become one with the spiritual source of greenness, God. "Such," he says, "was that happy Garden-state"; but of course the old Eden, "beyond a Mortal's share," is lost. To the loss of Eden with which stanza eight is concerned, stanza nine poses the new alternative:

How well the skilful Gardner drew
Of flow'rs and herbes this Dial new;
Where from above the milder Sun

---

11. On the connection between shade and the grace permitted by Christ's sacrifice, see the discussion in Stewart's chapter on "Shade," *The Enclosed Garden*, pp. 60–96. In brief, the connection arose from the attempt to explicate 1:5–6 of the Song of Songs: "I am black, but comely . . . Look not upon me, because I am black, because the sun hath looked upon me." The Bride's blackness represents our natural deformity: "since all men suffered the consequences of the Fall, all were open to the discoloring effects of the sun of God's justice" (p. 62). Christ's Sacrifice provides the Bride and all men with the shade of grace whereby man is protected from the sun of God's justice.

12. One does not, I think, have to turn to the Song of Songs to see the parallel; but even so, Stewart's discussion of the *imitatio Christi* within the *hortus conclusus* (*The Enclosed Garden*, especially pp. 91–95 and p. 178) provides useful supporting evidence.

Does through a fragrant Zodack run;
And, as it works, th' industrious Bee
Computes its time as well as we.
How could such sweet and wholesome Hours
Be reckon'd but with herbs and flow'rs!

The "skilful Gardner," Milton's "Sovran Planter," God, has drawn "this dial new." It is, symbolically, a new scheme and order, redeeming fallen man through the Passion and grace of "the milder Son." The classical withdrawal of the speaker from the chase of the world to contemplation of the sensuous green garden thus reaches a climax with a meditation on the highest significance of the garden emblem, the promise of that last and greatest withdrawl, promised by the Son, of man from the earth to the new Eden and full contemplation of "the skilful Gardner," the primal source of all greenness.

Although the ultimate resolution of the speaker's relationship to time comes through eternity and the Son's promise, at the same time his actual experience within the garden has provided a foretaste and prefiguration of his ultimate triumph over the mortal chase. What the garden is to the outside world, so the new Eden is to the garden. For within the garden, though time exists, it is no longer the time of the social chase, the time of those pursuing earthly ambitions. It is a time different from the time that, measured so precisely by man's clocks, binds man to the "uncessant Labours" of earth instead of freeing him from earth. The man of Christian meditation, communing with the green garden of the eternal Gardener, experiences a temporary suspension of his *sense* of time as a boundary; and when he returns to an awareness of time, he returns not to the time computed by the clocks of the social chase but time computed by and within nature itself. The bee can therefore compute the time as well as we because the time of the social chase has been replaced in the garden by natural time, a time that attempts to imitate and anticipate the eternal time of the celestial zodiac in the same way that the green garden attempts to imitate and anticipate the new Eden. The natural time of thyme makes the artificial time of the earth-bound chase irrelevant. With the new binding of time to heaven rather than to earth, the meditator simultaneously experiences a psychological slowing down of time by his indifference to time as part of the chase of the active life. Such a tentative victory over time through a shift in psychological perspective is not unique in Marvell. "To His Coy

Mistress" has a related psychological resolution to the problem of time:

> Rather at once our Time devour,
> Than languish in his slow-chapt pow'r.
> Let us roll all our Strength, and all
> Our sweetness, up into one Ball:
> And tear our Pleasures with rough strife,
> Through the Iron gates of Life.
> Thus, though we cannot make our Sun
> Stand still, yet we will make him run.

Both "The Garden" and "To His Coy Mistress" achieve, or look for, a triumph over time through a private withdrawal from an outer world. But in "To His Coy Mistress" the lovers would try to triumph over time *against* nature through their psychological reordering of nature, whereas the speaker of "The Garden" triumphs through a psychological integration of himself *with* nature, and thereby with God. The "Milder Sun" that is an image of man's hope of redemption from time in "The Garden" becomes in "To His Coy Mistress" an image of the ineluctable natural time that the lovers must, by rolling themselves into "one Ball," rival and defeat. Thus, while the speaker in "The Garden" triumphs over the time of the outer world by psychologically slowing down the passing of time through meditation, the speaker in "To His Coy Mistress" would reverse that process: since man cannot actually slow down the progress of real or natural time, he must master time subjectively and psychologically by making it seem to go faster through the intense experience of pleasure (the sun thus becomes, subjectively, "our" sun, the lovers mastering and controlling it rather than vice-versa). The resolution of this poem, then, is really quite simple, by no means so complex as it is sometimes made. Like many "metaphysical" poems, it works with a kind of rigorous absurd logic to establish a conclusion that, while logically absurd, is subjectively and psychologically true. The logic of the intellective mind and of the world of objective fact is thus perversely placed in the service of the private world of psychological experience. "The Garden," while divorcing social and private experience, discovers an alternative resolution of the conflict of private desire and objective limitations through religious promise and hope.

In "The Garden," the speaker's relationship to the earthly garden is placed analogically within the context of other gardens, the classical garden of retirement and pastoral *otium,* the pagan golden age, the old Eden, the *hortus conclusus,* the paradise within, and the new Eden. The synthesis of the multiple forms of the central image of the garden amplifies the significance of Marvell's garden in the same way that the synthesis of the poem's ideas into idea-patterns endows them with a far-reaching significance they would not have as a mere poetic translation of a single philosophic system. What is mere eclecticism in many seventeenth-century writers becomes in Marvell the source of far-reaching moral and artistic reverberation. This is equally true of "Bermudas," where two analogues are involved, Exodus and the garden of Eden. Though the literal events of the poem are no doubt influenced by the colonizing activities of the English Puritans,[13] the events are for the most part, and I think purposefully, kept exotic and rather unspecific. For however much "Bermudas" may have been suggested by and patterned on historical events, its principal concern, like that of "The Garden," is to depict man's perennial desire to recapture his lost paradise. As in "The Garden," there is a withdrawal from a hostile or at least an undesirable world to a garden retreat of repose and sanctity. The Bermudians have escaped from a land of "Prelat's rage" to a land "far kinder than our own" across a deep terrorized by "huge Sea-Monsters." Their journey is clearly analogous to that of the Hebrews, that is, an escape from a hostile land by an elect and holy people, providentially guided through dangers to a land of milk and honey. The isles of the Bermudians are of course a partial realization of the ideal harmony of the garden of Eden, to which they are an analogue. (Perhaps the pagan golden age is involved here as well, though it is now a Christianized golden age: it is a world of "eternal Spring"; nature offers her fruits to man without his toiling for them; arduous labor is abolished; and a world of social harmony and peace has replaced a world of social conflict.) As in "The Garden," the harmony of man, nature, and God is suggested by the humanizing and the artistic remaking of nature. The art, of course, quite unlike that the Mower castigates in the forced and artificial gardens, is a divine art. Providentially, God has humanized nature, so that the Bermudas "ride" in the ocean's "bosom"; and the winds are "listning Winds" that "receive" their song. The images of nature artistically reordered suggest the providen-

13. Rosalie Colie, "Marvell's 'Bermudas' and the Puritan Paradise," *Renaissance News (RN),* 10 (1957), 75–79.

tial reordering of nature by God the artist for his elect, just as He reordered the waters for an earlier exodus. Just as the divine artist (or, if one prefers, God acting through the human artist) provides an artistic zodiac of flowers to resolve the quest in "The Garden," so in "Bermudas" the divine artist has created a grassy "stage"; he "enamells every thing," "hangs in shades the Orange bright, / Like golden Lamps in a green Night," and has pomegranates enclose "jewels more rich than *Ormus* show's." The function of art, as in "The Garden," is not to reverse nature but to guide it to fulfill its purpose, so that just as the rocks form a natural temple of worship, all of Edenically ordered nature (unlike the more distant ocean) encourages a natural communion between man and God. God's role is the model for the artist's, a perfecting of nature. The Bermudians appropriately respond, *imitatio dei,* with an art of their own, a hymn of praise embodying their harmony with God and His creation:

> Thus sung they, in the English boat,
> An holy and a chearful Note,
> And all the way, to guide their Chime,
> With falling Oars they kept the time.

Like the bee and the herbs and flowers of the artistic zodiac, the Bermudians *"kept* the time" [italics my own]: though they have not really escaped time, they are in natural harmony with it and are consequently not mastered by it. In both "Bermudas" and "The Garden," then, the art of natural timekeeping contains an order and harmony that, in imitating absolute order, points to an ultimate triumph over fallen time. The temporal anticipates the eternal by imitating it.

As in "The Garden," some form of isolation and withdrawal seems essential to achieve spiritual well-being. In "The Garden," the withdrawal is a solitary one to a private and at least partly mystical end; it is a series of withdrawals to approximate an ideal private communion with God. In "Bermudas," on the other hand, the withdrawal takes the form of communal rather than private contemplation. One poem is the more mystical, the other the more evangelical. Moreover, the Puritans, rather than longing for the ultimate exodus of man from this world, content themselves with their garden counterpart of the Promised Land. Although the Exodus analogue does implicitly relate the Bermudians' exodus to the final exodus of man from earth to the new Eden, it is more by anticipation than identification. The Bermudians, still in this world and committed to it by their role as evangelists, have not allegorically realized the new Eden. The Exodus and Edenic analogues define and amplify the literal experience, on the one hand reflecting back on the lost Eden, on the other anticipating the exodus to the new Eden. Their exodus and their earthly Eden are thus an integrated pattern within, not an escape from, history and time.

In "The Garden," and possibly in "Bermudas," the pagan and Christian gardens are easily synthesized, with the classical garden and golden age readily subsumed within their Christian counterparts. In the next poem we will examine, this synthesis is less easily attained. The assumed harmony of the garden of the mind with the garden of nature in "The Garden" and "Bermudas" disintegrates in "Clorinda and Damon": the subject of the poem becomes a quest for a Christian synthesis of *hortus naturae* and *hortus mentis*, of the pagan-naturalist garden with the Christian-spiritual garden. The conflict of naturalist and spiritual gardens is the locus of the poem's wit and dialectic: Clorinda, the naturalist who participates in nature solely as nature, is appropriately for the most part a literalist;[14] whereas Damon, the spiritualist who will accept nature only when it is transformed into an emblem of the spiritual (when the fountain of water becomes the fountain of grace), is appropriately a worker in metaphor, a transformer of the letter of nature into spiritual metaphor. From this conflict of pastoral perspectives and garden-forms emerges a dialectical antagonism of letter and metaphor, of which the following exchange is typical:

C. Seest thou that unfrequented Cave?
D. That den? C. Loves Shrine. D. But Virtue's Grave.
C. In whose cool bosome we may lye
      Safe from the Sun. D. not Heaven's Eye.

The synthesis of Clorinda's pagan indulgence in nature-as-nature with Damon's Christian spirituality occurs through the metaphoric conversion of nature into art: "For all the World is our Pan's Quire." Damon rejects Clorinda's self-indulgent approach to nature. Indeed, it is more Clorinda's pagan perspective on nature, and less nature per se, that is the temptation; otherwise nature's enthusiastic joining

14. Clorinda's one venture into metaphor (the cave as "Loves Shrine") is, while artistically metaphorical, still literal in terms of her actual relationship to nature.

in the Chorus at the end of the poem would be inconsistent, she should be celebrating her own failure. Ultimately, Damon's argument directs itself not to a repudiation but to an assimilation of the pagan garden of natural delights with the Christian garden of the spirit; the natural garden must be harmoniously related to the spiritual garden of Pan-Christ, the good shepherd. The temporal garden, once it is perceived as "our Pan's Quire" and thus in harmony with the Christian garden, is consecrated, so that both poetically and morally it points toward, not away from, the Christian garden. The synthesis and reconcilation of garden-forms thus parallels the reconcilation of Damon and Clorinda, who when converted participates in temporal nature as an anticipation and a preparation for the eternal garden. Ultimately, then, "Clorinda and Damon" reaches the same Christian synthesis attained by "Bermudas" and "The Garden."

The reversal of roles in the poem further reinforces its allusive, analogical ramifications. In the "unconsecrated" pastoral genre, Damon would generally tempt Clorinda, and his metaphorization of the physical world, like that by Created Pleasure, would be only temptation's deceptive guise for seduction, not conversion. The dual meanings within the images (temples and the fountain, for example) would involve duplicity rather than a potential unity and synthesis. By reversing the role of tempted and tempter, the poem's events ask to be seen within the context of the archetypal temptation of man by woman, Eve's temptation of Adam to a nature separated from the words of Pan. Damon's obedience to Pan's words becomes the triumph of individual man following the pattern set by the new Adam. In refusing Clorinda's temptation, Damon imitates the new Adam. Damon's evangelistic spreading of Christ's "good news," His "Words that transcend poor Shepherds skill," and his triumph over temptation carry out the moral imperative, *imitatio dei*, whereby man may take advantage of the good news of His grace and triumph over the limitations of his purely natural being. The events of the poem, then, ask to be interpreted as analogous to the relationship of the old Adam and the new Adam to which the poem alludes: the triumph of Damon-Adam over Clorinda-Eve's temptation parallels and morally imitates the triumph of the new Adam over the temptation to which the old Adam succumbed.[15] The allusive technique of

15. The role of Christ-Pan, the good shepherd, is reinforced by Damon's allusion to Isaiah 40 in his remark to Clorinda that "Grass withers; and the Flow'rs too fade":

"Clorinda and Damon," with its moral cross-reference of analogues, is similar to that used in a related situation in *Samson Agonistes,* minus typology, in which Samson's original succumbing to the temptation of Dalila-Eve refers back to the archetypal temptation of Adam by Eve, and his subsequent victory over her second temptation, along with his regeneration, looks ahead to the victory of the new Adam, Christ. Both Samson and Damon, then, in their conversion and regeneration at once look back to the old Adam of the lost garden and ahead to the new Adam: what is foreshadowing in one is obedience and imitation in the other. Neither *Samson* nor "Clorinda and Damon" is an allegory; but both, by allusion, have their literal events related to and defined by the archetypal events of Christian moral history.

The use of the Eden analogue is considerably simpler in "The Mower Against Gardens." The opening couplet of the Mower's denunciation of artificial gardens alludes specifically to Eden and the Fall:

Luxurious Man, to bring his Vice in use,
   Did after him the World seduce.

Man's relation to nature alludes to and defines his relationship to Eden and the Fall. Three gardens are involved here: the lost garden of Eden; the ideal pastoral world of the Mower, imitating unfallen

---

The voice of him that crieth in the wilderness, Prepare ye the way of the LORD, make straight in the desert a highway for our God . . .

The voice said, Cry. And he said, What shall I cry? All flesh is grass, and all the goddliness thereof is as the flower of the field.

The grass withereth, the flower fadeth: because the spirit of the LORD bloweth upon it: surely the people is grass.

The grass withereth, the flower fadeth: but the word of our God shall stand for ever.

O Zion, that bringest good tidings, get thee up into the high mountain; O Jerusalem, that bringest good tidings, lift up thy voice with strength; lift it up, be not afraid; say unto the cities of Judah, Behold your God!

Behold, the Lord GOD will come with strong hand, and his arm shall rule for him: behold, his reward is with him, and his work before him.

He shall feed his flock like a shepherd: he shall gather the lambs with his arm, and carry them in his bosom, and shall gently lead those that are with young.

(verses 3-11)

In "Clorinda and Damon," Damon has assumed the evangelistic role of "the voice of him that crieth in the wilderness," John the Baptist. As in Isaiah, too, there is a contrast between Christ-Pan's eternal "Words that transcend poor Shepherds skill" ("the word of our God shall stand for ever") and the transient withering grass. Isaiah's "lift up thy voice with strength; lift it up" is fulfilled in "Clorinda and Damon" by Damon's announcing His coming and by the Chorus' celebrating Pan.

Eden, where man lives harmoniously with a "willing nature [that] does to all dispence / A wild and fragrant Innocence"; and finally, the square and unnatural garden of society's art. For the Mower, the artificial garden of society is an image of the recurring nature of the Fall, the continuing expansion of postlapsarian vice; whereas his own plain, unsquared nature permits an Edenic free communion with God through green nature ("The *Gods* themselves with us do dwell")—an attitude parallel to that taken in "Bermudas," "The Garden," and "Clorinda and Damon." The square gardens reduplicate the same sins that brought about the original Fall: man's efforts to square the garden (the square was traditionally conceived as symbolizing earth, and was often used in contradistinction to the divine circle) is in effect the presumptuous imposition of the human image on nature rather than an obedient worship of God's image. "Man, that sov'raign thing and proud" thus reproduces the presumption and pride of the original parents who succumbed to the temptation of being masters of nature apart from God. The modern horticultural mastery of nature is a perverse parody of the unfallen parents' role as masters of nature and a parallel to their own subsequent perversion of that role. For the Mower, horticulture is another aspect of Satan's recurring false promises. In the Mower's own pastoral world, however, the image of God within His creation is preserved intact by a humility before creation that counters the original pride and the narcissistic imposition of man's image on God's. The Mower's stance is therefore similar to Damon's: it is a rejection of Clorinda's use of nature for *self*-gratification and an assertion of the value of nature as divine revelation.[16]

16. John Rosenberg, however, "Marvell and the Christian Idiom," *Boston University Studies in English* (*BUSE*), 4 (1960), 159, has claimed that "the hyperbole of his indictment stresses a certain ambivalence in Marvell's attitude towards his Mower," and Harold Toliver, *Marvell's Ironic Vision*, pp. 104–106, has argued that the Mower has destroyed "the compromise between nature and art" found in Marvell's pastoral poetry of success, and that "if the Mower's point of view has Marvell's sympathy, it is a momentary and limited sympathy." Both Rosenberg and Toliver seem to be caught up in their own preconceptions about Marvell's characteristic "voice" so that they naturally find the Mower's hyperbolic voice not characteristically Marvellian. Though the Mower's position is more extreme, the basic values that motivate his tirade are precisely those of "Bermudas," "The Garden," and "Clorinda and Damon." The Mower is concerned less with the rejection of art and more with the rejection of the artificializing of nature. In his only reference to art in the conventional sense (the statues), art is simply granted an inferior function beside the natural art of the divine artist ("But howso'ere the Figures do excel, / The *Gods* themselves with us do dwell"). This position is certainly compatible with that in the other Christian pastorals, all of which celebrate nature as a place for meditation on and communion with the divine.

"The Nymph Complaining for the Death of Her Faun" differs from the Christian pastoral lyrics in that it does not involve an examination of man's relationship to God, and it does not use the natural retreat as a vehicle for communication with God. Yet it is concerned with one of the central themes of the Christian pastoral lyrics, the threat to the integrity of the garden by the nonpastoral (or false pastoral) world (the active life in "The Garden," England in "Bermudas," sophisticated society in "The Mower Against Gardens," and pagan naturalism in "Clorinda and Damon); and it does employ the characteristic poetic technique of these pastorals, the interpretation of the poem's events through allusion to archetypal events of Christian history. Peripheral though the poem may be to the overtly Christian pastorals we have examined, and although it shares with Marvell's amorous pastorals an interest in the psychology of love, its pastoral theme and allusive technique would seem to require our considering it. If in "Bermudas" and "The Garden" the attempt to recapture Eden is seen as a recurring pattern of human experience, in "The Nymph Complaining for the Death of Her Faun," as in "The Mower Against Gardens," the intrusion of vice into the pastoral world suggests by analogy the fallen Eden and, by extension, the recurring nature and consequences of the Fall. In both the latter poems, the central theme is the precariousness of "fragrant Innocence" within a fallen world indifferent to it.

"The Nymph Complaining for the Death of Her Faun" is one of Marvell's simplest poems, though it has been subjected to such a spate of allegorical or quasi-allegorical interpretations that it has become one of his least understood poems.[17] The two main problems

---

Moreover, Toliver's contention that the Mower's position is uncritical, that he might sensibly be warned by Candide that "cela est bien dit, mais il faut cultiver le jardin," seems slightly unfair. The Mower does not assert, as Toliver claims, that "the meadows . . . have no need of cultivation." The Mower is attacking unnatural cultivation, not natural cultivation. What does a mower do if he does not mow?

17. M. C. Bradbrook and M. G. Lloyd Thomas, *Andrew Marvell*, p. 50, argue that "the love of the girl for her fawn is to be taken to be a reflection of the love of the Church for Christ." E. H. Emerson, "Andrew Marvell's 'The Nymph Complaining for the Death of Her Faun,'" *Etudes Anglaises* (EA), 8 (1955), 107–110, elaborates on Douglas Bush's remark in his *English Literature of the Earlier Seventeenth Century, 1600–1660* (Oxford, 1945), p. 161, that if the poem has any ulterior meaning it may be "an Anglican's grief for the stricken Church." Emerson, while disclaiming to be allegorizing the poem, finds in it "Marvell's emotional reaction to the fate of the Church of England in the 1640's." The gift of the fawn is thus parallel to Christ's establishment, the death of the

that surround it have arisen from a dispute over the value of the Nymph's own experience and over the role of religious allusion. The poem has become for some a lament for the Anglican Church of the 1640's, or a symbolic analogue to the Crucifixion; Silvio's gift of the fawn has been likened to Christ's establishment of the Church; and the Nymph's love for the fawn has been taken as a reflection of Christ's love for the Church. The problem of having the fawn "equal" the Church or Christ is that the unconstant Silvio is, respectively, either Christ or God—which is either sacrilege or nonsense, if not both. Nonetheless, although the poem as a whole does not seem to call for a strictly allegorical reading, the biblical imagery cannot be cavalierly dismissed. This imagery focusses primarily on the fawn: the martyrdom of its white innocence seeming to allude to the martyrdom of the *agnus dei,* and the image of the Nymph mourning over her slain fawn resembling the Pietà. The deer, roses, and lilies images, moreover, seem to refer back to the Psalms, the Song of Songs, and to the *hortus conclusus* of the Virgin Mary. The function of this imagery has been aptly described by Karina Williamson, who observes that while the poem has religious overtones they are "not meant to supply another level of significance parallel to, or expressed through, the literal surface meaning but to intensify that 'meaning.' "[18] D. C. Allen also remarks, with equal sanity, that this "subsurface suggestion is metaphoric rather than symbolic,"[19] that while the fawn is *like* Christ, he is not Christ. The technique that Williamson and Allen observe is one that I have suggested is characteristic of Marvell's Christian pastorals: that technique of in-

---

fawn parallel to the sacking of the churches. (For another attempt to extract a topical meaning from the poem, see Earl Miner, "The Death of Innocence in Marvell's *Nymph Complaining for the Death of Her Faun,"* MP, 65 [1967], 9–16.) A recent attempt to revive the allegorical interpretation of the poem is Geoffrey Hartman's, " 'The Nymph Complaining for the Death of Her Fawn': A Brief Allegory," EIC, 18 (1968), 113–135. Hartman argues, among other, and frankly to me inscrutable, things that the poem is "an apotheosis of the diminutive powers of poetry" (p. 117), that "the fawn . . . is to Sylvio as the Comforter is to Christ," (p. 121), that the troopers are "the spirit of activism wishing to speed redemption, or ruin—in short, to force the issue—by an act directed in a sense against time itself" (p. 123), a characteristic apparently shared by the Nymph whose haste to die shows the "impatience" of "the expectant soul" (p. 122).

18. Karina Williamson, "Marvell's 'The Nymph Complaining for the Death of Her Fawn': A Reply," *MP,* 51 (1953), 271.

19. "Marvell's 'Nymph,' " *ELH,* 23 (1956), 102.

terpreting an event analogically, as part of an historical patterning of experience. The allusions to Christ and His Passion are reminders of the continuity, typicality, and universality of this injustice. Both the Crucifixion and the penetration of intruding vice into the Edenic garden of innocence are continuous and recurring aspects of the human condition.

In her martyrdom, the Nymph progresses from one withdrawal to another.[20] She is herself aware, however, of the loss that has accompanied both withdrawals, especially the last, the transformation of warm life into cold stone. For the Nymph, art is not so much a replacement for reality as a memorial to it: "For I would have thine Image be / White as I can, though not as Thee." The poem, then, is less about the failure of innocence than it is about the imperfection of reality. This emphasis, it seems to me, works much better with the religious allusions and the echoes of the Crucifixion of Innocence. To shift the focus of the poem even slightly away from the victimization of the Nymph toward her supposed failure is to blur the emotional and artistic focus of these allusions. "The Nymph," with its allusion to the martyrdom of supreme innocence to the world's savagery, thus suggests the recurring destruction through history of beauty and innocence. The wanton hunters can no more perceive the true value of the innocence of the Nymph and the fawn than they can the "fragrant Innocence" of plain nature. The tragic irony of this life is that only its tears are permanent (the rest is destroyed by the wanton hunt) and that man's closest approximation to permanence, art, while the more permanent is the less life. The allusions

---

20. As in "The Mower against Gardens" there has been some controversy over how completely we are to accept the speaker's own evaluation of his experience. D. C. Allen, *ELH*, 23 (1956), 93–111, and, to a much greater extent, Harold Toliver, *Marvell's Ironic Vision*, pp. 129–137, have both tended to shift the poem's emphasis from the Nymph's victimization to her failure to come to terms with actual life. Toliver quotes approvingly Allen's observation, in itself perfectly sound, that the Nymph enlarges "the token of love into a life symbol," that is, a virginal withdrawal from real life and love to its symbol, the fawn. The creation of the statue becomes the second stage of the Nymph's withdrawal from life, in which art becomes a life-surrogate just as the fawn was a love-surrogate. The statue, for Toliver, continues to embody the Nymph's conflict of cold passivity and warmth, and her supposed wishing to become a statue becomes "a rejection of the traditional pastoral compromise." "Marvell," he argues, "means to imply that it would be better if the red were not missing." The Nymph's tears suggest, however, that she feels the same way: the whiteness of marble is no really adequate substitute for the redness and whiteness of the living fawn.

emphasize that this is not the first time and it will not be the last: the martyrdom by wanton hunters of the only spirit that would redeem them is a recurring pattern within human history.

Marvell's Christian vision is curiously bifurcated. The poems we have just examined represent only one side of that vision; Marvell's other Christian lyrics—"A Dialogue Between the Resolved Soul, and Created Pleasure," "A Dialogue Between the Soul and the Body," "On a Drop of Dew," and "Eyes and Tears"—contradict the philosophical flexibility and synthesis of the Christian pastorals. In the pastorals, physical nature is spiritually therapeutic; pastoral setting and existence are potentially, if not always successfully, a means for the soul's development and its communion with God. The pastoral vision is not predicated upon a duality, but upon a continuum, of the natural and the divine or spiritual. The four nonpastoral Christian lyrics, however, reject this pastoral vision and its synthesis of Christian and pagan, the spiritual and the natural; and for this reason they may suitably be called "anti-pastoral." They portray the total incompatibility of nature and spirit, body and soul, and an other-worldly abnegation of the potential spiritual therapy of the natural world. "I have through every Garden been," says the speaker of "Eyes and Tears," "And yet, from all the flow'rs I saw / No Hony, but these Tears could draw." In the pastorals, the world is good or evil according to man's use of it, but in the anti-pastoral lyrics, the world is inherently a tempting snare, and the world of physical love and sensuous pleasures is repudiated altogether for a life centered solely on the Christian's moral and eternal responsibilities.[21] The conflicting pastoral perspectives in Spenser's *Shepheardes Calender* are in the pastorals of Marvell potentially and ideally reconciled: the perspective of earthly *otium* exists harmoniously with, and even supports, the spiritual and other-worldly perspective. This reconciliation in the anti-pastoral lyrics disintegrates in the presence of an ascetic and other-worldly ideal. Indeed, despite the subtlety and sophistication of their art, the moral vision of these poems is perhaps even more rigid than that of Mantuan, for at least in Mantuan while pagan pastoral may be rejected, pastoral itself is not; whereas in Marvell's

21. The Christian pastorals are ambivalent on the question of love in the garden. The speaker in "The Garden" prefers a solitary existence without amorous passion and women, but the same is not true of "Clorinda and Damon."

anti-pastoral lyrics, not only is the pastoral reconciliation rejected as unattainable and undesirable but so is the genre itself.

In the anti-pastoral lyrics, not only does the allusive world of pastoral greenness cease to provide the background for the poems, but it is also transformed from the locus and means of potential spiritual regeneration, a foretaste of the new Eden, to a road to damnation. Neither recalling Eden nor anticipating Heaven, it ceases to be the most select of earthly places, most thoroughly revealing divine presence, but is instead merged indistinguishably with the rest of the tempting physical universe. Nature stimulates man to meditation in the pastoral poems because man sees God's image there; but, perversely, nature stimulates the soul in the anti-pastoral poems to meditation precisely because God's image is not there; the soul's meditation is an escapist response to the unpleasantness of the physical world. The pastorals' distinction between analogues and perspectives is abandoned, and all gardens are reduced to a single *hortus tentationis*. The pastoral synthesis of the temporal and the eternal, the natural and the spiritual, is no longer even desirable, were it possible. This synthesis in fact becomes part of the lure of the Tempter. In "A Dialogue Between the Resolved Soul, and Created Pleasure," the five senses and all things of this world are subsumed under the abstraction Created Pleasure. Creation instead of potentially leading the Soul toward God its Creator would lure the Soul from its Puritan militancy. Earthly things appeared in this guise once before in "Clorinda and Damon," but in that poem creation could be consecrated by Pan and the holy mind, it could be integrated with the eternal and spiritual. In this dialogue, however, the pastoral synthesis, where the "Souls of fruits and flow'rs" can heighten the soul of man, becomes the argument of the tempter Pleasure:

Welcome the Creations Guest,
Lord of Earth, and Heavens Heir.
Lay aside that Warlike Crest,
And of Nature's banquet share:
Where the Souls of fruits and flow'rs
Stand prepar'd to heighten yours.

The pastoral world has become the Circean temptation of the Christian epic warrior. But the Soul refuses to be sidetracked by the temptation of pastoral from its quest. Like Damon when confronted with Clorinda's temptation, the Soul replies laconically, reweaving the images of his tempter:

> I sup above, and cannot stay
> To bait so long upon the way.

The Soul, like Damon, replies to temptation with a spiritual metaphorizing of temptation's images; but whereas spiritual metaphorizing and double meaning in "Clorinda and Damon" suggested a potential synthesis of nature and spirit, in the "Dialogue" it only reinforces the irreconcilable conflict between tempting wit and divine insight.

This same irreconcilability of opposites, which has supplanted the pastoral ideal of a progression between the temporal and the eternal, also determines the theme and form of "A Dialogue Between the Soul and Body." The dialogue is divided into two exchanges. In the first, the Soul laments its being tyrannized by the dungeon of the Body, and the Body laments its being impaled by upward movement of the Soul ("this Tyrannic soul. . .stretcht upright, impales me so"). In the second part, the complaint is framed in terms of disease rather than tyranny: the Soul laments that not only must it experience the pain of disease, it must also experience what is worse, the cure; and the Body laments that the Soul teaches it the maladies of human emotion, hope and fear, love and hatred, and so on. In essence, each disputant is complaining that the "art" of the other destroys the free "nature" of itself: the Soul's nature is heaven-bound, the Body pulls it downward; the Body's nature is earth-bound, the Soul pulls it upward.

Despite the fact that the debate form really speaks for itself, some readers have been disturbed by Marvell's apparent failure to take a stand in the debate. The Body speaks last, but that means nothing: the Soul speaks first. Moreover, the Body's witty and casuistic reversal of the commonplace neo-Platonic arguments directed against it can be interpreted in two ways: it may indicate the superiority or equality of the Body's just complaints or, to the contrary, its basic earth-bound morality. The latter seems to me more likely. The Body's word play in justification of the merely natural leads it to withdraw from its heavenly creator, to exalt the earthly over the heavenly; and however genial the Body may seem to us in its comic wit, it is nonetheless sinning. The ingenuity and wit of the Body, while more engagingly insidious than that of Created Pleasure, is nonetheless fundamentally akin to the ingenuity and wit of Created Pleasure. With both, verbal sophistry sets a barrier between themselves and the Creator; with the Soul in this poem and the Resolved Soul in the other, however, word play is exercised in the service of militant truth to permit their return to the Creator. The genial and comic *appearance* of nature should not cause us to lose sight of the fact that, for all its charm, the Body's argument is in fact sinful. To accept the Body at face value, to attribute equal or superior truth to its sophistry is to be deceived by the engaging but false appearances of the merely natural. The poem's complex artistry, its subtle presentation of a serious debate in a dance-like and sometimes comic fashion, in no way entails a comparable moral complexity. We have all been schooled in the doctrine of Marvell's moral complexity, but that doctrine is only partly true. What is complex in Marvell, even in the pastorals but especially in the anti-pastorals, is not the complexity of his moral vision but the complexity of his art. Marvell's complexity lies more in the process whereby his vision is reached and asserted, and less in the vision itself. Marvell takes complicated philosophical routes to the simplest of conclusions, and these philosophical convolutions and explorations were useful to Marvell less because they expressed the complexity of his moral vision than because they lent themselves to the complexity of his art. What is lost between the lyrics and the later satires is not so much moral complexity—that was never entirely there in the first place—but probing art. The overt contrast in this dialogue between moral simplicity and artistic complexity, then, should not disturb us; it is characteristic of Marvell, only here more obviously so. What is subtle about the dialogue we are examining is not the equal truth of Body and Soul but their *appearance* of equal truth. What we are witnessing in this little drama, after all, are the conflicting claims within a human being of his dual nature: one part of him is speaking to the other, fighting for supremacy. The dialogue of the poem is directed to the will that must chose between the Body, advocate for the life of the flesh, and the Soul, advocate for the life of the spirit. If we realize that the debate is a battle of the Body and the Soul for the will of the meditator, if we understand that what is involved is a choice of life in which the witty arguments of the Body are every bit as much a temptation as those of Created Pleasure, it becomes clearer, I think, where morally the will's choice must lie. The genial and persuasive sophistries of the Body, brilliant advocate of the libertine life of the flesh, are a reflection not of Marvell's moral complexity but of the psychological aptness of his art. The apparent lightness of the debate is thus part of a very serious wit. Essentially, then, this poem is concerned with the battle for the will of man by the Soul and the Body and with the sober theme of the irreconcilable incompatibility between the ways of life they represent. With such incompatibility, the pastoral synthesis inevitably cannot be attained, and no alternative exists except the complete withdrawal of one from the other. The conclusion, then (though the art is more subtle), is substantially the same as that in "A Dialogue Between the Resolved Soul, and Created Pleasure."[22]

The two other anti-pastoral poems, "Eyes and Tears" and "On a Drop of Dew," both espouse the rigid Manichaean divisions of body and soul, matter and spirit. "Eyes and Tears" opens with the assumption of the universal vanity of earthly things:

> How wisely Nature did decree,
> With the same Eyes to weep and see!
> That, having view'd the object vain,
> They might be ready to complain.

The poem is constructed as a systematic exploitation of the symbolic potential of the imagery of eyes and tears: the eyes become, for example, balances with tears "paid out in equal Poise" as an emblem of "the true price" of earthly joys. The poet seeks out other symbolic analogues to the eyes-tears relationship and finds parallel symbolism in the sun's distilling water only to return it back in showers; stars, inevitably, are "tears of light." In "Eyes and Tears," eyes and tears have no real, no inherent significance beyond what they signify symbolically about the world and man's relationship to it. From the world of gardens the speaker of "Eyes and Tears" can draw only tears:

> I have through every Garden been,
> Amongst the Red, the White, the Green:
> And yet, from all the flow'rs I saw,
> No Hony, but these Tears could draw.

In the world of "Eyes and Tears," all aspects of the natural world are transmogrified into the symbol that renounces them.

---

22. A detailed reading, reaching very different conclusions from mine, is Kitty Scoular Datta, "New Light on Marvell's 'A Dialogue Between the Soul and Body,'" *Renaissance Quarterly (RenQ)*, 22 (1969), 242–255. A useful survey of critical opinion on the poem can be found at the beginning of Mrs. Datta's article.

"On a Drop of Dew" makes the same systematic exploitation of symbol found in "Eyes and Tears," but whereas "Eyes and Tears" contains a series of parallel forays into symbolic, emblematic analogy, "On a Drop of Dew" is structured around two sustained similes: a longer simile between the progress of the soul and a drop of dew, and a shorter one resolving the dilemma of the soul by comparing the progress of the soul-dew to the ascent of the manna. Like the other three anti-pastorals, "On a Drop of Dew" is deeply rooted in the conflict of matter and spirit, body and soul. The soul's aversion to its descent and incarnation is based on its revulsion for even the most delicate, fragile, and lovely thing in the earthly garden, the rose; thus the dew

> Remembering still its former height
> Shuns the sweat leaves and blossoms green;
> And, recollecting its own Light,
> Does, in its pure and circling thoughts, express
> The greater Heaven in an Heaven less.

The "little Globes" circular extent expresses "the greater Heaven in an Heaven less": the circle of dew reflects the circle of God. The reflection of the greater circle in the lesser circle of the dew does not, however, suggest the synthesis that would be meant by the same phrase in the Christian pastoral lyrics. From one perspective, the dew itself is the "heaven less," a lesser heaven opposing its divine or heavenly image to fallen matter. From another perspective, the dew expresses "the greater Heaven" in a "heaven-less," the earth. From either perspective, the soul shuns its body, however lovely the "sweat leaves and blossoms green."

The resolution to the soul's nostalgia for its origins is provided in the last four lines:

> Such did the Manna's sacred Dew destil;
> White, and intire, though congeal'd and chill.
> Congealed on Earth: but does, dissolving, run
> Into the Glories of th' Almighty Sun.

The possible resolution of the soul's predicament was intimated earlier, with the dual suggestion of the word "orient" in "Orient Dew" (referring both to the dew's morning descent, being "shed from the Bosom of the Morn," and to its eventual ascent, anticipating the orient, or rising, motion of return) and with the multiple suggestions in the statement that the dew "gazing back upon the Skies, / Shines with a mournful Light." The dew literally shines with "mournful Light" simply because it reflects the light of the morning sun. But the soul-dew is also "mournful" because it mourns its separation from its "native Element." And finally, in that being full of morn means being full of sun, the "mournful Light" suggests further the soul's intimate and unbreakable connection to the sun, one that even its incarnation will not sever (the soul is "that Ray / Of the clear Fountain of Eternal Day"). It is this connection to the sun that ultimately redeems the soul from time and matter, returning it from "its Mansion new" to the eternal Mansion promised by the Almighty Son. The promise of return is developed through the typological significance of the manna in the last four lines. The apparent neo-Platonic action of the opening simile now takes on fully Christian meaning. The descent or distillation (*destillare* = to drop) of the manna, its smallness and roundness agreeing with the smallness and roundness of the soul-dew, parallels the soul's ascent and reunion with its origin, the Almighty Son. Moreover, the episode of the manna in Exodus in Christian typology foreshadows the coming of Christ, the bread of life, a significance reinforced by the manna's being said to run "into the Glories of th' Almighty Sun [Son]." The Platonic-Christian progress of the soul thus parallels the progress Christ endured for the soul's salvation. The resolution of the soul-dew's nostalgia for the Son is thus appropriately placed within the Christian context of the Passion and grace.[23]

"The Coronet" functions as a kind of intermediary between the two groups of poems. Like "The Nymph," "The Coronet" deals with the problem of innocence; but whereas in "The Nymph" innocence is subverted by external forces, in "The Coronet" it is subverted by the ambiguous morality of man's own nature. Both poems, moreover, employ the Crucifixion analogue to define the relationship of innocence and evil:

When for the Thorns with which I long, too long,
  With many a piercing wound,
  My Saviours head have crown'd,
I seek with Garlands to redress that Wrong . . .

23. J. Saveson, "Marvell's On a Drop of Dew,' " *N&Q*, 203 (1958), 289–290, has a similar interpretation to mine.

As in "The Nymph," the Crucifixion in "The Coronet" is a recurring event, continuously reenacted. The speaker, in his meditation, intends to terminate this reenactment by himself transforming the crown of thorns with which he has perpetuated Christ's agony into a crown of praise. His intention, however, is thwarted by the ambiguity of his own motive. Ironically, his very effort to escape sin involves him more deeply in sin: he may sin in the pride even of his submission. The new crown of thorns may indeed, therefore, "re-dress," not re-dress, the wrong and the wound. Pursuing his intention to escape sin, the speaker goes "through every Garden, every Mead. . . / Dismantling all the fragrant Towers / That once adorn'd my Shepherd-esses head." The Christianization of poetry is of course involved here: the poet thinks to triumph over his past sins simply by reweaving old flowers into new garlands, thus in a sense imitating Christ's own role but at the same time dangerously rivalling it. The mere Christianization of poetry is not enough. The translation of the flowers of the secular gardens into those of a religious garden may, perversely, actually return one to Eden and to the original sin:

> Thinking (so I my self deceive)
> So rich a Chaplet thence to weave
> As never yet the king of Glory wore:
> Alas I find the Serpent old
> That, twining in his speckled breast,
> About the flow'rs disguis'd does fold,
> With wreaths of Fame and Interest.

Ironically, in his efforts to prevent the recurrence of the Crucifixion, the artist—through his own pride in mastering nature by making a crown "as never yet the king of Glory wore"—repeats the Edenic sins that necessitated the Crucifixion in the first place. This son of Adam, in reenacting the original presumption, perpetuates the old Adam's role as crucifier of Christ. As a result, the speaker has only added one crown of thorns to another. The resolution to the poet's dilemma comes, as it must, not through himself alone, for that was the mistake of Adam, but through Christ:

> But thou who only could'st the Serpent tame,
> Either his slipp'ry knots at once untie,
> And disintangle all his winding Snare:
> Or shatter too with him my curious frame
> And let these wither, so that he may die,

179

> Though set with Skill and chosen out with Care.
> That they, while Thou on both their Spoils dost tread,
> May crown thy Feet, that could not crown thy Head.

The problem of the impure motive, the dilemma that the wreathing of a crown of praise may also be the wreathing of the Serpent, is resolved only through the grace of the divine artist. Allying himself with those who, on Palm Sunday, sacrificed palms and garments before Christ on his way to Jerusalem, the poet thus sacrifices his pride in his art to his humility before Christ. Christ, then, must ultimately mold the poet's work, like his life, into a perfect and sinless end; or, that failing, destroy it. The poet thus submits his imperfections to the perfection of Christ and to the higher art of divine grace.

I suggested before that "The Coronet" acts as a kind of intermediary between the pastorals and anti-pastorals. This is true more of theme than technique. The poet's experience is interpreted, as in the pastorals, within the context of a continous cross-reference of analogues—the Fall of man, the Crucifixion, primarily. The poet's relationship to Christ is seen as part of a recurring situation, the Crucifixion, with himself as the son of the old Adam crucifying Christ. The meditator's decision rests on whether to crown the King with the old thorns of the old Adam, thinking them new, or whether to join those who humbly threw palm leaves before the new Adam as he entered Jerusalem for them. The poet's problem involves a renunciation of his paternity by the old Adam and a submission to the paternity of the new Adam. His dilemma is thus defined by a cross-reference both to Adam's fall in Eden and Adam's traditional role in the crucifying of the new Adam. The poet's meditative experience is a psychological counterpart to the traditional relationship of these events in Christian history.

The vision of the poem, however, seems to fall between the two groups of Christian lyrics. The major difference between "The Coronet" and the pastorals is that in "The Coronet" nature has ceased to afford man a way of communing with God. Yet the poem does not reject the natural world, as do the anti-pastorals, except as it is the pastoral world of Clorinda, that is, the world of purely amorous and secular pastoral. The Serpent that lurks in the wreaths does not represent, as it would in the anti-pastorals, the sinfulness of matter; the sin lies in the poet himself. The poet, like Clorinda, must come to see his relationship to nature no longer in terms of self but in terms of his submission to Christ. In addition, in "The Coronet" the pastoral synthesis of pagan and Christian breaks down; the pagan cannot be accommodated to, and instead must be rejected by, the Christian. There is obviously in "The Coronet" the desire to attain the synthesis of the pastorals, but the imperfectness of man makes that synthesis impossible to achieve.

Different though they are, in certain highly general respects the pastoral and anti-pastoral Christian lyrics are similar. Both groups are concerned with a nostalgia for primal experience, whether it be the old Eden or the birthplace of the soul. Both groups are concerned with man's or the soul's relationship to the outside world (which may take the form of society, the monster-filled ocean, artificial gardens, the forest, or simply the World), and most of the poems of both groups postulate some kind of withdrawal from this undesirable outside world. In the pastoral poems, of course, one withdraws from the nonpastoral in order to come into communion with the highest aspects of nature, morality, and God; withdrawal within nature can be a preparation for and an anticipation of eternity. But in the anti-pastoral poems, the garden and the forest, the plain fields and the square gardens, merge. The world is one and tempting, so that inevitably man has no choice but to submit (which is the death of the spirit) or to withdraw finally and absolutely (which is the death of the flesh). What is for one the withdrawal of the pastoral primitivist becomes for the other the other-worldly withdrawal of the ascetic. Similarities, then, there are; but for the most part they are general more than specific. What remains the most impressive fact about Marvell's moral poems is their division in thought. The philosophical division that characterizes the pastoral genre characterizes the two conflicting groups of Marvell's Christian lyrics, but with a difference. The pastoral poems share the flexible and assimilative vision of most pastoral. It is clear that for Marvell pastoral involved synthesis. This is true of the anti-pastoral poems as well. Both groups of poems, then, associate pastoral with synthesis, but they look at this synthesis from totally different perspectives. In the pastorals, this synthesis permits and in fact encourages man's closer approach to God; it is in the end a means to redemption. Precisely the opposite is true of the anti-pastorals; such synthesis becomes a form of temptation, a deception for the other-wordly soul. Behind this division in thinking is, as I suggested earlier, the Renaissance ambivalence about man's relationship to nature. The pastorals accept the premiss that closeness to nature encourages the moral and spiritual perfection of man; within nature man can meditate on the divine image. The anti-pastorals take a view diametrically opposite from this; nature becomes equivalent to the body that the aspiring and other-worldly soul must repudiate or lose itself. Similarly, in the pastorals classical thought can be subsumed within Christian thought, the latter bolstered and confirmed by this assimilation; while in the anti-pastorals, the classical becomes transmuted into the merely natural, the Christian into the spiritual, and there can be no reconciling of this duality.

The bifurcation that characterizes Marvell's Christian vision would seem to fall within the same bifurcated tradition Spenser inherited, not simply the bifurcation of pastoral but also the bifurcation that characterizes Renaissance humanism in general. On the one hand, humanism represented the great Renaissance attempt to assimilate the classical tradition within the Christian, morally as well as aesthetically. The analogical thinking that was characteristic especially of Christianity, and perhaps of most moral and mythic systems, was used to bring classical and Christian ethics into tandem (for example, Ficino's *Theologia Platonica*) and classical and Christian myth (for example, Boccaccio's *Genealogia*). This coexistence, as we all know, was often precarious. While to consider Pan a pagan type of Christ might on the one hand suggest the universality of Christian truth, it might on the other debase the uniqueness of Christian truth. For this reason and many others beyond the province of this work, humanism could lead at once both to a synthetic assimilation of pagan and Christian and to a duality of pagan and Christian. Within the pastoral tradition, Mantuan, despite his use of classical poetic convention, represents the philosophic disintegration of the pagan and Christian synthesis; and so to a great measure does the young Spenser of the *Shepheardes Calender*, who, recognizing the merits of both the classical and the Christian, can nonetheless not find, except mythically, the reassuring synthesis. Marvell does attain this synthesis; and yet, curiously, in the anti-pastorals this synthesis disintegrates, and we return to the moralistic humanism of Mantuan, Barclay, and Googe, without the pastoral form itself.

4. The Amorous Pastorals

Approaching Marvell's amorous pastorals by way of his Christian pastorals, one may well be tempted to assume a similar pastoral meaning and poetic technique.[1] What Marvell did with pastoral in these poems, however, is something quite different from what he did in "The Garden" or "Clorinda and Damon." In those poems, events are placed within their proper perspective by being perceived in terms of analogy: the experience of the speaker in "The Garden," for example, is related analogically to the experience of the other gardens, the garden of the lost Eden, the classical garden of retirement, the *hortus conclusus* and the promised garden of the new Eden. From this cross-reference of analogues the full meaning of the events emerges. The amorous pastorals do not lend themselves to this critical approach. The pastoral world Damon the Mower inhabits does not,

1. Within the category of amorous pastorals I include the amorous Mower poems ("Damon the Mower," "The Mower's Song," "The Mower to the Glo-Worms"), "Ametas and Thestylis Making Hay-Ropes," and "Thyris and Dorinda." (The authenticity of "Thyrsis and Dorinda" has been questioned. See the Introduction to *Andrew Marvell: Complete Poetry*, ed. George deF. Lord (New York, 1968), p. xxxii, and the note to the poem, p. 261: the major arguments against its inclusion in the canon are that (1) it does not appear in the Bodleian MS.; (2) it seems inferior to Marvell's other works; and (3) "the advocacy of suicide is completely unlike anything in Marvell's other verse." Once we understand the poem's comic and ironic perspective, however, it does not seem quite so inferior and unusual.) Unlike Harold E. Toliver, *Marvell's Ironic Vision* (New Haven, 1965), pp. 103–112, I do not consider the Mower poems a psychological and narrative progression. For Toliver, the Mower's intransigent quest for innocence in "The Mower Against Gardens" leads to an increasing personal alienation from innocence by breaking "the machinery for compromise" between art and nature: "The unqualified quest for innocence," he writes, "leads to a quest for death, to the Mower mowing himself." The innocence the Mower defends in that poem, however, is not asexual. On the contrary, part of his objection to artificial gardens

it seems to me, ask to be seen in terms of Eden, nor does his experience ask to be seen in terms of Adam's; whereas the pastoral world of "The Garden" clearly does ask to be seen analogically. By referring Damon's pastoral world to Eden, one runs the risk of seeing his love for Juliana as a succumbing to Eve's original temptation and thus as a counterpart to the amorous proclivities that precipitated Adam's fall. Within this context, the portrayal of love, in the Mower poems especially, must seem considerably more antierotic than is actually the case. The soundest approach to these poems is not through "The Garden" but through Theocritus, Virgil, and Spenser; for the amorous pastorals belong to that special breed of pastoral, of which Spenser's "March" and "August" are representative, in which an ironic perspective is taken on rustic love. Rather than a sober commentary on the penalties of loving, the amorous pastorals are instead a witty and sophisticated play with, and an exploration of, both the psychology of sexual experience and the traditional formulas of pastoral and amorous poetry. The wit of these poems emerges from the irony and paradox found not only in actual experience but also in the genre itself. The amorous pastorals are a witty and often comic portrayal of the contradictions, the topsy-turviness, of the amorous mind.

"Damon the Mower" follows the conventional structure of the amorous pastoral eclogue as it is illustrated by a host of works from Theocritus' third idyll to Sannazaro's second piscatorial eclogue, from Virgil's second eclogue to Spenser's "January." The movement of the eclogues of amorous complaint is roughly tripartite: first, the

---

is that, in addition to its removing the spiritual image of God from nature, they destroy the "nature" of nature by desexualizing it:

His green *Seraglio* has its Eunuchs too;
  Lest any Tyrant him out-doe,
And in the Cherry he does Nature vex,
  To procreate without a Sex.

There seems to me only a slightly better case for a narrative progression in the amorous Mower poems. All of them have a mower in love with Juliana, and all deal with the disorienting effects of love on the mind of the frustrated lover and how it effects his relationship to nature; but this is similarity not progression. To be sure, the third poem, "Damon the Mower," concludes with the Mower's deciding that only death will relieve him, but for that matter that is also the conclusion of the first. It seems to me soundest to regard the amorous Mower poems as companion-pieces, three witty variations on a mower's theme, his love for Juliana.

complaint to the reluctant mistress (usually involving either a contrast of the shepherd's misery with the happiness of the rest of nature or a correspondence of the shepherd's mind with nature and his flock, and a lament that the mistress has refused his pastoral gifts); second, the shepherd's self-evaluation, including the merits of his profession, his material prosperity, his looks, his piping; third, some form of resolution, consisting sometimes of a repudiation of the mistress (as in Virgil's second eclogue) and sometimes of a decision to die (as in Sannazaro's second piscatorial).

In "Damon the Mower" the complaint to the reluctant mistress occupies the first five stanzas. The conventional assumption of a correspondence between the objective world and the world of the Mower's own mind provides Marvell the occasion for what Mia Gerhardt has aptly called "la rhétorique amoureuse."[2] Marvell's ironic and witty perspective on the Mower and his amorous rhetoric is established in the opening stanza:

Heark how the Mower *Damon* Sung,
With loue of *Juliana* stung!
While ev'ry thing did seem to paint
The Scene more fit for his complaint.
Like her fair Eyes the day was fair;
But scorching like his am'rous Care.
Sharp like his Sythe his Sorrow was,
And wither'd like his Hopes the Grass.

Marvell's perspective on the Mower is not unlike that of Willye on Perigot in Spenser's August eclogue. Like Perigot, the Mower, caught up in his amorous frustration, lacks the detachment and objectivity to see himself as others see him. While he portrays himself as the tragic martyr to love, we see him self-indulgent in his passions, as he "paints" the scene for his complaint, the verb suggesting the Mower's self-posturing. Like Perigot, too, the Mower portrays his experience as unique and tragic but the conventionality of his gestures and sentiments ironically undermine this self-posturing. Like pastoral lovers before him, the Mower reaches out into nature to find analogues to his amorous situation: inevitably, the day is fair like his mistress' eyes, but also hot like his own passions; his scythe is as sharp as his sorrow, and the withered grass (the Mower's counterpart to the shepherd's mourning flock) is as withered as his hopes. In his "paint-

2. Mia I. Gerhardt, *La Pastorale* (Assen, 1950), p. 296.

ing" of the scene, then, we sense the Mower's emotional and poetic exaggeration of his experience, and we realize that Marvell is playing with both the Mower's experience and the conventions of the genre itself. We are not to take the Mower's sentiments and gestures at face value.

Stanzas two and three continue the Mower's conventional examination of the landscape of his suffering. The "unusual Heats" of the July day are an extension of the Mower's "hot desires," and are a result not of the sun but, as we would expect, of a higher sun, Juliana (as her name suggests, a creature of July):

> This heat the Sun could never raise,
> Nor Dog-star so inflame's the dayes.
> It from an higher Beauty grow'th,
> Which burns the Fields and Mower both:
> Which made the Dog, and makes the Sun
> Hotter then his own *Phaeton*.
> Not *July* causeth these Extremes,
> But *Juliana's* scorching beams.

The compliment is as conventional as the Mower's love: the Mower is simply following the conventions of Renaissance amorous rhetoric, whereby the mistress always puts the sun to shame, though Marvell makes a witty variation on the formula by making Juliana's heat, not her light, the rival of the sun's. And in the fourth stanza, the Mower, continuing to follow convention, looks for a "cool Cave" or "gelid Fountain" where he may "pass the Fires" of his "hot desires." But the affliction of course is interior, and the physical world can provide no remedies. The fires of passion might be put out by water, but, alas, "No moisture but my Tears do rest"; and the heat might be countered by cold, but, alas, "Nor Cold but in her Icy Breast." The situation is hopeless, unless of course the mistress will relent. The complaint thus concludes with the pastoral convention of the Mower's offering his mistress his rude and rustic gifts.

In the first stage of the amorous eclogue, the shepherd laments his own deprivation, and the comedy emerges from the exaggerated rhetoric and gestures whereby he expresses this deprivation. In the second stage, the shepherd has a perfectly natural human reaction: he shifts from his being deprived of his mistress, to her being deprived of him. In this second stage (stanzas six to eight in Marvell's poem) the comedy emerges from the shepherd's exaggeration of his own merits: the mistress surely must not realize just how important a man she's turning down! His sense of self-importance injured by her rejection, he understandably reacts by blowing that image up a bit. "I," he says with charming pretentiousness and pomp, "am the Mower *Damon*, known / Through all the Meadows I have mown." Quite an impressive fellow, a big shot in the rustic world, and nature herself knows it:

> On me the Morn her dew distills
> Before her darling Daffadils.
> And, if at Noon my toil me heat,
> The Sun himself licks off my Sweat.
> While, going home, the Ev'ning sweet
> In cowslip-water bathes my feet.

Of course nature does this for anyone in the fields, but that unsettling thought does not occur to the Mower; as far as he's concerned, he's the center of creation, and nature the handmaiden of a rustic demigod.

In his defense of his merits, the pastoral lover is often forced to defend his profession: if he is a shepherd, he must defend himself against the goatherds; if he is a fisherman, he must defend himself against the landdwellers; if he is an orchardist, he must defend himself against the shepherds. Marvell's Mower is also caught up in this comic professional rivalry. As a Mower he is forced to defend his mowing and its prosperity against the shepherds' sheep and their prosperity:

> What, though the piping Shepherd stock
> The plains with an unnum'red Flock,
> This Sithe of mine discovers wide
> More ground then all his Sheep do hide.
> With this the golden fleece I shear
> Of all these Closes ev'ry Year.
> And though in Wooll more poor then they,
> Yet am I richer far in Hay.

With equally charming braggadocio, the Mower praises his looks:

> Nor as I so deform'd to sight,
> If in my Sithe I looked right;
> In which I see my Picture done,
> As in a crescent Moon the Sun.

The Mower's seeing his image reflected in the scythe is a counterpart to the more usual situation of a shepherd's seeing his image reflected in a pool. The narcissism of the Mower's fascination with his own looks in the mirror, which is perhaps a comment on the narcissism that underlies his love, or any love for that matter, is extended by the simile, "As in a crescent Moon the Sun." Just as the sun's light is so much greater than its reflection in the moon, so too, the Mower hopes, is his own face to its picture in the mirror: if the image was fair in the mirror, how much more fair he himself must be! The Mower's comic narcissism is reinforced by his comparison of himself to the sun. In the first stage of the poem, the beloved is the sun; here—in keeping with the narcissism of the second stage of the poem—the Mower is the sun.

Having established his great reputation in the meadows, his importance as nature's darling, his wealth and prosperity, and his good looks, the Mower completes the conventional catalogue of merits by praising his abilities as pastoral songster:

> The deathless Fairyes take me oft
> To lead them in their Danses soft;
> And, when I tune my self to sing,
> About me they contract their Ring.

The fairies here are probably a counterpart to the Muses with whom the shepherd, either in amorous pastoral or in the singing-contest, claims a special affiliation, and their surrounding him in a ring is possibly an echo of a similar situation in the *Faerie Queen,* VI, x, where Colin Clout, the chief representative of English pastoral, is surrounded by the Graces. The Mower lays claim to being the center of art as well as nature.

The final three stanzas provide the resolution of the poem. Like Virgil's Corydon, who asks himself "quin tu aliquid saltem potius, quorum indiget usus, / viminibus mollique paras detexere iunco?" (II. 71-72) and a host of other shepherd-lovers who turn to their work as an escape for love's anguish, the Mower "all the day complain[s], /Joyning [his] Labour to [his] Pain; / And with [his] Sythe cut down the Grass." The Mower tries through physical means to "mow" his psychological grief—but to no avail:

> Yet still my Grief is where it was:
> But, when the Iron blunter grows,
> Sighing I whet my Sythe and Woes.

Again, the conventional irony emerging from the contrast of the physical and the psychological: the physical scythe dulls, the psychological scythe does not. The same contrast of the outer and the inner world concludes the poem. The Mower, having mown himself with his own scythe, reports that

> Alas . . . these hurts are slight
> To those that dye by Loves despight.
> With Shepherds-purse, and Clowns-all-heal,
> The Blood I staunch, and Wound I seal.
> Only for him no Cure is found,
> Whom *Julianas* Eyes do wound.
> 'Tis death alone that this must do
> For Death thou art a Mower too.

Having attempted to make work an escape from passion and in his frenzy to "depopulate all the Ground" and having failed in that attempt, Damon turns to the second conventional escape of the pastoral lover, death.[3] But we need not mourn: this, too, is one of love's postures of self-pity and self-glorification. The tragic gesture is exactly that, a gesture; for the Mower is modelled not on a Colin Clout but on a Perigot.

3. The Mower's characterizing Death as "a Mower too" does not mean that the Mower himself is Death, or his cohort. Joseph H. Summer, "Marvell's 'Nature,' " *ELH*, 20 (1953), 121–135, recognizing the Mower's traditional relationship to death, remarks that the Mower "symbolizes man's alienation from nature" since "he cuts down for human ends what nature has produced." (By Summer's line of reasoning, a grazing cow could become an image of death, symbolizing bovine alienation from nature.) Harold E. Toliver, *Marvell's Ironic Vision*, p. 109, finds "a more complete identity of the two mowers implied" since "Damon and Death work side by side in the once innocent meadow." The relationship between Damon the Mower and Death the Mower does not seem to me all that serious. In pastoral, the shepherd usually perceives the world and himself in terms of his profession (as the Mower also does in "The Mower's Song," where he makes Juliana a mower). The limitations of such provincial rustic perception is often comic, as I think it is here. The Mower's characterizing Death as a mower is a comic diminution of the traditionally awesome figure when seen with the eyes of the innocent rustic, while at the same time his calling upon Death to relieve his suffering is a comic blowing up of his misery beyond all reasonable proportion. In a universe that is a hierarchy of mowers, Death becomes a fellow member of the union who will come to his rescue. The Mower's characterization of Death as a mower, then, is meaningful for what it tells us about the Mower's psychology, the partially pathetic disorientation of the mind in love.

While it is tempting to find something symbolic like the Mower as Death in Marvell's substitution of the Mower for the usual shepherd in pastoral, in all probability there is nothing more behind this substitution than his desire for a fresh set of witty variations on pastoral conceits and ideas. The substitution of

I have insisted at some length on the conventionality of "Damon the Mower" not to suggest that it is a weak poem—actually, it is rather successful, I think—but to indicate that it is using the conventions of the amorous complaint as a device of characterization. What is purely artificial and unconvincing if taken at face value is actually quite natural and quite human when viewed from the ironic perspective that I believe Marvell intended us to view the Mower's gestures. Marvell's purposeful conventionalizing of the poem permits him to play with the genre and with pastoral love, and indeed all banally idealized love. The serious amorous pastoral possesses at once both artificiality of convention and truthfulness of psychology. Marvell, following the procedures of all comic amorous pastoral, exaggerates even further the artificial conventions to attain a greater psychological truth. Those conventional and tragic lovers of pastoral who are always mourning their love in lofty platitudes, falling into despair, going mad, and throwing themselves from cliffs are highly conventional and artificial in their gestures of expression and sentiment. Theirs is a tragic idealization of love and its consequences, and their experience and the way in which they express it are considerably removed from reality; and indeed, if we enjoy this kind of pastoral at all, we expect it to be unreal. Nonetheless, behind the artificiality of convention and idealization, there is a basically sound psychology: love can indeed disorient us, cause us to doubt our merits if rejected, lead us into melancholy and despair. Serious amorous pastoral simply takes these commonplaces of our psychology and exaggerates them to the end of tragic elevation and loftiness. In comic amorous pastoral, on the other hand, the same psychological assumptions are exaggerated and artificialized even further, and become as a result a kind of comic *reductio ad absurdum* both of the conventions of serious amorous pastoral and of our own reactions to love. The exaggeration that seems artificial in serious amorous pastoral is vastly more convincing in comic amorous pastoral because it is rooted in a psychological truth that serious amorous pastoral, if it is to succeed, simply cannot face: that is, the absurd manner in which we all exaggerate our totally commonplace experiences and sentiments. In serious amorous pastoral, we must see the tragic lover very much as he sees himself, a tragic

---

a mower for a shepherd is, after all, no more unique that Sannazaro's substitution of fishermen for shepherds. Both have precedent in Theocritus, the tenth idyll for the mower, the twenty-first for the fisherman.

martyr to love; otherwise he seems a fool. In comic amorous pastoral, entirely to the contrary, we are required to see the lover as he cannot or does not see himself; we must place ourselves at a remove from his passions, assume an ironic perspective. Comic amorous pastoral, then, while admitting and assuming the commonplace psychological truths of its serious counterpart, moves to an even greater awareness of the psychology of love by admitting as well the commonplaceness of the experiences that, when caught up in the throes of love like Damon, we blow up out of reasonable proportion. The human animal tends to deal with unpleasant circumstances either by diminishing their importance or by exaggerating them, and it is the latter mode that Damon pursues. His own ego damaged by his rejection, he salvages some of it by exaggerating his misery and his fate and thus making himself the focus of a drama of apparently enormous consequence. Damon's tragic pose is thus a means of rebolstering an ego whose sense of importance has been pretty much shattered by Juliana's rejection of him; and one has only to know the amorous hysteria of the spurned adolescent female to realize how psychologically true Marvell's portrayal of Damon is.

"Damon the Mower" is an ironic and witty examination of the contradictions and absurdities of the amorous mind, and should thus be seen in terms not of "The Garden" but of comic amorous pastoral such as Theocritus's tenth and eleventh idylls or Spenser's "March" and "August." However, if we are to be objective, I think we must consider the possibility of an alternative reading, even though we may ultimately find it untenable, along the lines of the analogical vision and technique of the pastoral Christian lyrics. If we read "Damon the Mower" in terms of "The Garden," we would assume that Damon's pastoral world is a counterpart to Eden, and that Damon's experience within that world is analogous in some way to Adam's: Damon's love for Juliana alienates him from the paradise of his innocence just as Adam's love for Eve alienated him from Eden; and Damon's wounding himself and falling into grass, and his prophesied death, are analogous to the consequences of the Fall.[4]

---

4. Barbara Everett, "Marvell's 'The Mower's Song,'" *Critical Quarterly* (*Crit Q*), 4 (1962), 219–224, agreeing with Ruth Nevo, "Marvell's 'Songs of Innocence and Experience,'" *Studies in English Literature* (*SEL*), 5 (1965), 18–20, that the amorous Mower poems portray the progress from innocence to experience, relates the Mower's experience to Adam's: "This discovery of experience, whether the experience of Society in any wider sense, or merely the society of Eve, is

There are, however, only three possible specific allusions in the poem to Eden, none of them very plausible. Two of these possible allusions are to the snake. In the second stanza of the poem, the snake is singled out as the only creature who can venture out into the hot meadows:

> The Grass-hopper its pipe gives ore;
> And hamstring'd Frogs can dance no more.
> But in the brook the green Frog wades;
> And Grass-hoppers seek out the shades.
> Only the snake, that kept within,
> Now glitters in its second skin.

I cannot think that the serpent's Edenic symbolism of evil is any more relevant here than its symbolism of immortality (like the Phoenix, the snake, emerging from its dead form, was often taken as a symbol of immortality). Like the fact that in hot summer days frogs seek out water and grasshoppers shade, this is a natural fact and nothing more. The second appearance of the snake as one of the gifts Juliana has refused, provides no more substantial suggestion of Eden than the first:

> To Thee the harmless Snake I bring,
> Disarmed of its teeth and sting.
> To Thee *Chameleons* changing-hue,
> And Oak leaves tipt with hony due.

The "harmless Snake" may have phallic significance, and the color-changing chameleon and honey-tipped oak leaves may be an ironic commentary on Juliana—but none of the gifts has mythic, or Edenic, significance. The snake is like the chameleon and the oak leaves, simply an absurd gift to offer a mistress. The Mower's offering these gifts to Juliana reflects not Eden but his comically bumbling ignorance of feminine psychology: nothing could be more incongruous and ludicrous than to offer a woman oak leaves, a snake, and a lizard! Damon, of course, does not see this, and this is why he is so funny; for him these are things of great price, and he is annoyed that "Thou

---

the Mind's Fall in Marvell." The Mower is thus "much more of an Adam than a confused peasant," though this is a comic pretension of the Mower's. Harold E. Toliver, *Marvell's Ironic Vision*, pp. 103–109, also tends to see the Mower in terms of Adam, but more soberly, finding Edenic analogues in the Mower's reaction to Juliana, his falling into grass, and his desire (in "The Mower's Song") to reduce nature to "one common Ruine."

ungrateful has not sought / . . . what they are." The love offerings, then, are part of a comedy as old as Theocritus, reflecting the comic and charmingly naive simplicity of the amorous rustic.

A third possible allusion to Eden occurs in stanza ten:

While thus he threw his Elbow round,
Depopulating all the Ground,
And, with his whistling Sythe, does cut
Each stroke between the Earth and Root,
The edged Stele by careless chance
Did into his own Ankle glance;
And there among the Grass fell down,
By his own Sythe, the Mower mown.

The Mower's falling into grass is perhaps analogous to the Fall in Eden, but I doubt it.[5] Even in "The Garden," there is considerable doubt as to whether the falling on grass has Edenic meaning, and that poem clearly functions within a religious context. How much more circumspect, then, should we be in this poem in invoking religious analogues! In the Christian pastoral lyrics like "The Garden," the relevance of Eden is specific and concrete; it does not have to be manufactured solely by double-meaning (the fall) or vague similarity (the Juliana's effect on Damon paralleling Eve's effect on Adam). In "The Mower Against Gardens," the moralistic Mower himself establishes specifically the relevance of Eden to the gardens and the plains; and in "Clorinda and Damon," the moral characterization of Clorinda and Damon, the definition of Clorinda's temptation, and the ensuing conversion through Pan-Christ's words, establish a religious context that makes the Eden analogue specific, congruous, and relevant. But there is really nothing of the sort in "Damon the Mower," nor, I would suggest, in any of the amorous Mower poems. Simply for Damon to be upset by a woman is not enough to justify our invoking Eden, nor the fact that the grass falls or that Damon falls in grass. The falling in grass has no thematic relevance to the original Fall; the similarity is verbal, not real. We are clearly dealing with two quite different versions of pastoral, the one Christian and religious,

5. For Harold E. Toliver, *Marvell's Ironic Vision,* p. 103, "in the Mower's accident, the fall is re-enacted, bringing death once again to Arcadia." Lawrence W. Hyman, *Andrew Marvell* (New York, 1964), p. 21, finds "Damon the Mower," like the other amorous Mower poems, revealing an ambivalent attitude towards sex. The grass is flesh (we are to recall Isaiah) and a phallic symbol. Consequently, cutting down the grass becomes the punishing of the sinful flesh, while falling in the grass is "symbolic of the Fall of man."

the other comic and amorous. And if one insists upon introducing Edenic analogues into the poem, they would have to be thought of as comic and ironic, not moralistic, something along the line of the music-hall comic handling of woman's sexual temptation of man, that ever since creation began, woman has been doing this to man. To apply them moralistically to Damon's love is to disrupt the whole thrust of the poem, its witty exploration of the comedy of the amorous mind. Instead, it seems to me that the tenth stanza is best understood in terms of the comedy of amorous psychology. In the previous stanza, the Mower has decided to escape his inner torment by labor, and that he does in this stanza with the exaggeration characteristic of him; in a frenzy of activity, "his whistling Sythe" depopulates all the ground. His excess in labor parallels his excessive reaction to Juliana, and not surprisingly, just as Juliana's rejection of him causes his psychological scythe to cut his mind so his physical scythe cuts his flesh. The cutting of himself with his scythe is thus an analogue to what is going on in his mind. When the Mower cuts himself and falls, he is not re-enacting the Fall but revealing how much his love for Juliana has shaken him up. Conceivably, his cutting himself suggests something of the psychology of frustration, the self turning against the self, and would thus fit in with the feelings of inferiority and self-aggrandizement that alternate in the poem. Be that as it may, the Mower's mowing himself and his falling down in the grass are chiefly significant as a comic portrayal of the topsy-turviness of the lover's irrational world: his actions are a comic analogue to the confusion in his own mind, not an analogue to Eden. The poem is not an antierotic homily, speaking out against the dangers of sex and the recurring temptation of Eve; for though we sympathize with the Mower's mowing himself, we are amused, and do not mourn.

"The Mower's Song," like "Damon the Mower," takes an ironic and witty perspective on both the conventions of amorous pastoral and the behavior of the amorous mind. The Mower's love for Juliana has broken the once happy correspondence of mind and meadow: "My Mind was once the true survey / Of all these Medows fresh and gay"; but Juliana has come, "and She / What I do to the Grass, does to my Thoughts and Me." But while the Mower withers, the grass grows "more luxuriant still and fine" and flowers. The Mower's response to the flowering of the grass is a witty play on the conventional pastoral assumption of a correspondence between the shepherd and his flock, the assumption, as Colin says, that "thou . . . art made a myrrhour, to behold my plight." The Mower, furious that the "Unthankful Medows, could . . . / A fellowship so true forego," resolves that

> . . . what you in Compassion ought,
> Shall now by my Revenge be wrought:
> And Flow'rs, and Grass, and I and all
> Will in one common Ruine fall.

The Mower's violent insistence that the grass should cease to grow and flourish, defy the natural cycle and come to his defense, is a comically literal-minded enforcement of the pathetic fallacy of pastoral poetry. The literate Mower seems to have taken the poetic convention a bit too seriously. Marvell is obviously employing the Mower's childlike reaction to play ironically with the conventions of the pastoral genre. At the same time, however, the Mower's reaction is meaningful in terms of human psychology as well as literary convention: the Mower's exaggerated responses manifest the absurdity and irrationality of love. The Mower's violent revenge against the grass and his resolve to die in the final stanza should not be taken too seriously, however.[6] Admittedly there is some pathos in his frustration, but the chief perspective is comic not tragic. The Mower's taking revenge against the grass, his insistence that all will "in one common Ruine fall," is no more a reenactment of the Fall than is Damon's falling in grass because of his frustration in love. How comically absurd, after all, the Mower's threat to the grass is! The only difference between slaughtering and mowing the grass is entirely in the mind of the Mower. The grass has flowered and is ripe for mowing, and the Mower, despite the comically grandiose pretensions of his threat to the grass, is really doing nothing more than what he's supposed to do when the grass is ripe—to mow it. We smile at the naiveté in his transforming his simple task into cosmic proportions, just as we smiled at his cosmic pretensions in the previous poem. The Mower's "revenge" is simply a comic way of getting rid of his frustration and anger. The revengeful, and for all that rather

6. Lawrence W. Hyman, *Andrew Marvell*, pp. 20–21, pursuing the idea that the amorous Mower poems reflect the Mower's ambivalence about sex, finds a double implication in the death: the death morally deserved and the death sexually desired. For Harold E. Toliver, *Marvell's Ironic Vision*, p. 112, in the arranging of the grass for his tomb, "the successful shepherd's mastery of nature through art, mastery especially of love and death, is . . . fully inverted."

pointless, mowing of the grass becomes, morever, a comically vicarious way of getting back at Juliana. The Mower, like the shepherds of traditional pastoral, perceives the world as a hierarchy of mowers: he mows the grass, and Juliana mows him. No matter how much Juliana annoys the Mower, however, she is still a Petrarchan mistress, a "higher beauty," upon whom he certainly cannot take direct revenge. The only way he can mow Juliana the way she mows him is vicariously, and so the Mower transforms the grass into an image of Juliana: it has no "compassion"; it is "unthankful"; it forgoes "a fellowship so true." Like a punished child, he kicks the cat; and however said this may be for cats, there is a comedy in it depending on the childish lack of logic underlying the mind upset by love. Thus, in a comic distortion of true reason, the Mower argues that if he cannot force Juliana to his desire, he will at least force nature to do his bidding; if the grass will not mirror his grief, it will be forced to mirror his death. "The Mower's Song," like "Damon the Mower," is thus a serious comedy of the devasting effects of woman on the male animal.

"The Mower to the Glo-Worms" is a simpler poem than the other two Mower poems, it is more straightforward than comic; yet it shares with its companions the same theme, the disorienting effects of love on the amorous mind.[7] The poem is structured around a contrast of the order within the natural world and the disorder within the Mower's mind. Representing the order within the natural world are the glowworms; appropriately, the opening three stanzas of the poem are parallel apostrophes in praise of their ordering power in the physical world. Each stanza praises a single function. As "living Lamps" in stanza one, glowworms cooperate with the nightingale to make "Her matchless Songs"; as "Country Comets" in stanza two, they portend not the disorder of war or a prince's funeral but "the Grasses fall"; and as "Glo-worms" in stanza three, they offer their "officious Flame / To wandring Mowers" who have lost their way at night and stray after foolish fires. The glowworms are thus involved with three aspects of natural order: the order of music in stanza one;

7. For Lawrence W. Hyman, *Andrew Marvell*, p. 16, "The Mower to the Glo-Worms" is an exemplum of the consequences of foolish passion replacing the truth of the mind. Man loses his way from home as a consequence of his fall into sin (the cutting of the grass). For Charles Mitchell, however, "Marvell's 'The Mower to the Glo-worms,'" *Explicator* (*Expl.*) 18 (1960), item 50, the poem represents the incompleteness of both physical love (symbolized by the glowworms) and intellectual love (represented by Juliana, who affects the mind of the lover).

the order of the harvest in stanza two (typical of pastoral, the orderly harvest of the pastoral world is contrasted with the tragic and disorderly "harvest" of war and a prince's death); and the reordering of lost mowers to the way home in stanza three. The first three stanzas, then, describe the power of the glowworms to order the physical world. The final stanza contrasts their ability to order the physical world with their inability to order the Mower's mind:

> Your courteous Lights in vain you wast,
> Since *Juliana* here is come,
> For She my Mind hath so displac'd
> That I shall never find my home.

The wit of this poem, like that of the other amorous Mower poems, depends largely on a contrast of the objective world of nature with the internal world of the Mower's mind. Just as "Damon the Mower" concludes with a contrast between the curable physical wounds and incurable psychological wounds, so "The Mower to the Glo-Worms" concludes with a contrast between the ordering and reordering of the physical world (sound reordered into music, grass into mown hay, the lost wanderer to the wanderer at home) and the impossible reordering of the Mower's mind. "The Mower to the Glo-Worms" is, like its companions, a witty play on the ironies inherent in both amorous experience and the systems of correspondences traditional in pastoral and Petrarchan poetry (between shepherd and landscape, between outer world and inner world).

The portrayal of love in Marvell's amorous Mower poems is witty and ironic; it is not moral. Whereas in the Christian pastoral lyrics, love (and all experience, for that matter) is evaluated within a religious or quasi-religious context, in the amorous Mower poems love is examined in terms of the paradoxes of human psychology. Marvell is playing with the wit of sentiment. Consequently we are looking in the wrong direction when we try to discover an antierotic meaning in images of the grass's fall, the Mower's falling down into the grass, and his forcing all into a "common Ruine" by relating these images analogically to Eden. Each of these images, which in the Christian pastoral lyrics might very well have analogical significance, is significant as a characterization of the Mower's state of mind: in "Damon the Mower," the Mower falls because Juliana has upset him so much that his mind is not on his work (his mowing himself is a comic extension of the confusion and conflict in his mind); in "The Mower to the Glo-Worms," the grass's fall is an orderly process defining by contrast the Mower's own internal disorder; and in "The Mower's Song," the Mower's desire that everything "in one common Ruine fall" is an attempt to get even with Juliana vicariously. These images describe the comedy and pathos of man's passion for woman. Marvell's aim is witty and descriptive, not moral and prescriptive. Neither in intention, nor technique, nor vision do the amorous Mower poems resemble Marvell's other major kind of pastoral. Marvell is obviously working with a different species of pastoral. Instead of being related to the pastoral Christian lyrics, the amorous Mower poems should be related to Marvell's two other "light" amorous pastorals, "Thyrsis and Dorinda" and "Ametas and Thestylis Making Hay-Ropes."

Another amorous poem of hay-making, one which although obviously lighter in tone (it is not concerned, as are the amorous Mower poems, with the fine line between the comic and the pathetic) nonetheless also deals in a comic, nonmoral way with the irrationality and ironies involved in sexual experience, "Ametas and Thestylis" is a witty reversal of the seduction poem, with the tempted woman by deft agility ending up tempting her temptor. Ametas opens the temptation with the argument to constancy which pervades the poem: his love will not last if Thestylis continues to "say me nay." Like the Mower, he reasons with the images of his profession:

> Love unpaid does soon disband:
> Love binds Love as Hay binds Hay.

But Thestylis, like Marvell's other tempted figures (Damon of "Clorinda and Damon" and the Resolved Soul, for example), takes her temptor's imagery and reweaves it:

> Think'st Thou that this Rope would twine
> If we both should turn one way?
> Where both parties so combine,
> Neither Love will twist nor Hay.

Thestylis' witty retort to Ametas' threat of transience or inconstancy is that the ropes that bind love, making it enduring and constant, are made just like the ropes of hay, by contrary-motion, not by yea-saying. To which Ametas retorts:

> Thus you vain Excuses find,
> Which your selve and us delay:

And Love tyes a Womans Mind
Looser then with Ropes of Hay.

Ametas thus continues the wit-by-reversal: Thestylis really does not
want constancy; her image of hay-making as going in different directions was only a ruse for her inconstancy. A woman's mind can be
bound by love no more than it can be bound by hay. Ametas has
thereby reversed his temptation from the threat of his own inconstancy
to accusation of hers. The reversal works:

IV.
Thestylis.
What you cannot constant hope
Must be taken as you may.

V.
Ametas.
Then let's both lay by our Rope,
And go kiss within the Hay.

The outcome of this temptation was of course never really in doubt.
It is part of the sexual game's ritual that Thestylis tempts while
being tempted. Correspondingly, when she finally assents, it is amusingly in the form of Ametas' original temptation to seize the moment;
but whereas Ametas had twisted *carpe diem* to mean a lasting relationship (a standard male ploy, as Thestylis apparently realizes), Thestylis
brings his comment down to earth, making it clear that she has understood all along his stratagem: they'll take it when they can get it.
The argument about constancy was only a rhetorical ruse, a kind
of formal dance and pretense for the assumed indulgence of the
passions. The rhyme-patterns themselves reflect the foregone conclusion of their sexual rope-making: the first three stanzas are all linked
by a common "long *a*" rhyme, one of which in each stanza is contained
in the word "hay." The final stanza completes the weaving rhymes:
it is divided equally, and its *abab* rhyme-scheme reflects the binding
of the two sexual partners. In rhyme and rhetoric, the sexual rope-
making was assured. "Ametas and Thestylis," therefore, is a witty
play on the comic ritual and ironies underlying the psychology of
the male-female relationship. It is thus not unlike the amorous Mower
poems. Both are concerned with the comic irony emerging from the
psychology of man as a sexual animal. Sex is not treated with moral
disdain. The poem is not interested in the fact that the two rope-makers

trick each other and are perhaps a bit deceitful; it is not concerned with the dubious morality of their making love in the hay. What it is concerned with is the psychology of love, the "wit" inherent in human relationships.

Discussion in "Thyrsis and Dorinda" is not a rhetorical ruse for assumed indulgence in pleasure as it is in "Ametas and Thestylis"; but it does, amusingly, come to the same end. The moral exchange between Thyrsis and Dorinda is meaningful not because of any conclusions it comes to in terms of theology and morality but because of the comedy of these rustics' naive and limited perspective on the abstract issue of Elizium. "Thyrsis and Dorinda" handles some of the same themes found in the pastoral Christian lyrics, but in an entirely different way. The idea, for example, of this life ideally antedating the after-life, as we find it treated quite seriously in "The Garden" or "Clorinda and Damon," becomes in "Thyrsis and Dorinda" a kind of psychedelic anticipation of heaven on earth by drinking poppies steeped in wine. This perversion of what is meant abstractly by this life's anticipating the next stems from Thyrsis and Dorinda's limited, literalist perception of heaven; theirs is a pagan conception of heaven as simply an extension of earthly pleasures but more comfortable and timeless. It is a literal-minded conception of a theological concept, and their reaction to it is appropriately literal-minded. In this respect "Thyrsis and Dorinda" differs most appreciably from the pastoral Christian lyric that is most similar to it, "Clorinda and Damon." In both poems, a female protagonist blind to the eternal must be illuminated by the greater wisdom of her male lover. But whereas in "Clorinda and Damon" Damon persuades Clorinda to a spiritual and symbolic perception of nature, in "Thyrsis and Dorinda" Thyrsis himself has only a limited command over spiritual perception; he is only a bit less literal minded than Dorinda. He knows that "a Chast Soul" can never miss Elizium, that "Heaven's the Center of the Soul," but his notion of Elizium is that of a physical pleasure palace, the good of life without its attendant evils. Such a conception of Elizium is part of the pastoral genre's traditional comedy of limited rustic perception, as is Dorinda's naively literal-minded fear that, no bird with wings, she cannot fly to that great Elizium in the sky. Thyrsis' naiveté is both comic and quaint. Since in Elizium there is "No need of Dog to fetch our stray, / Our Lightfoot we may give away"; it is as though Thyrsis' passing on to eternal bliss were simply moving to a new neighborhood, leaving his neighbors with the things he no longer needs. And quaintly, in Elizium "every Nimph's a Queen of *May*," as though heaven were a perpetual May festival. There is, furthermore, a kind of comedy in the exaggeration of their sentiments, just as there was in the Mower's reaction to Juliana; and just as the Mower seems to ape the lofty tragic sentiments of his social superiors, Dorinda and Thyrsis also imitate the blown-up tragic phrasing and language of their masters: "Ah me, ah me," weeps the overly protesting heroine, "I'm sick, I'm sick, and fain would dye: / Convince me now, that this is true; / By bidding, with mee, all adieu." This is a bit of mock-melodrama, and Thyrsis replies in kind, "I cannot live, without thee, I / Will for thee, much more with thee dye." The poem thus concludes with a kind of psychedelic suicide:

> Then let us give *Carillo* charge o'th Sheep,
> And thou and I'le pick poppies and them steep
> In wine, and drink on't even till we weep,
> So shall we smoothly pass away in sleep.

If this is a parody of the withdrawal found in the Christian pastorals, it is also a distortion of the transformation of earthly nature for eternal and spiritual purposes, as we see that theme in "Clorinda and Damon" in particular. But while Thyrsis and Dorinda, paradoxically and contradictorily, withdraw from nature only to participate further in it, this contradiction is not, as it might be in "Clorinda and Damon" and as it would certainly be to the Resolved Soul, immoral. What would ordinarily be a form of immoral self-deception, a confusion of spirit and senses, from the perspective of the anti-pastorals, becomes here simply the traditional comedy of rustics' partial perception and misperception of abstractions, a comedy with a lineage from Theocritus to the *Shepheardes Calender,* including as well the rustic comedy in Elizabethan drama. The comedy of course is a gentle one; it is not satirical and it is not moralistic. It is a portrayal of innocence in a double sense, and our reaction to it is correspondingly double, as it frequently is in pastoral: we have an admiration for the intuitive innocence of the rustic at the same time that, in finding it comic, we feel superior to it. In summary, the framework for our perception of "Thyrsis and Dorinda" must not be the same as that for our perception of "Clorinda and Damon" or "The Mower Against Gardens." We are no more concerned here, than in "Ametas and

Thestylis," with the morality of theological misperception, self-deception, or (depending upon the meaning we ascribe "dye") sexual promiscuity. Dorinda is not a type of Eve, tempting Adam to suicide, nor Thyrsis a type of Adam, succumbing to Eve's temptation because "I cannot live, without thee." These analogues, if they exist at all, are incidental not formative, comic not moral or Christian in their emphasis. The amorous-psychedelic resolution of the poem is no archetypal or mythic evasion by the passions from spiritual responsibilities. For in this poem the amorous pastorals' comedy of sexual experience, with its serious and witty exploration of psychological contradictions, carries over into another dimension, the comedy arising from the contradictory and ironic relationship of the abstract ideas of the mind and the basic sexual and physical desires that so often give them birth.

The analysis of Marvell's amorous pastorals has brought me back once again to my central point: for Marvell, as for Spenser, pastoral did not always mean the same thing; there were different perspectives on pastoral, different perspectives within pastoral, different uses of pastoral. The same pastoral synthesis of classical and Christian, body and spirit, the natural and the supernatural into a unified Christian vision in the Christian pastorals could, in the anti-pastorals, become a form of deception and temptation. So, too, with the amorous pastorals, we find Marvell less concerned than he was in the Christian pastorals with reaching out into history and philosophy to bring analogues—Eden, the *hortus conclusus,* the Exodus, and so on—to bear upon pastoral experience; rather, he looks internally, he looks within at the psychology of love and its wit. Pastoral could thus serve Marvell, on the one hand, to explore man's relationship to morality, God, and history; yet it could, on the other hand, serve as a vehicle whereby he might portray the comedy of human experience and psychology. To consider Marvell's pastorals all of a piece is to blind ourselves to the diversity that pastoral could have in the Renaissance; and to ignore the multiple possibilities inherent in this diversity is to ignore a lesson that both Marvell and Spenser had learned well.

Bibliographical Note
Index

Bibliographical Note

The bibliography for pastoral is, of course, immense; fortunately, most of the more important items are included in J. E. Congleton's bibliographies in his discussion of pastoral in *The Encyclopedia of Poetry and Poetics,* ed. A. S. Preminger et al. (Princeton: Princeton University Press, 1965), pp. 603–606. The best historical survey of pastoral from its beginnings into the Renaissance is still W. W. Greg's *Pastoral Poetry and Pastoral Drama* (London: Sidgwick and Jackson Ltd., 1906), though the work is admittedly dated. On the history of pastoral in the Renaissance, the two works which should probably be first consulted are Mia I. Gerhardt's study of Renaissance vernacular pastoral, *La Pastorale* (Assen: Van Gorcum, 1950) and W. Leonard Grant's *Neo-Latin Literature and the Pastoral* (Chapel Hill, N. C.: University of North Carolina Press, 1965), though these two works must be supplemented by such older but still standard works as A. Hulubei, *L'Eglogue en France au XVIe siècle* (Paris: Droz, 1938), Jules Marsan, *La Pastorale dramatique en France* (Paris: Hachette, 1905), and Enrico Carrara, *La Poesia pastorale* (Milan: Vallardi, 1909). On the theory of pastoral, the best beginning is the articles of Renato Poggioli: "The Oaten Flute, *HLB,* 11 (1957), 147–184; "The Pastoral of Self," *Daedalus,* 88 (1959), 687–699; "Naboth's Vineyard or the Pastoral View of the Social Order," *JHI,* 24 (1963), 3–24; "Dante *Poco Tempo Silvano:* Or a 'Pastoral Oasis' in the *Commedia,*" *Eighteenth Annual Report of the Dante Society* (Cambridge, Mass.: Dante Society of America, 1962), pp. 1–20. Other studies especially to be recommended include: Erwin Panofsky, "Et in Arcadia Ego," in *Philosophy and History,* ed.

Raymond Klibansky and H. J. Paton (Oxford: The Clarendon Press, 1936); Hallett Smith, *Elizabethan Poetry* (Cambridge, Mass.: Harvard University Press, 1952), pp. 1-63; Frank Kermode, ed., *English Pastoral Poetry* (London: Harrap, 1952); William Empson, *Some Versions of Pastoral* (Norfolk, Conn.: New Directions, 1950); E. W. Tayler, *Nature and Art in Renaissance Literature* (New York: Columbia University Press, 1964); H. M. Richmond, " 'Rural Lyricism': A Renaissance Mutation of the Pastoral," *CL,* 16 (1964), 193–210; Bruno Snell, "Arcadia: The Discovery of a Spiritual Landscape," in *The Discovery of the Mind* (Cambridge, Mass.: Harvard University Press, 1953), pp. 281–309. Finally, I would strongly recommend Gilbert Lawall, *Theocritus' Coan Pastorals: A Poetry Book* (Cambridge, Mass.: Harvard University Press, 1967); and John S. Coolidge, "Great Things and Small: The Virgilian Progression," *CL,* 17 (1965), 1–23; both have many fine things to suggest about how pastoral works and have done much to stimulate my own thinking about pastoral.

Index